Praise for *Travels in the Greater Yellowstone*

"Jack Turner is a truth-teller. In a world of spin, doublespeak, and lies, his writing becomes a path of clarity. *T*   be compared to John Steinbeck's *Log f*   d-edged, and loving. Whether it's cut   a, Turner is an impassioned chronicler   -pher. Bureaucrats, nature-fakers, and   h out, Jack Turner's words will hunt you   e-cause it is an offering of honest joy in America's first national park: an en-lightened text for an enlightened land."

    —Terry Tempest Williams, author of *Finding Beauty in a Broken World*

"There have been legendary Indians, mountain men, and mystics, but the West has never been loved by a greater poet-warrior than Jack Turner. In *Travels in the Greater Yellowstone*, he reveals treasures and threats to the Greater Yellowstone Ecosystem while taking us on the most intimate and in-formative tour of America's wildest lands."

    —John Passacantando, executive director of Greenpeace USA

"Champions of Yellowstone and the truly wild West already know Turner's work. This one merits a wide audience, particularly in the Department of the Interior."   —*Kirkus Reviews*

Praise for *Teewinot*

"Bursting with a sense of place . . . a rewarding experience replete with rav-ishing observations of nature."   —*Publishers Weekly*

"A measured luxuriance in the landscape, a love song to the natural history of a place . . . Turner's writing is muscular, never swaggering, and almost lyrical, sum-moning a Teton Range in its rightful, sublime austerity."   —*Kirkus Reviews*

"*Teewinot* is a rare book. The wonderful accounts of mountaineering serve as armature not only for Turner's meditative reverence for the Grand Tetons and his often evocative prose but also for an uncommon density of knowl-edge of place."   —Peter Matthiessen, author of *Tigers in the Snow*

"This is, simply stated, a wonderful and utterly engaging book."
    —Jim Harrison, author of *Dalva* and *The Road Home*

"Each place must find its muse. The Tetons have found theirs and his name is Jack Turner."   —Terry Tempest Williams, author of *Coyote's Canyon*

Also by Jack Turner

Teewinot
The Abstract Wild

Travels

in the

Greater

Yellowstone

←--→

JACK TURNER

Thomas Dunne Books
St. Martin's Griffin ⚏ New York

THOMAS DUNNE BOOKS.
An imprint of St. Martin's Press.

TRAVELS IN THE GREATER YELLOWSTONE. Copyright © 2008 by Jack Turner.
All rights reserved. Printed in the United States of America. For information,
address St. Martin's Press, 175 Fifth Avenue, New York, N.Y. 10010.

The poem on page 156 is from *Saigyō: Poems of a Mountain Home,* translated by
Burton Watson. Copyright © 1991 by Columbia University Press.

www.thomasdunnebooks.com
www.stmartins.com

The Library of Congress has catalogued the hardcover as follows:

Turner, Jack, 1942–
     Travels in the Greater Yellowstone / Jack Turner.—1st ed.
          p. cm.
     Includes bibliographical references.
     ISBN-13: 978-0-312-26672-1
     ISBN-10: 0-312-26672-3
     1. Yellowstone National Park Region—Description and travel. 2. Natural
history—Yellowstone National Park Region. 3. Cahill, Tim—Travel—Yellowstone National Park Region. I. Title.

     F722.T875 2008
     978.7'52—dc22

                                                                        2008002211

          ISBN-13: 978-0-312-56095-9 (pbk.)
          ISBN-10: 0-312-56095-8 (pbk.)

First St. Martin's Griffin Edition: May 2009

10   9   8   7   6   5   4   3   2   1

For

Dana, wife, friend, companion on the path

and

Rio, teacher from another tribe.

Contents

Acknowledgments

I thank my companions on these travels for their fellowship and good spirits, sometimes under trying conditions: Boots Allen, Renee Askins, Dan Burgette, Greg Goodyear, Charlie Craighead, Dick Dorworth, Joe Kelsey, Rod Newcomb, Bob Schuster, and Dana Turner.

Friends and family often provided generous and timely support during the five years it took to write this book. My heartfelt thanks to each of you.

Change in Greater Yellowstone is so rapid that books on the subject are often out-of-date. I have relied instead, for the most part, on the Web sites, newsletters, reports, bulletins, and alerts from conservation groups. The following organizations track events and conduct research and promote conservation in Greater Yellowstone. Each and every one deserves the support of everyone who loves the ecosystem: Alliance for the Wild Rockies, Audubon Society, Biodiversity Conservation Alliance, Biodiversity Legal Foundation, Campaign for the Snake Headwaters, Cougar Fund, Defenders of Wildlife, Earthjustice, Federation of Fly Fishers, Friends of the Teton River, Foundation for North American Wild Sheep, Grand Teton National Park Foundation, Great Bear Foundation, Greater Yellowstone Coalition, Henry's Fork Foundation, Jackson Hole Alliance, Jackson Hole Land Trust, Predator Conservation Alliance, National

Resources Defense Council, Nature Conservancy, Rocky Mountain Elk Foundation, Snake River Fund, Wilderness Society, Wyoming Outdoor Council, Trout Unlimited, Trumpeter Swan Society, Upper Green River Valley Coalition, Whitebark Pine Ecosystem Foundation, Wildlife Conservation Society, and Yellowstone Park Foundation.

The following publications are essential reading for anyone who wants to understand Greater Yellowstone and I have profited from the depth and breadth of their journalism: *High Country News, Jackson Hole News and Guide, Wyoming Wildlife,* and *Yellowstone Science.*

The following artists, writers, teachers, and warriors supplied inspiration: Russell Chatham, Nelson Foster, Jim Harrison, Ted Kerasote, Tom McGuane, Peter Matthiessen, John Passacantando, Andrea Peacock, Doug Peacock, Flo Shepard, Paul Shepard, Gary Snyder, Casey Walker, Louisa Wilcox, Terry Tempest Williams, Brooke Williams, Todd Wilkinson, Ted Williams, and George Wuerthner. They are my heroes.

Dan Burgette, former sub-district ranger at Grand Teton National Park; Steve Cain, chief resource biologist at Grand Teton National Park; Mark Gocke, regional public information officer at the Wyoming Game and Fish Department; and Lloyd Dorsey, at the Jackson Office of the Greater Yellowstone Coalition answered many of my questions over the years, and when they could not answer my questions, always directed me to a knowledgeable source. Though from different institutions, they all serve the cause of Greater Yellowstone. Joe Kelsey, Steve Kobylski, and Tom Mangelsen kindly provided photographs.

My companions on these journeys read the chapters they appear in and offered incisive comments. Dick Dorworth and Joe Kelsey read the entire manuscript. Their vast knowledge of the ecosystem, their many journeys through it over the years, and the fact that they are accomplished writers made this a better book than I ever could have written alone. Diane Meitz reviewed the final manuscript and offered felicitous suggestions. My wife, Dana, read the book more times than I am prepared to admit, always with thoughtfulness and care. My debt to her is infinite.

Nine bows to all.

Opinions expressed here are mine. So are the mistakes.

—JACK TURNER
Lupine Meadows
Grand Teton National Park

The moral duty of the free writer is to begin his work at home: to be a critic of his own community, his own country, his own government, his own culture. The more freedom the writer possesses the greater the moral obligation to play the role of critic.

—Edward Abbey, "A Writer's Credo"

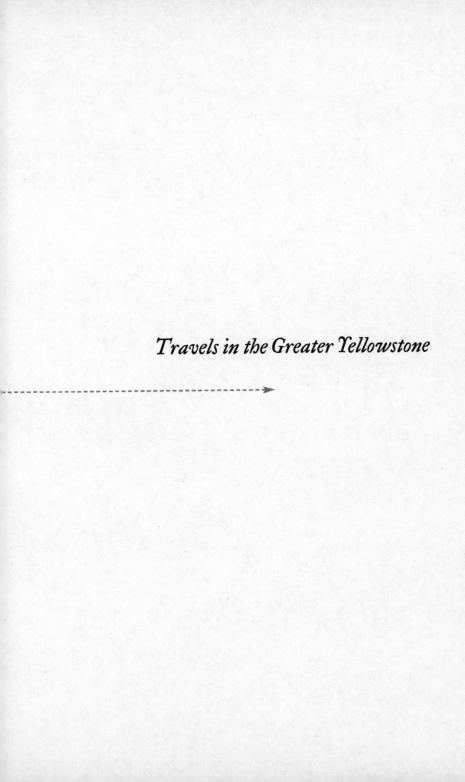

Travels in the Greater Yellowstone

Introduction: The Greater Yellowstone Ecosystem

It is a place of superlatives and fame. Home of the first national park and the world's largest concentration of geysers and hot springs; the largest relatively intact temperate ecosystem in the United States; the youngest range in the Rocky Mountains, the oldest exposed rock in North America, the highest peak in Montana, the highest peak in Wyoming, and the largest glaciated region in the contiguous states; the source of the three largest rivers in the West; the largest elk herd, the largest bison herd, the largest number of grizzlies and wolves, the largest winter concentration of big game animals; the best big game hunting and fishing; a United Nations Biosphere Preserve and World Heritage Site; a place traversed by the Lewis and Clark Expedition and the Oregon Trail; home of the mountain men; the place where Owen Wister wrote the first Western—*The Virginian*; home to some of the fastest growing counties in Idaho, Montana, and Wyoming, to the wealthiest county in America, and to the most intense energy development in the nation. The list goes on and on. Some items are merely curious, some surprising, some are legendary and laden with emotion. It is a list that suggests both the extraordinary and the contradictory nature of a mass of land that in the last few decades has come to be known as Greater Yellowstone.

Greater Yellowstone encompasses about 18 million acres—the size of West Virginia—comprising parts of Idaho, Montana, and Wyoming. Of that, Yellowstone

National Park is 2.2 million acres, or roughly 12 percent. My subject is the larger entity, the Greater Yellowstone Ecosystem.

I first came into this country forty-seven years ago. At first I came and went as a tourist. Forty years ago I began to work here as a mountain climbing guide. Thirty years ago I began to live here full-time. It is, in the deepest sense of the word, my home. I really don't like being any place else. I've climbed, hiked, skied, canoed, kayaked, fished, hunted, and explored it in all seasons, always with pleasure. Like anyone who lives here and has a baseline of memories extending over nearly half a century, I've watched it change in ways that casual visitors would not notice, change in ways that will profoundly affect its future. The ice climbs I did as a young man are gone, and many of my favorite fishing holes have been closed by NO TRESPASSING signs; the mountains and rivers are often unpleasantly crowded, lands that were once open space are now glutted with houses. Bugs have arrived from Egypt, pollution from China. Even the seasons have changed: summer is longer, winter is warmer, and spring is earlier.

With recognition of those changes came a desire to understand the place where I live, what made it what it is, what made it different and unique, and what made it the object of such intense love. What is this place? What is its essence, its identity? The more I've understood the answers to these questions, the more dismayed I've become—and angry.

Greater Yellowstone is defined by similarities, affinities, and shared histories across many biological, geological, and geographical categories. We call it an ecosystem because the parts—whether a mountain, a river, a rock, a moose, or a fish—are not just a totality of things, but a functioning whole held together by an extensive series of mutual dependencies and interactions. It includes two national parks, part or all of seven national forests, three national wildlife refuges, lands under the jurisdiction of the Bureau of Land Management, an Indian reservation, state land, and private lands held by individuals and corporations. No single institution is devoted to its interests; no single person or group has authority over its destiny. Its heart is Yellowstone National Park, but in much the same way as a heart is dysfunctional without a body, the Park will become dysfunctional without the protection of a much vaster area surrounding it.

The original boundaries of Yellowstone National Park were arbitrary and had no relation to biological or ecological processes. Hiram Chittenden, one of the park's early superintendents and author of its first notable guidebook, is clear on this point: "At the time when the bill creating Yellowstone Park was before Congress there had been no detailed survey of that region, and the boundaries, as specified in the bill, were to some extent random guesses." Early visitors and park staff soon realized that the park was too small to safeguard its wildlife, most obviously because it failed to protect essential migration routes and winter grazing grounds outside the park that were used by elk, deer, antelope, and bison.

In 1880, only eight years after the park's creation, Superintendent Philetus W. Norris recommended that the park's boundaries be extended. In 1917, a writer named Emerson Hough first used the term "Greater Yellowstone." Since then a combination of philosophy, science, history, and empirical data has made it apparent that adjoining lands required some form of protection in order to fulfill the park's mission. For the past ninety years a variety of individuals and groups have struggled to resolve this issue. I have watched these struggles; in a few cases I played an active part in them. Some of my friends have devoted their lives to its resolution.

The sea change began with conservationist Aldo Leopold's insistence that the land be treated as a whole, an idea he first set down in a 1944 rough draft entitled "Conservation: In Whole or in Part?"

There are two kinds of conservationist, and two systems of thought on the subject.

One kind feels a primary interest in some one aspect of land (such as soil, forestry, game, or fish) with an incidental interest in the land as a whole.

The other feels a primary interest in the land as a whole, with incidental interest in its component resources.

The two approaches lead to quite different conclusions as to what constitutes conservative land-use, and how such use is to be achieved.

The first approach is overwhelmingly prevalent. The second approach has not, to my knowledge, been clearly described.

Now the land as a whole—an ecosystem—has been described, but most conservation efforts still focus on the parts. We fret, argue, and create management plans for many species, one for an endangered species of trout, another for the nearly extinct lynx population, another for a creek destroyed by cattle grazing. These efforts to conserve Greater Yellowstone have encountered formidable obstacles: conflicts with traditional uses of the land, such as ranching, resource extraction, and real estate development. Most visitors to the Yellowstone country do not realize how serious the conflict has become. And there is a deeper problem. Management plans treat the ecosystem as a machine whose parts are maintained as we wish (elk populations) or removed and replaced at will (wolves), instead of a whole whose parts are created and maintained by one another without our assistance—a wild ecosystem.

To gain public acceptance of the ecosystems conservationists created new maps that represented biological reality instead of political reality, maps that required thinking at new spatial scales about the complex interactions among flora, fauna, and the nonbiological world of rock, water, fire, and climate. The first maps of the Greater Yellowstone Ecosystem made the *idea* of Greater Yellowstone real to the American public. I remember seeing those first maps and feeling we had made a quantum leap in understanding the natural world. But it was only the first step and, ironically, conservation organizations are now less and less inclined to publish such maps.

With the publication of *The Theory of Island Biogeography* by Robert H. MacArthur and Edward O. Wilson in 1967, scientists realized that species diversity on an island was related to two factors: the distance of the island from the mainland and the size of the island. Isolation and small size limited species diversity.

The theory was not limited to islands surrounded by water. It included any area of land separated from similar habitat. Since Yellowstone National Park and the Greater Yellowstone Ecosystem are mountainous, and are both encircled to varying degrees by steppe and human development, they, too, are islands whose species diversity is affected by isolation and size. To emphasize this new reality I often speak of the ecosystem as "Island Yellowstone" or "Yellowstone Island."

The park's boundaries were fixed, but the wildness of much of the surrounding land had protected it beyond the mere measure of those boundaries. Greater Yellowstone was tenuously connected by so-called land bridges to similar habitats to the west via the Centennial Range in southern Montana and to the south by the Wind River and Wyoming ranges. The upshot of island biography was that connections to surrounding habitat were as important as places that had been formally protected by legislation as parks, wilderness, and refuges. In particular, mammals in both the park and the ecosystem depended on surrounding public lands and private property for their survival, lands that often lacked long-term protection.

Between 1959 and 1970 Frank and John Craighead studied the behavior, population dynamics, and habitat of Yellowstone's grizzly population. At that time the park's grizzly population was declining. Using newly developed radio collars, the Craigheads documented how grizzly bears often wandered or hibernated outside the park's boundaries. A population adequate for the long-term survival of Yellowstone National Park's grizzlies would require a much larger protected habitat. Reducing their habitat would lead to their extinction. How large would this protected habitat have to be? Roughly the size of Greater Yellowstone.

In 1987, William Newmark published in the journal *Nature* his discovery that thirteen of the fourteen national parks he studied had lost some of their mammal species since they were established. Parks such as Yosemite and Mount Rainier had lost more than a quarter of their original species, and smaller parks had lost even more. Newmark predicted that as the national parks and other nature preserves became more isolated, the number of extinctions would increase, and that this increase would be related to both the size of the park and its age—the smaller and older the preserve, the higher the number of extinctions.

Yellowstone is the world's oldest national park. For nearly a century experts had said it was too small. Some species—such as the wolf—had been exterminated, and many others—the grizzly, fisher, lynx, and wolverine—were threatened and deserved protection. The buffers of undeveloped land—forests and ranch lands that have so far protected it—faced an alarming rate of real estate and energy development. Further isolation of the park would lead to a bleak dialectic, for species loss leads to aggressive human manipulation of natural processes, the very thing the parks were supposed to protect. Preservation and conservation became artificial, human constructs masked as natural systems. Yellowstone National Park would survive, but it would become a cross between a zoo and a prison.

Anyone who thought about this situation realized that the health and integrity of the world's first national park was at stake. The writer David Quammen entitled an article on the subject "National Parks: Nature's Dead End." I prayed he was too pessimistic, but after traveling in the ecosystem for this project these past five years, I began to think he was right.

So if Yellowstone National Park and Greater Yellowstone were islands, how much land around them would have to be protected for them to remain healthy? Everything? No, but we would have to protect corridors between similar habitats to the north and south— north to the Yukon, south to the Colorado Rockies and the Uinta and Wasatch ranges of Utah—and to do so would require a visionary approach to preserving huge parcels of land.

To preserve Yellowstone National Park in a semblance of its current form we would need to preserve Greater Yellowstone, and to preserve Greater Yellowstone would require three things: genuine protection of flora and fauna inside the representative sections of the ecosystem that buffer the national parks, preservation of the current size of the ecosystem from fragmentation or outright destruction, and the reestablishment of corridors to areas by which resident species could maintain contact with their own kind to ensure genetic enrichment. In 2001, Conservation Science, Inc., produced a biological conservation assessment of Greater Yellowstone for the Greater Yellowstone Coalition that was detailed, exhaustive, and persuasive. No one who reads it can deny that Greater Yellowstone is in trouble. We've known this, in theory, for decades. Now we know the particulars. And although the fact that species in Yellowstone and Grand Teton national parks depend on unprotected lands outside the parks may not occur to visitors, it is obvious to anyone who lives, as I do, in Jackson Hole.

Grand Teton's mountain sheep, whose numbers decreased considerably in the past few decades, often spend most of their year in the adjoining Jedediah Smith Wilderness, where they are hunted and harassed by back-country skiers. The antelope in Grand Teton migrate 200 miles south for the winter through national forests and across Bureau of Land Management lands where habitat protection is minimal or nonexistent, lands that are being plundered by oil and natural gas development. Elk seek winter range on other federal, state, and private lands. Ninety percent of our mule deer winter on private lands, as do 80 percent of trumpeter swans. Sixty-four percent of our native cutthroat trout spawn in waters on private land. Wolves from packs in Yellowstone have colonized Jackson Hole and reached Colorado and Utah. Perhaps most spectacularly: in the summer of 2002 a radio-collared wolverine trapped near where I live in Jackson Hole wandered north to Tower Junction in Yellowstone, then southwest to within miles of Pocatello, Idaho, then across the Salt River and Wyoming ranges, back to Jackson Hole, and south again to the Wind River range, where it threw its collar— all within six weeks. It traveled hundreds of miles through national parks, national forests, BLM land, and private property. Its journey demonstrates better than theory or abstract terminology what will be required to keep Yellowstone healthy and whole.

Tragically or ironically, depending on your philosophical druthers, as our understanding of the importance of Greater Yellowstone grew, forces inimical to its integrity grew, too. Greater Yellowstone has become a battleground that in the years to come will make the conflict over drilling in the Arctic National Wildlife Refuge seem like child's play. It is the one great chance for us to preserve a large, relatively intact ecosystem that is embedded in our history and our hearts. But Greater Yellowstone faces problems—some might call them challenges, but I think they are problems.

First and foremost is the American public's ignorance of ecology. According to a June 2007 *USA Today*/Gallup Poll, only 18 percent of Americans believe evolution is "definitely true." Evolution is the foundation of biology, biology the foundation of ecology, and ecology the basis of informed conservation. How can we expect public support for sound conservation policy against a background of such ignorance?

Second, development continues to fracture Greater Yellowstone at an alarming rate. Roughly a third of Greater Yellowstone is vulnerable to real estate development; perhaps a quarter is vulnerable to industrial energy development. If you believe that an ecosystem can withstand that level of fracturing and disturbance, then you are probably putting your dentures under your pillow for the tooth fairy.

Third, most of the ecosystem is within the state of Wyoming, unfortunately—a state that depends on mineral extraction for its economic welfare because it lacks a personal income tax and a corporate tax, a state that is as reactionary, fundamentalist, and rightwing as any in the nation.

The billion-dollar surplus budgets the state has been enjoying for the past few years are a direct result of energy development. Wyoming produces a third of the coal used in the United States and nearly half the natural gas. At present there are about 63,000 functioning gas and oil wells in the United States. The federal government plans to approve 50,000 new wells in Wyoming alone, most of them in the western and northern parts of the state, either in Greater Yellowstone or its environs. Not to mention the development of wind power, increased coal mining, and new power plants and power lines. Can we do this without irretrievably destroying much of Wyoming? The government, as usual, says, "Trust us." I trust them about as far as I can spit a brick.

Over the past few years I've heard Wyoming referred to as the Saudi Arabia of coal, the Saudi Arabia of natural gas, and the Saudi Arabia of wind power. "We're gonna have cowboy sheiks!" they exclaim. Well, I reply, go to Saudi Arabia and take a good look. Saudi Arabia is butt-ugly from energy development. Do you want the Yellowstone country to look that way? I don't.

And I'm not so sure about those cowboy sheiks, either. The energy companies stand accused of bilking the U. S. Treasury out of billions of dollars—that's *our* money for developing *our* resources on *our* land, and many of those companies are subsidiaries of foreign corporations whose headquarters are in places like Canada and the Barbados.

Fourth, climate change will aggravate the situation. I hope by now everyone realizes that our climate is warming, and that a warming climate will drastically affect all mountain ecosystems. Since it is surrounded by warmer ecosystems, Greater Yellowstone can be imagined as a cool island surrounded by a thermal sea of warmer habitats. As the climate warms, this thermal sea rises, fracturing the island into a chain of even smaller islands and separating them further from the mainland. This will aggravate precisely the two conditions that island biogeography predicts will deplete species diversity: isolation and small size.

Perhaps no one of these problems will be devastating, but common sense suggests that their accumulation will be. It takes only one pernicious event to cascade through an ecosystem, only one falling domino that sets the other dominos in motion, creating change faster than the system can adapt. Ecosystems do collapse, usually, though not always, because of human activity. Could something like that happen to Greater Yellowstone? You bet.

Do we care? Who weeps now for the passenger pigeon, the once-fertile delta where the Colorado River enters the Sea of Cortez, the grizzlies that fed on beached whales along the California coast, or Daniel Boone's vast Eastern hardwood forest, across which a squirrel could hop, tree to tree, from the Atlantic Ocean to the Mississippi River? There may come a time when Americans will no longer weep for the loss of Greater Yellowstone, either, but that time is not now. The considerable love, understanding, and legislation that exist can still be harnessed for its protection.

I have watched these changes in Greater Yellowstone for most of my adult life. Given the many problems confronting the ecosystem, I decided to revisit corners of the island that I have known and loved. I also wanted to visit a few places I have never been in order to see what is at stake. I hold the old-fashioned view that to understand how nature works in a particular place you have to spend many years there on the ground and in the water, in all seasons, creating a baseline by which to measure change. Theories, models, and statistics are of limited use; indeed, they are often a place to hide from reality. You have to see things with your own eyes—no one can do it for you. New arrivals and tourists passing through cannot understand what has been lost. As a character in Ernest J. Gaines's *A Gathering of Old Men* says, "You had to be here then to be able to don't see it . . . now. But I was here then, and I don't see it now."

I am neither a scientist nor a historian. My intent is neither comprehensive coverage nor definitive detail. What I sought in these travels was much more personal, my own reckoning of how this place where I've lived most of my life is doing, whether its soul is indeed intact, as authorities and experts would have it, or unraveling. I wanted to walk and drive, float rivers, paddle lakes, fish, study trees and critters, filter past memories through present events, and write a bit about what I saw and felt. It is this modest project that has been recorded here.

I. The View from Blacktail Butte

Your love of spring is proportional to the depth of your winter. My wife, Dana, and I live with our Australian shepherd, Rio, at the base of the Teton Range, at the edge of Lupine Meadow and along Cottonwood Creek in Grand Teton National Park. It is a place of extreme winters, a place where geography is destiny. Snow often covers the ground for six months a year. Wyoming's record low temperature is 63 degrees below 0 at Moran, twelve miles northeast of our cabin. Nights in the cabin are cold, often painfully cold. Timbers in the walls crack like a gunshot close to your head. There is also a blend of silence and serenity that is rare in the modern world. And uncommon beauty: walking in the dark with a headlamp, we sometimes see ice crystals falling from a clear sky.

Home is four miles from the trailhead for Taggart Lake, across a sagebrush-covered plain buried beneath deep, windswept snow. For several miles it is flat as a table, bare and uncluttered.

Once a week Dana skis home from work at dusk in temperatures that are often well below zero. Rio and I go out to meet her halfway. At times we all break trail for miles through encrusted, dazzling snow. At times the plain is a monotonous gray, dim and dreary. At times falling snow unifies land and sky into a subtle pale gray bleached of reference and coats us until we assume the hue of the place through which we pass. At times the moon rises above this snowy plain into a translucent violet sky like a silver orb rising from the sea.

When Rio and I see Dana, Rio runs ahead, lunging through chest-deep snow until Dana greets her; then back to me and back to Dana again, back and forth until we—her flock, her family, her responsibility—are together. Dana and I slurp sweet tea from a thermos and Rio dances about, whimpering with joy.

In early November, snowshoe hares change into their winter coats and we follow their example. Winter clothes will be standard fare until at least late April. During winter at the cabin we have no running water, no television, and no music; we do have an abundance of solitude and time. Summer returns us to the jet train of modern life.

Color is a luxury in a white world. I fall inordinately in love with my oil paints. Dana, who loves flowers, nurses various bulbs to provide relief from what we refer to as "the great white." Our favorite is a gaudy, shocking red monster of an amaryllis named Zelda that fills half a window and glows briefly in defiance of the colorless world. She dies eventually; the great white lingers. Protesting winter is like beating a stone drum and expecting to hear rhythm.

However beautiful our winters, sometime in February we begin to yearn for spring, for color, for something other than the metallic smell of cold, and most important, perhaps, the freedom to walk. By March the bare aspen, cottonwood, alder, and willow bore all but the most devoted skiers. Then, always suddenly, spring winds shred old, frozen snow from the limbs of conifers and the snow on the ground begins to melt.

Every year spring comes earlier. The runoff from western rivers peaks ten days sooner than it did fifty years ago. This year the Snake River in Jackson Hole peaked nearly a month earlier than it used to, and the ice went off Jenny Lake three weeks earlier than it did two decades ago. And the seemingly hard winters that we have known are nothing compared to the epic winters Wyoming once knew. They are history now, and soon the memories of them will be history, too.

In April the ski areas close and many restaurants and shops in Jackson follow suit. Locals depart for friendlier climes. If they are wealthy they go to Baja, Belize, Hawaii, and France; if they are not they go to Arizona, Death Valley, and southern Utah. Those who remain in April inhabit a delicious seclusion unknown in any other month in the ecosystem. We believe that solitude is a function of distance, but it's more complicated than that in the modern world. Being alone in Greater Yellowstone requires a bit of cunning, the absence of trails, and the absence of profitable recreation. Even that solitude—satisfying, healing, and spiritually renewing—is marked by an awareness of how much care and thoughtfulness is required to find qualities that should, one thinks, be normal in national parks or designated wilderness.

As the snow melts off Lupine Meadow—our front yard—we wander about looking at the ground, appreciating dirt. Until you have lived without dirt for six months you do not appreciate its rich hues and aroma, the Godiva-chocolate umber, the gold ochre, the camel tan. Dana kneels and smells the dirt. It has, she says, "the smell of life."

Flowers begin blooming early in the spring, and our appreciation of them is heightened by knowing that trees and bushes will not leaf out until May. Flowers are among the first species to return, beginning the perpetual cycle of return and reinhabitation that permits Greater Yellowstone to flourish each summer in all its abundance and magnificence. Without these returns and reinhabitations, the ecosystem would be impaired and impoverished. We celebrate that homecoming.

First to arrive, regardless of fluctuating weather patterns, is the sagebrush buttercup. Finding the first one is a pleasant game. It usually appears along the edges of receding snow, sometimes even piercing a thin layer of ice. The lemon yellow petals are so bright you neglect its green leaves—the first new green of the year, earlier than the grasses.

We walk toward Jenny Lake and search a favorite area for orogenia. Orogenia is not ubiquitous in Jackson Hole, but where it occurs it is prolific. The umbel of white florets is so inconspicuous among the glacial grit and cobbles of our meadows that many residents never notice it at all. The flower is rarely two inches tall, and it tends, like many spring flowers, to droop. Each floret is smaller than a pin head. From it rise diminutive anthers, which, together with the top of the ovary, are a rich, dark purple. Its name is from Greek: *oros,* "mountain," and *genos,* "race," so: "of a mountain lineage." I like that. The local names are equally charming: turkey peas, snowdrops, Indian potato. As the last suggests, the root is edible, crisp and tasty.

Slightly later, fields of pink and white spring beauties bloom, interspersed with an occasional steershead. Steershead also droops and its hues are so akin to the spring beauty that one wonders if they are a camouflage. Yellow fritillaries boast a delicious petal, enjoyed raw, and edible bulbs the size of rice. Yellow violets appear, a few lavender waterleafs, and, alas, swarms of dandelions, the earliest blooming of many alien species that have invaded the ecosystem, much like viruses invade a body. Dana forgives them. "We are rich," she says. "We have flowers."

The return of other species is reassuring because many species avoid Greater Yellowstone's winters. Our winter birds are few in kind. Chickadees, both mountain and black-capped, spend so much time at our feeder one wonders how they get along without us. A few ravens are about, Clark's nutcrackers, several Stellar's jays, blue and ruffed grouse, great horned owls, and our favorites, a pair of white-breasted nuthatches. Along the creek—never away from water—are dippers and belted kingfishers. Mergansers, an occasional mallard, a few swans. Goshawks cruise the winter forests like ghosts. Snow buntings, wintering here from the Arctic, flutter about in groups, feeding on windblown seeds.

Mammals are also rare. Moose, coyote, pine marten, snowshoe hare, sometimes a wolverine just passing through. Shrews, mice, and voles move about under the snow; picas live deep in the talus, eating grasses they collected all summer. Insect species are uncommon or absent.

If we could be said to have companions, they are moose. They seem not only tolerant of our presence but interested. Nor does Rio's growling intimidate them. After she charged a moose when she was a puppy, she decided she was not cut out for herding moose. She sits on the porch and growls; the moose ignore her.

Sometimes they are indifferent to our presence. Once when Dana was meditating out on our picnic table, a bull moose walked past, perhaps five feet in front of her. She remained still; the bull studied her and went his way.

At other times they seem genuinely curious. One moonlit night we heard a moose walk by the cabin on frozen snow until it reached the window next to our bed and stood towering above us, the bottom of its chest level with the sill. Slowly its head dropped down until its face appeared next to us, perhaps eighteen inches away, the massive nose quivering as it sniffed, an enormous eye reflecting moonlight. Rio, on the bed as always, growled softly, her most serious warning, but the moose paid no mind. Then ever so slowly it backed away and wandered north a few yards to feed on branches of subalpine fir. In the morning we found a shallow depression where its warmth had melted the snow. The depression's depth and shape showed that it had spent the night watching us.

Despite the presence of winter residents, tens of thousands of other beings must return if this island of Greater Yellowstone is to flourish. Each returns in its own manner.

Ground squirrels and bears have been here all winter—in hibernation. Ground squirrels return, so to speak, from the dark, digging out from their burrows to the surface of the snow and braving long journeys across unmarked expanses to feed on new greens. Great gray and great horned owls await them. Grizzlies and black bears leave their dens when melting snow reveals winter kills and red squirrel middens filled with whitebark pine nuts. Trout leave the depths of the lakes and feast on bugs washed down the feeder creeks into the holes at each inlet.

The majority of critters return via a migration indexed to what they eat. Some migrate from within the ecosystem, both vertically and horizontally, others travel thousands of miles. They are nomads with summer and winter homes connected by established corridors to the island of Greater Yellowstone.

Pronghorn that will raise calves in Grand Teton National Park's meadows travel two hundred miles from southern Wyoming, one of the longest mammal migrations in North America. Elk return from a national wildlife refuge near Jackson. Mule deer arrive from warmer, exposed buttes at the southern end of Jackson Hole. Swainson's hawks return from Argentina, redtail hawks and mountain bluebirds from Mexico. Wilson's warblers, a tiny being weighing about a quarter ounce, come back from Costa Rica. Robins return from the southwestern United States and Mexico when worms are about in the just-melted earth. Ospreys return from winter habitats ranging into South America when ice leaves rivers and lakes, exposing fish. An osprey nest at the end of Lupine Meadow has been occupied for as long as I can remember. The first time I see an osprey flying along Cottonwood Creek with a fish in its beak I wonder where it's been all winter—Panama, Ecuador, Chile?

Ticks, mayflies, butterflies, and squalla stone flies appear; mosquitoes begin to emerge, though they are never numerous. Geese, ravens, loons, and kestrels lay eggs. Fungi emerge from the wet earth. The planet tilts toward the sun, trillions of bacteria go to work, photosynthesis proceeds.

All these returnees are essential parts of a vast complex whole that is itself unseeable, the web of life constituting the Greater Yellowstone Ecosystem, and their arrival reveals how the integrity of Greater Yellowstone depends on corridors—in the air, on the land, and in the rivers—and on environments, habitats, human acts, and policies at the other ends of these corridors in places far from our national parks and wilderness areas.

We greet the visible returnees with acts of appreciation because we are a species that valorizes the eye and many of our judgments are visual. The very small is seen only with specialized equipment, usually by those experts with specialized interests. The very large—the entire ecosystem—is virtually ignored except by other experts with other specialized interests. Human perception is restricted to a certain scale, just as it is restricted to certain wavelengths of light. The spectrometer and varieties of satellite imaging allow us to see more, each in its own mediated manner, but in general we are indifferent to other spectrums or scales (and there are ecosystems at every scale)—indifferent, that is, until things begin to go wrong.

It's sort of like a body. When things go wrong with the body (itself a collection of ecosystems at various scales) we ask for X-rays and magnetic resonance imaging, swabs and biopsies. Similarly, concern for the health of an ecosystem requires us to adopt different scales of view than those derived from a casual afternoon drive through the landscape. One of the least technical ways of seeing things at a larger scale is to climb a summit and look around.

Although Dana and I are committed to greeting each new arrival, it is difficult for humans to get around in April, especially if you want to climb a summit. Many of the roads in Grand Teton and Yellowstone remain closed. Large sections of Jackson Hole and the surrounding mountains are designated critical winter habitat for game animals and will not open to public entry until May 1. Then, too, cycles of freezing and thawing convert dense snow into large loose crystals that collapse beneath your skis or snowshoes, leaving you crotch-deep in junk, which discourages snow travel in the valleys. Axle-deep mud defends the dirt roads. Places open to the public concentrate people. A dedicated community of skate-skiers, in-line skaters, runners, and cyclists crowd the newly plowed road through Grand Teton National Park while it is still closed to vehicular traffic. But we do not want be on pavement; we want dirt and life, a place to hike, and that means our valley's buttes.

Our prevailing winds are from the southwest, or west, so the southern-facing ridges on the valley's buttes are swept by winds that remove snow, and the direct sunlight melts what little remains. These southern ridges are the first places where you can do steep hikes, even though you must sometimes ski to reach the bottom of them.

One named Blacktail Butte is protected inside Grand Teton National Park, near the community of Moose. Its southern ridges are my first hike each spring. Dana has just moved here from Hawaii and is particularly keen to see greenery and flowers. I've described the hike up one of its southern ridges and down another. As April drifts toward May and the days get warmer, she insists, as though she is affected by photosynthesis, "Let's go to Blacktail Butte."

"That means we have to walk uphill. Horrible thought." I'm a mountain-climbing guide. We've been skiing on the flats all winter and aren't in shape for hills, but I have to get in shape for hills and Blacktail is one of my workouts.

The butte rises next to the main highway through Jackson Hole. It is roughly three miles long and two miles wide, the south section being wider than the north, so that on a map it resembles an arrowhead. The top is 7,688 feet high. Most of its summit and sides are covered with forest, but many of its western flanks are partially bare ridges that extend downward like fingers of a hand.

"Butte" doesn't sound spectacular and Blacktail Butte isn't. It is devoid of alpine environments for which the Tetons are famous; there are no lakes, no streams, and precious few springs. And since it is so near the highway and its constant noise, few people are familiar with its charms. This is unfortunate, since the summit of the butte is an excellent place to survey the valley's structure and communities—both nature's and our own. It is a particularly fine location for seeing the result of geological processes in Jackson Hole. Faulting induced by earthquakes and the consequences of glaciation jump out at you—even amateurs like us can make sense of what happened.

Faults have raised the Teton mountains six miles. Studies over the past several decades by the geophysicist Robert Smith show that thousands of major earthquakes lifted the Teton Range into its towering setting while simultaneously making the valley of Jackson Hole sink. Strangely, his most recent measurements suggest the movements have reversed: the mountains are falling and the valley is rising!

Two of the more recent glaciations have been carefully studied. The first, called the Bull Lake Glaciation, buried the land upon which the town of Jackson now stands beneath 1,500 feet of ice. The second, called the Pinedale Glaciation, retreated only 14,000 years ago, a mere blip in geological time. Plants and animals returned to the rock-filled valley, and the first Native Americans followed them.

Other processes—plate tectonics and hot spots—are less apparent and require knowledge of modern geology. The movement of the earth's crust over Yellowstone National Park's active volcano—the "Yellowstone Hotspot"—leaves earthquake epicenters. Earthquakes rated 7.5 on the Richter scale have occurred in Greater Yellowstone, and it is only a matter of time before a quake of equal magnitude strikes Jackson Hole.

Blacktail Butte is probably the product of complex secondary faults, a medley of limestone, siltstone, claystone, sandstone, and shale, plus generous amounts of loess and debris from glaciations, surrounded by a plain of quartzite cobbles. No one knows why it survived glaciation, but there it stands, isolated, with the dignity that attends isolation.

The base of Blacktail Butte is only a half mile from the main highway. It is one of those warm, luminous spring days you dream of in January, a day for ambling and contemplation. Dana and I hike toward the butte, pausing often to enjoy new flowers and birds. Although our elevation here is only 300 feet lower than the meadow near our cabin, spring is more advanced. The slightest increase in warmth is a difference that makes a difference. Dana begins her welcomes. "Purple delphinium!" "Scarlet gilia!"

Few trees inhabit this plain; there is little soil and the glacial till is so porous water immediately drains into underground reservoirs. Trees present, usually cottonwood, grow along either waterways or irrigation ditches. Two plants of similar height are prominent: sagebrush and antelope bitterbrush. However, interspersed between these bushes are twenty species of grasses and more than one hundred species of flowering plants—a richer community than one would think.

We climb an alluvial fan at the bottom of a dry gulch that suggests that rain was once more abundant than at present. At the top we spot our first Indian paintbrush of the season. After gaining a ridge, one of the "fingers," descending from the summit, we recognize concentric irrigation ditches climbing up the fan beneath us, and faint outlines of fields, probably a homestead that failed in this harsh country.

The 1,200-foot difference in elevation between the sagebrush flats and the top of the butte, plus the many different planes of fingerlike ridges, each receiving different amounts of sunlight, produce a variety of microhabitats, each with its own set of wildflowers. At each new bloom we stop and Dana shouts an appropriate welcome.

"Shooting stars!"

"Phlox!"

"Bluebells!"

As we climb higher, it gets cooler and the variety of flowers changes to those we first saw in Lupine Meadow this spring. Walking uphill is like walking back in time and reminds me that what is natural is always indexed to time. Hence the arrival of flora and fauna is one way of tracking time (technically known as phenology), one used by humans for millennia before the arrival of mechanical clocks in the twelfth century.

The sound of the highway is lost to the wind. The same cannot be said of the noise from airplanes. Beneath us lies the most conspicuous artifact in Jackson Hole, the Jackson Hole Airport, infamous for being the only airport in the nation located entirely in a national park. More than sixty thousand planes land in Grand Teton Park every year, at least seven thousand of them private jets.

The major flight path from the north goes down the Snake River through Grand Teton National Park, right over the float trips, the anglers, the park visitor center, its offices, and a clutch of homes. Many people want to get rid of the airport, but every year it becomes less likely as development and its beneficiaries subvert the national park ideal.

"It hasn't always been this way. I can remember when there were no subdivisions, no log castles, and the airport was slated for removal," I remark.

"Why wasn't it removed?" Dana asks.

"James Watt, former secretary of interior."

The roar of a Gulfstream jet landing at the airport destroys my composure. It glides by, improbably close, a mechanical goose approaching a concrete pond.

The ridge is edged with Douglas fir and with aspen that have been dwarfed by the wind. As we climb higher, the fir diminishes and limber pine becomes more common. The deepest gullies contain patches of dirty snow. Many open areas are still brown—last year's foliage matted from the winter snow load. New flowers peek up through it, every one a phoenix rising from the dead.

We see the first mourning cloak butterfly of the season. A prairie falcon soars over the ridge, hovers momentarily in the updraft, and then dives out of sight. It is a particularly well-named migrant, since it retreats each winter to the Plains states, from the Dakotas south to Texas. A redtail hawk signals its presence high above with its characteristic screech.

The summit on the south end of the butte is capped with flat rocks. Mountains surround us on all sides—the Gros Ventre, Teton, Hoback, and Snake River ranges. The mountains are still white, the valley green with spring growth. The flat rocks are a perfect place to rest and snack. We are both beat. Every year Blacktail seems a bit harder to me.

A red-napped sapsucker lands obligingly in the limber pine next to us and pecks away for five minutes, providing the longest and best view I've ever had of the species. It has just returned from Mexico. We watch it with binoculars as it hops from tree to tree, admiring the bold colors—red, black, yellow, and white—and the intricate patterns on its back.

A fire swept up the lower reaches of the butte last summer. Through the glasses we see patches of larkspur and bluebells, and a yellow field of arrowleaf balsamroot. Fresh green sprouts of grass look like slivers of emerald against the black soil. Six bison graze sagebrush flats further south, and herds of elk roam the cottonwood forest along the Gros Ventre River.

I walk around, searching for cactus—*opuntia fragili*—a plant both widespread and uncommon. Few people know there is cactus in Jackson Hole, and fewer still can find it. An exacting combination of wind and exposure is required for its survival. It is an inappropriately named little plant that can survive sustained temperatures of 40 below 0, lives as far north as British Columbia, and is so tough that gardeners who have planted it claim it is virtually impossible to get rid of—a cactus weed, they say. Soon it will bear a pale yellow flower.

After a while we cannot help but notice the background magnified by our binoculars. The far away and unnoticed becomes near. As we sharpen the focus it becomes obvious that pine and bird and cactus exist within a matrix that is anything but wild and natural.

"Yonder lies Jackson Hole, last of the Old West." I'm quoting a famous sign. Right! Land of the trophy log house, hivelike motel rooms for the worker bees, the stretch Hummer, the Gulfstream jet, miles of irrigation ditches, roads, trails, and fences, a slew of golf courses, two ski areas, the largest building in Wyoming, thirty thousand people a day milling about town in summer, gridlock on the streets, the five-dollar latte, the arnica oil massage. And yet . . . what an interesting collection of people! The reclusive billionaires and the ski bums, the traditional Republican ranchers and a thriving Latino community, a slew of misfit writers and hundreds of nonprofit organizations.

This is my favorite place in the world. Many people find it the epitome of natural beauty, but it is about as natural as it is the last of the Old West—the delusional fluff of travel writers and the Chamber of Commerce.

The view from Blacktail Butte brings out my ambivalence about my home valley, a conflict between beauty and ecological health. I usually assume they go together, and the beauty of Jackson Hole is so overwhelming it's easy to ignore the crisis of its ecological health.

I cherish the parts—the spring beauties, the falcon, the stonefly, the wolf—yet the matrix in which these parts are embedded consists of many mutually interdependent processes—population dynamics, fire regimes, forest succession, river flows, climate, and so forth—all of which have been rendered so artificial from human intervention that I no longer have a sense of exactly what in Jackson Hole remains natural and exactly what it is I want to preserve.

Jackson Hole is not a special case. Development in other towns nibbling at the edges of Greater Yellowstone—Cody, Lander, Pinedale, Afton, Driggs, West Yellowstone, Gardner, Cooke City, Bozeman, Livingston—all artificialize (to coin a term) Greater Yellowstone. Despite its natural beauty I think of Jackson Hole as a *natural artifact,* more like a garden, a hothouse tomato, or a game preserve in Scotland than wild country in Canada or Alaska, a background for people's preferred version of fun—golfing, skiing, fishing, hand gliding, climbing, kayaking, rafting, in-line skating, mountain biking, hiking, snowmobiling, four-wheel driving, birdwatching, motorbiking, hunting, ATV-ing—the list seems endless.

"But it *is* so beautiful," says Dana.

"Yes, a beautiful artifact. It's been a natural artifact since the first Native Americans arrived twelve thousand years ago and exterminated dozens of species; since the mountain men killed off the beaver; since ranchers arrived in the eighteen-eighties and their cattle introduced alien diseases to elk and bison, and riparian lands were planted with alfalfa and other alien plants that changed the kind and distribution of indigenous plants; since those same ranchers and government agencies killed off wolves, bears, mountain lions, coyotes, and eagles to protect their livestock; since various irrigation projects siphoned water from the valley's creeks and rivers until they went dry, and they dammed the valley's artery, the Snake River, and flooded nearly thirteen thousand acres of riparian habitat in 1916, rendering river flows artificial for the past ninety years and leading to a constant juggling act by the Bureau of Land Management in a vain attempt to satisfy Idaho's farmers, local anglers and fly-fishing guides and white-water rafting companies, all the while refusing to insure adequate water levels for the river's insect life (once stonefly hatches coming off the river would cover you like snow, now they are gone); since real-estate development along the Snake River further diminished the riparian habitats and channeled the river into a narrow slot that destroyed fish habitat and jump-started the long-term destruction of the cottonwood forests, all courtesy of the Army Corps of Engineers who built dikes paid for by public monies, simultaneously subsidizing agriculture and real-estate interests and promoting environmental destruction, only to later spend additional millions for further interventions to correct the devastating ecological consequences of their previous efforts; since the quasi domestication of Jackson Hole's iconic animal, the elk, who found their historical winter habitat occupied by fences, cows, houses, people, and began to starve in such large numbers a national outcry led the Izaak Walton League to purchase land that eventually became the National Elk Refuge, a flawed model of compassionate conservation that lacked sufficient area and resources to feed the elk who wintered there so that they were fed tons of elk kibble each winter, kibble delivered by horse-drawn sleds; since keeping elk artificially close together increased the likelihood of wild animals transmitting brucellosis back to cows, causing the state to trap and kill elk and some fools to call for killing all elk and bison to save their beloved cows; since elk were integrated into the local economy as a commodity and hunters, many guided by outfitters, managed the number and sex of the population, and tours among the Serengeti-like winter elk herd on horse-drawn sleds daily plied the refuge habituating elk that would be hunted by humans and Scouts collected the racks cast by the bulls to auction to Oriental medicine manufacturers and crafts folks for knife handles and chandeliers; since we suppressed wild fires and thinned forest around the development to create 'defensible space,' further altering the natural processes of forest succession, even though the Forest Service repeatedly tells anyone who will listen that what the American West does in the summer is burn, that burning is not only natural but as essential to the ecosystem as water; since Grand Teton National Park conducted 'controlled burns' to simulate natural succession even though the controlled burns are never big enough or hot enough to maintain the historical landscape architecture caused by uncontrolled wild fires. And I don't know how to parse all that with the perception that Jackson Hole is an icon of natural beauty, that is my home and the place I love."

Dana is silent. She's lost me to a mind on fire and she knows it. I am exhausted from my rant. And I have said nothing about other scales. The Oxford entomologist J. M. Anderson says that temperate forest soil can support "up to a thousand species of soil animals . . . present in populations exceeding one or two millions per square meter." The mycologist Paul Stamets begins his masterwork, *Mycelium Running*, with this sentence: "There are more species of fungi, bacteria, and protozoa in a single scoop of soil than there are plants and vertebrate animals in all of North America." Can we meaningfully track the consequences of human activity at that scale? Trillions of events are occurring in Greater Yellowstone every second. Trying to understand them is like driving into a blizzard at a hundred miles an hour and trying to analyze each flake as it passes. The Dense Array of Being. Thinking about it makes me dizzy. Yet these multiple, complex, interrelated waves of human artifice have cascaded through Greater Yellowstone for at least 12,000 years, and now the most pervasive human influence is affecting everything—global warming. What's left of "natural"?

An ecosystem is like Humpty Dumpty: all the King's bureaucrats and all the King's biologists can't put an ecosystem back together again. Flora and fauna will adjust or depart for cooler regions farther north. Raccoons arrive from the south. No trout or mountain sheep, but great bass fishing and coon huntin' in Wyoming. And what about new butterflies arriving in the ecosystem? Will we take arms against a flock of butterflies?

Dana leaves for a subsidiary point on the ridge we will descend so I can take a photograph of her with the mountains in the background. This is all so new to her she wants pictures to send to her friends in Hawaii and to her parents.

On the summit she stands with arms outstretched in the universal sign of victory. Again the magnification of the photographic lens throws things into a different perspective. Beyond her stretches the Gros Ventre Wilderness; directly above her head is Jackson Peak, edges of the valley that still harbor wilder things— wolves, grizzlies, mountain lions. We wander into their mountains, they wander into our valley; we live together in a mixed community where the boundary of wild and tame, natural and artificial, is permanently blurred.

I study the Grand Teton with the binoculars. I've climbed it around four hundred times and I have an enduring interest in its being. I study the routes, the approaches, and the trails leading into the canyon beneath it, trails I will soon ascend again. Avalanche debris fills an area called the Meadow. Plumes of snow trail from the summit. Aloof, literally and metaphorically, it seems as timeless as anything I am likely to know.

But I am not seeing. I have left the moment, my lovely wife, the cactus at my feet, the mountain, everything present, to occupy my mind and fret. And since I think best when I am walking, I let my mind wander with my feet.

"Wild" and its cognates have become slippery words. *The Oxford English Dictionary* traces the history of "wild" to the *Corpus Glossary*, a Latin/Anglo-Saxon dictionary compiled in A.D. 725. Interestingly, the Latin equivalent in the glossary is *indomitus*, a word that suggests much of its consequent elaboration. Usage number 7, from A.D. 1,000, is: "Not under, or submitting to, control or restraint; taking, or disposed to take, one's own way; uncontrolled . . . going at one's own will; unconfined, unrestricted." This is Thoreau's sense of the word and why he wished his neighbors were wilder.

The opposite of "wild" is "control," which is defined as "purposive influence toward a predetermined goal." Since we became a distinct species we have influenced all life; it is impossible to be in a relationship without mutual influence. We see this in our own relationships. But influence is not control. Influence is quite compatible with "going at one's own will," or, to use a fancy word, autonomy. Control goes beyond influence; it is an increasing intervention with autonomy that travels along a spectrum, becoming controlling and, finally, abusive.

Why continue to apply the word "wild" to elk that eat kibble inside of fences, or to wolves whose ancestors arrived by air freight from Canada, or to trout whose ancestors were raised in hatcheries in California, or to mountain sheep imported from Oregon? Why call them "wildlife"? Can we use words any way we wish?

Humpty Dumpty is not only a character in a Mother Goose nursery rhyme, he is also a character in Lewis Carroll's *Through the Looking-Glass,* where he epitomizes a common contempt for ordinary language by saying that words mean whatever you fancy they mean. To wit:

> "When *I* use a word," Humpty Dumpty said, in a rather scornful tone, "it means just what I choose it to mean—neither more nor less."
> "The question is," said Alice, "whether you *can* make words mean so many different things."
> "The question is," said Humpty Dumpty, "which is to be master—that's all."

Indeed—who is to be master of the language of nature? Shall conservationists, biologists, and politicians call the shots, or should we start with the dictionary?

I think one distinguishes wild from its opposites the way one distinguishes master from slave. It is a matter of looking at your subject through the optic of control, a filter available to anyone who has ever experienced a relationship with a friend, a spouse, a child, a dog.

Biology and ecology are irrelevant to this practice. Wildness is not a branch of science. There is no biology or ecology course entitled "Wildness 101." The issue is freedom, whether in human nature or the rest of nature, a matter of philosophy, perhaps even religion, perhaps ontology, but it sure as hell can't be quantified. Computer models and statistical greed advance neither the cause of freedom nor wildness; indeed, there is a good deal of historical evidence to suggest they are antithetical to both. Who then is to decide what's wild?

Dana is waiting for me; I can tell from her posture. We have miles to go before we sleep. The ridge, its cactus, its colorful flowers beckon. We drop down the ridge, welcoming both, and then cut across into forest and alarm a cow moose. She snorts and ambles off into some aspen.

Walking down the southern ridge of Blacktail Butte I know,

because I am too old not to know, that one spring I will not return to my valley with the sagebrush buttercups, the ospreys, and the bears. I am, alas, not only an irrelevant part of the ecosystem but an irrelevant *kind* of part. Humans can disappear and the ecosystem will be just fine. Nonetheless, it is unlikely we will disappear anytime soon, and I would like this place to endure with some semblance of its current identity, though I am quite confused about what that might be. I have nothing against racoons and bass, but I prefer mountain sheep and cutthroat trout, grizzlies and our own butterflies, thank you. I realize, however, that I have little personal sense of how the rest of Greater Yellowstone is faring. This year the view from Blacktail Butte made me want to see how it is doing, preferably with Dana, Rio, or friends who know it better than I do, to make my own quite unscientific judgment as to how wild and intact it all is, to study the places I visit, and to bear witness to those travels.

2. Opening Day on the Firehole River

Every year on the Friday before Memorial Day I drive north from Jackson Hole to the Firehole River in Yellowstone National Park. Fishing season opens the Saturday before Memorial Day in the park. I want to arrive a day early to study the river before it is lined with anglers and to visit a favorite fly shop in West Yellowstone. The drive, the study, and the visit celebrate the start of my angling year.

The drive is pleasant, the road relatively free from the spectacle of America dragging its material culture into the last vestiges of the more-or-less-natural world. No procession of RVs towing SUVs, boats, or storage trailers, no gridlock when they stop to see an elk or a bear or a bison, no anxiety of watching people lead their kids up to bison for that fatal home video. The snow has disappeared from the valleys but lies deep in the mountains. The backcountry is devoid of people. The dirt roads are unusable. The snowmobiles have departed. The land and its inhabitants are enjoying a break from the burden of human presence.

Looking out over the mud flats of Jackson Reservoir, I see the Snake River flows, barely, amid swaths of fresh green grass. Serious runoff has yet to begin this year, even though some years it's nearly over by now. A line of white dots makes me pause at a turnout to watch my first white pelicans of the year, a bird Audubon found particularly beautiful and my favorite bird. They have just returned from parts south, the Gulf Coast and Mexico. Thirteen of them are snoozing, floating, their heads turned back toward their butts, their long yellow beaks buried in feathers. I imagine they are on their way to the Molly Islands at the south end of Yellowstone Lake, their only breeding ground in Greater Yellowstone.

Pelicans eat trout; they're predators. So are lots of other creatures, and we usually don't care unless they are eating something we want to pursue for our own pleasure, or if they are after us. Some anglers don't like pelicans. For a hundred years they've complained to the parks about pelicans eating *their* trout. They don't like the seagulls, grizzlies, mink, or otters much, either. Complying with tourist wishes, Yellowstone National Park and Bureau of Fisheries employees destroyed eggs and killed pelican chicks on Molly Island between 1923 and 1930 for roughly the same reasons they killed wolves, mountain lions, and coyotes—fewer predators meant more game and fish and enhanced recreation. In 1926 park employees crushed 200 pelican eggs; in the following two years they killed 200 baby pelicans. Few decisions in the history of the Park Service have been equally ill informed. We're lucky to have any white pelicans here at all. But we do and I look forward to again seeing their graceful flight.

After entering Yellowstone at the South Entrance, the road climbs steeply through lodgepole pine forests and then meanders along the Lewis River on the rim of the Pitchstone Plateau, a mass of volcanic rock that receives up to twenty-five feet of snow in winter. At times twelve-foot high drifts border the road and are cleanly sliced by snowplows.

The river is only occasionally visible, a sliver at the bottom of a narrow canyon 600 feet deep. Even later in the season, when the snow has melted, access is difficult—a nasty scramble on steep scree and talus. The fishing guidebooks say the descent is not worth the fishing, that the trout are neither more plentiful nor larger than in other, more accessible rivers in the area. In *Fishing Yellowstone Waters,* Charlie Brooks is vehement about Lewis Canyon: "[T]he section in the deep, steep, rough, dangerous Lewis Canyon does not hold fish worth either the labor or the risk of going after them.

I did once, when I was young, strong as an ox and just as smart. But never again."

True, but this ignores the beauty and solitude of the canyon's meadows, qualities I find more interesting than the number and size of the fish and well worth the labor and risk of reaching them. Perhaps the trip is more attractive to a mountaineer than to an angler, but I've never had company in this canyon—which is saying something in a national park. Then, too, grizzly bears are common and that virtually guarantees solitude. If someday you have nothing to do and a desire a minor adventure, you can walk beside (and often in) the river from the big meadow at the top of the canyon, beneath the falls, to the South Entrance, a distance of approximately six crow-flying miles. Plan on enjoying a long, arduous day—or two.

I pull over at another turnout to inspect my favorite fishing holes with binoculars. I have to climb up onto a snowbank to do so. The air is clear and cold. The Lewis Canyon is choked with snow. The river is low, its waters black as crankcase oil, and no sound of its passage reaches the rim. I think of this section of the Lewis as our own river Styx, a river worthy of mythology. It looks a bit scary this time of year. I will not venture down to its riffles until August, or later.

Native Snake River fine-spotted cutthroat trout inhabit the canyon, but I usually catch a pure strain of Scottish Loch Leven brown trout introduced, along with lake trout from Lake Michigan, into Lewis and Shoshone lakes in 1890. Waterfalls prevented the native cutthroats from ascending the Lewis from the Snake River to the lakes, but some of the browns survived the falls to inhabit the lower river and compete with the natives.

If the view into the canyon is grim, the view of the land above is grimmer. The great Yellowstone fires of 1988 burned thousands of acres along the Lewis River. Masses of young lodgepole pines cluster around the charred, cold skeleton of the old forest, their tips rising above the surface of the snow. Although the forest lacks its former beauty, it is healthier. Fire is as necessary as water for a healthy lodgepole pine forest because the lodgepole pine requires fire to reproduce. The lodgepole cones do not release their seeds, even after the tree dies. Heat of at least 113 degrees is required to melt the resin that bonds the cone's scales, which in turn releases the seeds. Without fire, a generation of pines matures and dies, leaving heaps of perfect kindling. Sooner or later, one way or another—a lightning strike or sparks from a campfire—lodgepole pine forests burn.

The longer natural fire regimes are suppressed, the larger the fire—the primary lesson of the fires of 1988. Since lodgepole pine is the most common tree in Greater Yellowstone, the entire ecosystem is dependent on catastrophic wildfires for anything remotely recognizable as "natural" regulation. Big fires preserve the landscape architecture we so admire in Yellowstone—especially the vast meadows. This is, of course, a problem, since human beings don't like catastrophic wildfires. And so a century of public policy that sought to prevent wildfire—remember Smokey?—has left plenty of dying trees in our forests, kindling that just can't wait to burn.

Furthermore, drought promotes wildfires. Forests are drier and that in turn reduces the resistance of trees to beetles. The warming climate has reduced the beetle's cycle of reproduction from two years to one year, which means more beetles. More beetle infestation means more dead trees, and more dead trees—an entire forest on the eastern side of the ecosystem near Cody—means more and bigger wildfires. And so it goes. Mother Nature bats last.

Lewis Lake is frozen solid; not a fracture line in sight, not a patch of clear water along the shore. It could be February in Siberia.

Like a commuter who knows each exit on the freeway, I know each side road and parking lot between Jenny Lake and the Firehole. I tick them off as I pass. Trailhead to Heart Lake. Trailhead to the Channel between Shoshone and Lewis Lakes—a fishing spot so beloved it is capitalized in angling literature.

The road climbs again to the first of three passes over the Continental Divide between Jackson Hole and the Firehole. This one is at an elevation of 7,988 feet. South of this gentle pass the water flows into the Snake and then the Columbia. Farther east along the Divide, it flows into the Green and then the Colorado. The water north of here flows into the Missouri and then into the Mississippi.

The headwaters of the West's circulation system lies at this juncture of planes, here a humble lodgepole pine forest that offers no indication of its significance.

Melting snow provides 75 percent of the water in Western streams, and much of that is stored in reservoirs for use farther downstream. In Greater Yellowstone arises the snowmelt that flushes toilets in New Orleans, provides drinking water in Phoenix, pumps fountains in Las Vegas, greens lawns in L.A., and generates electricity in Portland.

The years 2001 and 2002 were the worst two consecutive years of drought in Wyoming since 1896. Studies suggest that the current warming/drying trend will diminish snowpacks and alter the species composition in Greater Yellowstone. Major tree species will either disappear or "migrate" north, perhaps even out of the park, rendering Yellowstone a quite different place than the one we have strived to preserve. You would think folks downriver might be a bit concerned.

Trailhead to Riddle Lake.

Turn off to Grant Village, a horrible mistake of a tourist center the Park Service built in the middle of prime grizzly-bear habitat to appease the Winnebago crowd.

West Thumb, a parking lot with restrooms.

Yellowstone Lake is also frozen, though with binoculars I can see patches of clear water to the east. A long, cold spring this year.

The road climbs again. The second pass over the Continental Divide affords a view south to Shoshone Lake, the largest lake in the contiguous states not reached by a road. It, too, is frozen. Then yet another pass over the Divide and I begin the gradual descent into the headwaters of the Missouri River.

The road crosses the Firehole River above Old Faithful. It flows from Madison Lake, a pocket of water cradled by a curve in the Continental Divide, into the Upper Geyser Basin, where it doubles in volume after joining the Little Firehole and Iron Creek. The Firehole receives over 82 million gallons of water a day from these geysers, some as hot as 200 degrees F. Hence the Firehole is always a warm river.

By the dog days of August it is usually a hot river—dangerously hot for trout. Water temperatures above 77 degrees are lethal to trout, so they hide in the cooler feeder streams. On July 21, 2003, the park closed the Firehole, Madison, and Gibbon rivers to fishing because the trout were too stressed by high water temperatures. If Greater Yellowstone's climate continues to warm, as predicted, the Firehole may soon lack trout.

By the time the Firehole enters Biscuit Basin, where it can be legally fished, it looks like a river, albeit a small river. The snow has melted in Biscuit Basin. The first tints of green brighten the meadows. The grimness of the Pitchstone Plateau and the Lewis Canyon seem like another country, yet another reminder of Greater Yellowstone's diversity. Bison and elk graze alongside the road, year-round residents of this comparatively tropical paradise; others lie about, chewing, oblivious to the gawking tourists and traffic that have intruded on their paradise.

I stop at several places to study the river, which at this time of year is a tea-colored surge flooding the meadows, running high along the sinter banks near the geysers and sporadically inundating the lodgepole pine forest. I walk out onto a bridge and stare down into the water. Tiny blue-winged olive mayflies (*Baetis tricaudatus,* for those who worry about such things) flitter about in great numbers. There are a few yellow-green pale morning duns, a dignified little being blessed with the beautiful species name *Ephemerella.* Iridescent dragonflies soar by, gorging themselves on smaller insects—especially, I remind myself, mosquitoes and blackflies. The wind is blowing hard out of the southwest, ruffling the water. During strong gusts the mayflies cling valiantly to the logs and bridge before being blown away. Soon they cover my hands and face, though I can barely feel their presence.

The road up Fountain Flats—my favorite place along the river—is closed. In the past it was open all the way back along the west side of the river to a place named Goose Lake Meadows. Forty years ago the loop at the end of the road was a gathering place for Firehole cognoscenti. One could learn a lot by hanging around in the parking lot and listening to them talk, their conversations laced with expertise and wit. Now, even when the road is open, you can drive only a mile or so; the rest has been turned into a bike and hiking path. The park will open the road tomorrow morning.

Ninety-three bison graze the meadow. This year's crop of calves—to my eyes the most Pleistocene-looking babies on the planet—gambol and frolic, nurse, and sprawl on the grass so listlessly you might think them dead. Waterbirds float upon the river—mergansers and mallards, two trumpeter swans. A killdeer wanders along the shore, pecking. Canada geese have built their nests on islands isolated by the flooding river to make it harder for predators to reach them. Their creamy white eggs will be the size of avocados.

I usually drive the road up the Firehole Canyon to Firehole Falls for no reason other than to see them again, but the road is closed. A sign warns that a boar grizzly has taken up residence. I do not reach my reserved tent site in the Madison Campground until early afternoon. I have lingered, intentionally. The prelude, alas, is over.

The Madison River begins at the confluence of the Firehole and the Gibbon rivers. It should be one of the most beautiful meadows in the park but the Madison Campground, a monster facility with 277 campsites, occupies it. Dana, who is always more charitable than I am, calls the Madison Campground "a parking lot with trees." There are beautiful campgrounds in Yellowstone, but this is not one of them. It is, however, ground zero for some great fishing.

I have reserved a campsite with my credit card, which is quite a contrast to the old days when I simply drove in and slept on the ground close, very close, to my truck so I could roll under it if I was fondled by a bear—which has occurred twice.

While I set up my tent, four kids—my neighbors—stamp on every ant in sight. Their parents are figuring out how to erect their tent, a contraption nearly as large as our cabin. In its present state the tent looks like it was struck by a tornado. After watching me set up my tent—one pole, eight stakes, no floor—they glance hopefully in my direction. I ignore them but decide the kids need a sermon on food-chain dynamics.

I suggest to the kids, as kindly as I can, that if they stamp on all the ants, the fish and birds will have nothing to eat. They run to their mother, who scowls at me as though I've abused her children. Having momentarily given up on the tent, their father bashes a soggy log with a hatchet. I flee to West Yellowstone and the refuge of a fly-fishing shop.

Like every great fly shop, Blue Ribbon Flies is a sanctuary for obsessives, and one of the things obsessives desire is information about the object of their obsession. Before I reach the door of Blue Ribbon Flies I am confronted with a blackboard posting information of interest only to those attuned to an arcane language. Are there Flavs? PMDs?

I tempt the Fates by entering to look at gear, though I do not need any gear. I have enough fly-fishing gear for a platoon. But . . . fly-fishing gear is not a matter of need. How many poems by Rilke do we need? Soon I am in consumer mode: How can I possibly fish without Frog's Hair Tippet—the thin material attached to your fly? Won't Polar Bear Zelon—basically, white plastic—alleviate my primary failing as an angler: not being able to see my fly? Perhaps some new glasses; the thin, black, wraparound, polarized jobs that will make me look like a senile Batman. I gaze, I study books.

Blue Ribbon Flies is owned by Jackie and Craig Mathews. Jackie is an expert angler and serves on the board of the Greater Yellowstone Coalition, Greater Yellowstone's largest and most prestigious conservation organization. Craig has authored or coauthored the definitive books on fishing Yellowstone's waters, and was named Angler of the Year in 2005 by *Fly Rod and Reel*. He is also an ardent bird hunter, an elk hunter, a saltwater angler, and the former chief of police of West Yellowstone. Their charm and infectious enthusiasm have caused me to give them far too much money over the years.

Craig is behind the counter. We shake hands. He asks, "See any bugs?" He loves bugs and knows as much about the bugs in this region as anyone. He also knows how to imitate them, too. He's created a slew of memorable fly patterns—concoctions of fur, feathers, hair, and plastic that very loosely resemble various bugs. I tend to buy lots of them, most of which I do not need any more than the Batman sunglasses.

The truth of the matter is that I like to give Blue Ribbon Flies my business. Their catalog features membership forms for conservation organizations. In 1997 Jackie and Craig began self-taxing Blue Ribbon Flies 2 percent of its annual gross sales and giving it to local conservation groups. In 2001 they founded with Yvon Chouinard, of Patagonia, the "1% for the Planet" club, a collection of businesses that rely directly on natural resources and pledge 1 percent of their gross sales to help protect them. I prefer shopping at stores that support this fine program.

On the wall of the store is a commemorative plaque thanking the Mathews for helping preserve one of my favorite holes on the Madison River, a place with the charming name of $3.00 Bridge. Often unmentioned, but not unnoticed, is that Jackie and Craig have courageously opposed the use of snowmobiles in Yellowstone National Park in a town that bills itself as the Snowmobile Capital of the World. In short, Blue Ribbon Flies is a model of what stores in Greater Yellowstone, and everywhere else, could and should be. Business is simply too powerful a force not to play a key role in local conservation.

I escape with only one box of flies. A large new box, it is true, containing sixteen flies. And a package of Polar Bear Zelon. And only one spool of Frog's Hair Tippet.

On the drive back to the campground, I linger by the famous pools along the Madison. Other anglers are doing the same. From them emanates an ineffable sense of reverence. We stare intently at foam lines, calculating the drift of a fishing line in the strong currents, watching for bugs, for rises. The Madison and its upper tributaries—the Firehole and the Gibbon—are hallowed water, matched in fame by only a few American streams. They have a history, a literature, a tradition, and one behaves accordingly.

When I arrive at my campsite I find that my neighbors have left. The tent must have defeated them, or perhaps the kids ran out of ants. The disfigured log lies forlornly in the iron fire ring, memorialized by a halo of chips. Dinner consists of cold beer and a huge steak, barely cooked.

I first saw the Firehole River in August 1960 while driving through the park with a friend in a pink 1957 Ford convertible. We stopped at Biscuit Basin because it seemed—and still seems—the most beautiful little trout stream in the world. But we did not fish.

When I returned to the Firehole in July 1962, I was not what I would call an angler, even though as a child I had fished a lot with my father and grandfather. I was a klutz in hip waders with a handful of bright red "Humpy" flies in my shirt pocket and a 7½-foot Fenwick fiberglass pack rod. The Humpy, a concoction of deer hair, imitated no known insect. It was intended to attract trout with its flamboyant color and size—at least that was the theory. I thrashed the river, I lashed the air, and I lost Humpies to the weeds—all to no avail. I never caught a fish.

I would have preferred to believe there were no fish, but, unfortunately, several men around me not only caught fish, they occasionally caught big fish. Between bouts of frustration I sat on the bank and watched the scene through my binoculars. They resembled figures lifted from Norman Rockwell paintings—old hats, baggy chest waders, reading glasses, and vests stuffed with fly boxes. Their casts, their patience, and their gravity implied beyond doubt that flyfishing was a serious matter. Watching them I learned something important: they used tiny flies. When they finally quit, at twilight, I accosted one of them in the parking lot.

"Why do you use such little flies?" I asked.

"Little bugs," he replied.

"But how do you know which fly to use?"

My ignorance led to a lengthy lecture at the end of which he suggested I read Ernest Schwiebert's *Matching the Hatch*. When I got back to Jackson Hole I managed to find a copy. It had a sulfuryellow dust jacket with a line drawing of a man surrounded by swarming insects—a man not unlike the gentleman who had recommended the book to me. I read several pages and put it back on the shelf. It was too complicated, filled with Latin, illustrated by delicate watercolor paintings of what appeared to me to be nearly identical flies. There were no photographs. When I mentioned the book and its support of small imitations to a friend, he dismissed it with a laugh. "Fag fishing," he said.

I fished in Colorado when it was still possible, if you worked a bit at it, to spend a day on the Platte, the Frying Pan, the Gunnison, or the Roaring Fork without seeing another angler. I caught fish with my gaudy flies. But I didn't return to the Firehole.

When I went east to graduate school I felt like a hick who was in over his head. To cheer myself, I pursued the traditions I had brought with me from the West—rock climbing and fly-fishing. Eventually I drove down to the Beaverkill, another legendary river. I threw flies for a day. I was skunked.

Following that humiliation (neither the first nor last of my fly-fishing humiliations) I escaped to a diner in the town of Roscoe. When I left, I noticed the sky was filled with the largest hatch of mayflies I have ever seen, millions of them, all backlit by the sun. I was irritated that I had no idea what they were—they were simply . . . bugs. At that point I remembered the little sulfur-yellow book.

I bought a copy and was soon immersed in the esoterica of aquatic entomology. On page 121 I found the following paragraph on the genus *Baetis*: "The diminutive size of these May flies often leads anglers to consider them of little importance. No greater mistake could be made. My stream notes are filled with days that were successful because of this species. One morning on the Biscuit Basin stretch of the Firehole I moved forty-two trout of some ten to eighteen inches. They were all raised on the Iron Blue Dun and none were retained. The hook of my imitation was size twenty."

I studied Schwiebert as assiduously as I studied Plato, making copious interlinear notes and translations from the Latin with an extra-fine black pen. That copy lies at the bottom of Colorado's Blue River, the result, let us say, of a swim. My wife bought me a second copy. I gave it to a much better angler than I am in a moment of generosity—it had by then become a rare book. My third copy sits on a shelf, little read but fondly remembered. These days I admire

Schwiebert's delicate hand-painted plates of mayflies as much as I admire his elegant prose, for they retain a Victorian dignity most modern fly-fishing books lack. And his final chapter—"On Ethics and Philosophy Astream"—distills into a few pages the unique civility that should characterize our sport. I still begin each fishing season with a pilgrimage to Biscuit Basin.

Dawn is chilly, Homeric, rosy streaks of sky mixed with leaden clouds. I make coffee and oatmeal on my single-burner stove. Then I make more coffee for the thermos, cupping my hands around the stove for a bit of warmth. I stuff a dozen cookies into a fanny pack and break down the tent. My truck will be warmer than my campsite, and more pleasing. Soon I am cruising around, looking, parking, looking, walking. No hurry. There is no reason to arrive on the Firehole early except to avoid people; the fishing won't be good until the sun warms things up.

The Fountain Flats road is open now. The surrounding meadows are pale with frost, nearly matching the patches of snow in the forest. The white accentuates a group of ink-black ravens pecking at the bones of a winter-killed bison.

The cold increases the volume of vapor in Midway Geyser Basin; great masses of it billow across the sky to the south. The heavens are pearl gray, the Firehole a pewter gray, and the vapor ash gray, all of which makes the landscape vaguely martial. Howard Back, who served in the Royal Engineers in World War I, says in *The Waters of Yellowstone with Rod and Fly,* the first classic book on Yellowstone fishing, that Midway Geyser Basin reminded him "of the Somme as it appeared in 1918." Nothing has changed.

And yet all this gray and cold bodes well for fishing, especially if it begins to rain or snow, and it looks like it will. Patience.

Ten o'clock. I glass the river for hatches, waiting, savoring the Yellowstone tourist experience: elk and bison, a small black bear, two osprey that aren't catching fish, a red-shafted flicker, a muskrat, a group of ruby-crowned kinglets in the lodgepole pine, red-winged blackbirds, spotted sandpipers, and a greater yellowlegs in the shallows. The frost is gone, revealing flowers that were hidden earlier: dandelions (an alien weed), spring beauties, an unusually pale—as though bleached—lupine yarrow, mountain stars.

As always, the human element is also worth observing, too. My favorite find is a Peter Built truck-RV home, white and silver, heavy on the chrome, and the size of a long-haul rig—a fishing mansion for the postmodern trout bum who has everything.

Squads of anglers pour from vans, decked out in $5,000 worth of fashionable clothing and gear. They speak Latin with their guides, talking bugs. I find it disconcerting in that odd way that leads the mind to nostalgia. I remember those old somber men and their witty, down-to-earth discussions. I remember Sheridan Anderson, whose comic book—*The Curtis Creek Manifesto: A Fully Illustrated Guide to the Strategy, Finesse, Tactics and Paraphernalia of Fly Fishing*—remains the best introduction to the sport. I remember Sheridan sitting in a folding chair next to his truck in the parking lot of the Climber's Ranch, a hostel in the Tetons. He was tying flies on a simple C-clamp vise clamped to the tailgate, fetching what would now be considered a dismal collection of materials out of junky cardboard boxes. I remember when "trout bum" (and "dirt-bag climber") named an authentic form of life, not an advertising strategy. I remember my father's fishing gear, which he used all his life, gear that was cheaper and simpler than anything you can buy at Kmart. I remember the sacred respect accorded my grandfather's Granger bamboo rod and Hardy reel.

Whether from experience or from the dozen or so books on fishing the Firehole, everyone knows what bugs are hatching on opening day. What is revealing is how they are referred to. One possibility is *Hydropsyche cockerelli*. Or, rather than the seemingly Latin bug, a fly-pattern designed to imitate it—"Elk Hair Caddis" or "Tan X-Caddis." "Little brown caddis" suits me just fine. And "Mother's Day Caddis" is more pleasing to my ear than *Brachycentrus occidentalis*.

Unless I am fishing below the falls, my fly selection devolves into two kinds: mayflies and caddis flies. Instead of carrying the various sizes and color variations, I carry only the smaller options. Like my

unknown mentor said: little bugs. For the ubiquitous *Baetis,* I have
A. K. Best's classic Olive Quill Dun, a little beauty about the size of a
pencil eraser. Sometimes I can actually see it, or at least believe I can
see it. Hence I add, at the last moment, Craig Mathews's version, an
Olive Sparkle Dun, which I can see. Then an imitation of the spinner
stage, a Rusty Spinner, its outstretched wings made from a fluffy plastic something whose relation to the petroleum industry I would just as
soon remain ignorant of. The pale morning dun is larger and more
colorful.

Most other hatches will be caddis flies, tan, gray, or black. I use an
Elk Hair Caddis for the tan one, a Henrysville Caddis for the gray,
and a scruffy little black thing of unknown origin for the black varieties.

Only two kinds of nymphs—a trim Pheasant Tail and a shaggy
Golden-Ribbed Hare's Ear, both in size #16—will have to cover
both mayflies and caddis.

Enough? Nope. I need a Griffith's Gnat in size #22 for midges
and a tiny red Serendipity to imitate the larval stage. Why red? After all, Serendipities come in many colors. Because red is the last
vestige of my old Red Humpies and my totemic color. Fly-fishing is
not a rational activity.

I add a few Adams, the most beautiful of all mayfly imitations.
Just in case, though I cannot explain what "just in case" means. And
I must have a few Royal Wulffs, size #16. I can see Royal Wulffs
when I can't see anything else, and, besides, they have red bodies.

This all fits in one small black box that I carry in my fanny pack.
One side consists of tiny compartments, each with its own flip-up
top. The other side is lined with a sheet of foam into which I stick
the nymph imitations. The box cost as much as a case of wine.

This seems like a lot, but it is not. I'm a minimalist. Many anglers
carry hundreds of flies; some carry thousands. When Craig Mathews lost his fishing vest several years ago he lost *7,000* flies! Now it
is true that Craig is a fly tier par excellence, but on the other hand,
one of his competitors, and another great fisherman, George Anderson, maintains that he could catch 90 percent of his fish if he was

limited to two flies: the Adams and the Golden-Ribbed Hare's Ear. I think he's probably right. Do we need all these flies? How many poems by Rilke do we need?

What rod to use? This is another grave matter, one that bears only obliquely on questions of efficacy. For the Firehole, I favor my $8\frac{1}{2}$-foot Winston rod for a #4 line, a beloved object, even though the company's onetime motto—"Not just a fly rod, but an opportunity to redeem yourself for every compromise you've ever made"—made me puke. I've forgiven them, in part because the motto is gone, in part because I needed (as it were) to purchase more Winston rods.

Thus armed, I approach my prey, the wily trout, a critter with a brain the size of a BB and a long history of humbling large predators armed with high-tech rods and flies.

A big storm is brewing to the south. The air is still. I walk down the river past half a dozen anglers. One is talking on this cell phone, his head cocked at the telltale angle. His rod tip lies submerged in the river and a long arc of line is lodged in a weed bed. The cell-phone tower near Old Faithful—and four others that provide partial coverage in the park—has incurred the wrath of some—"the death of solitude in national parks"—and pleased those who claim cell-phone access is required for emergencies. This chap's emergency features the weather and his commodity futures.

The park is addressing the issue in predictable fashion by developing an "antenna management plan" and studying the possibility of more cell-phone towers, wireless Internet access, and perhaps even TV and radio service throughout all of Yellowstone. Fortunately, a great group called the Coalition of Park Service Retirees is gnawing on the butts of the current park administration, trying to prevent this dismal piece of "progress." May they prevail. Otherwise . . . welcome to the Yellowstone National Cyber Park!

I walk faster, praying that no one is at my spot. Unless you are weird, privacy is essential to fly-fishing, hence the angler is one of the four kinds of recluses venerated by Taoists. Have you ever seen an advertisement for fishing gear featuring a horde of anglers?

Tee-hee: the river is lined with people but no one is within a hundred feet of my hole—as much privacy as I can hope for here on opening day. Insects carpet the water. The banks here are steep and undercut, perfect for sitting and perfect for big trout to hide under. They are also indicative of a healthy stream.

I sit on the bank with my legs in the water and look. Two bison bulls, 2,000-plus-pound monsters, are lounging near the river. They ignore me. There is a faint hum of insects. I get out my binoculars. Soon my waders are covered with tiny black caddis. Indeed, three kinds of caddis are fluttering about in characteristically frenzied fashion, along with an occasional blue-winged olive. I believe, without careful examination, that most of them are gray. I tie on a Henryville caddis.

The storm is closer. The clouds are an ominous steel blue that painters know as Payne's Gray. Peals of thunder somewhere near Old Faithful seem to be moving in my direction. The wind gusts and then suddenly goes calm. Darkness descends. I take off my sunglasses to better see what I'm about.

Fish are feeding on caddis flies along the banks. I select a sipping shadow along the bank and cast across and slightly up, trying, without much success, to track my dark fly in the failing light, all the while wishing I was fishing a Sparkle Dun with that glittering little fuzz of white plastic made from the oil that starts wars in the Middle East. But it's OK. A twelve-inch rainbow takes the fly and jerks to the side, hooking itself with no effort on my part. Soon it is at hand in the shallows. I roll it over and release the barbless hook with a hemostat. It darts into the nearest weed bed. My first trout of the year.

As the wind dies, the sky fills with snow, big gentle flakes the size of quarters. Everything is hushed. The anglers in the meadow above me disappear into a murky pallor.

> *How timely*
> *the delight of*
> *this snowfall,*
> *obliterating the mountain trail*
> *just when I wanted to be alone!*

Obliterating this mountain river, too. Old Saigyo knew.

Though I can barely make out the surface of the river, I know a hatch is underway. The water around my boots is covered with *Baetis*. Swallows are diving madly at the surface. Anglers have been known to hook swallows under these conditions. Visibility is too poor to use the Olive Quill, so I tie on an easy-to-see Olive Sparkle Dun and cast into the falling snow. Between the flakes and the dimples they make when they hit the water, I can occasionally see my fly.

Cast. Cast. Cast. The delicate green line drifts upon the flowing water, the limp gossamer tippet faithfully ignores eddies and swirls, the fly fades into a white blur, the universe shrinks. I watch, mesmerized. Then the tug.

The storm passes, the sun shines, the wind freshens, blows hard, then harder still, so hard my fly line quivers in the air like a banner. I have to thrash the rod downward to get the fly on the water, which is very unpleasant.

I spend the afternoon fishing near the Nez Perce picnic area. I nap, and then I watch heartier anglers flail. A bison bull nearby is doing much the same in a mud wallow. But I grow bored, so I wade the river to a spot where I once caught a large fish—eighteen inches long, I like to think, though that was long ago and an angler's memory inflates all victories. It has been a long time since I've caught a fish that large in the Firehole, though Blue Ribbon guides who know the river well still help clients catch twenty-inch browns. This is catch-and-release fishing, but I presume they are not catching the same fish. Never know about guides, though—cunning folks with a vested interest in catching fish.

I drift nymphs into the eddy, without success.

Time for dinner. On a picnic table with a view of Fountain Flats I heat a can of soup on my stove, drink a glass of wine, and watch the action. Bison hairs flutter from the planks of the table where they have rubbed their backs. There are elk droppings in the grass. I smell both animals, though neither is present. Several women wrapped in blankets are nestled in chaise lounges along the river bank, watching their husbands cast erratically into a stiff wind.

Another nap, another contemplation.

For a place central to the history and traditions of American fly-fishing, the Firehole River is a study in irony and tragedy. Irony, because before 1889 the river above the falls in the canyon contained no fish. Rudyard Kipling, who visited Yellowstone is 1889, wrote, "There is a stream here called Firehole River. It is fed by the over-flow from the various geysers and basins,—a warm and deadly river wherein no fish breed."

We stocked the trout in the upper river. Adding an alien fish to a stream is bad; adding three alien fish crosses a threshold that exceeds an ecosystem's resiliency. It can't continue to organize itself in its own manner, and the cumulative consequences of this change cascade up and down the food chain in ways that soon affect nonbiological factors, like the amount of oxygen in the water. Another ecosystem's integrity is lost, though the landscape—the scene we find so compelling—remains the same visually.

A tragedy, because the stocking of the aliens affected fish that were indigenous to the river below the falls. The westslope cutthroat and the Montana grayling are gone: there are no viable populations.

In short, no stretch of the Firehole River is the same as it was when Yellowstone became the world's first national park in 1872. Nor can we do anything about this situation now. Removing the alien trout will not reestablish the original flora, fauna, and nonbiotic relations in the stream. It's the Humpty Dumpty Deal: once you screw up an ecosystem, all the King's bureaucrats and all the King's biologists can't put it back together again. It's gone. Finito.

How could such an ecological disaster have happened, especially in a national park?

A coterie of fish culturists and anglers, abetted by the U.S. Fish Commission, began, in the second half of the nineteenth century, to redistribute trout populations according to human desire rather than evolution's verdict. Devoted to the now-common technological premise that if something can be done then it should be done, and eager to leave no body of water free of favored prey, they transported fish stocks all over the planet. Beginning in 1889, brook trout from the Northeast, brown trout from Scotland and Germany, and rainbow trout from California were stocked in the Firehole, the Madison, the Gibbon, and in most other rivers and lakes in the park.

This massive redistribution of trout went both ways. The Commission created three cutthroat trout egg collection stations in the park and a hatchery on Yellowstone Lake. By 1915, five million Yellowstone cutthroat trout eggs were shipped to other ecosystems and disrupted natural processes there just as much as their indigenous trout disrupted Yellowstone's ecosystem.

Thus the hallowed Firehole is a completely artificial fishery, and to call the trout here wild is absurd. I reserve that classy appellation for: (a) populations that arrive in their habitat under their own power and not by cargo ships, trains, strings of pack animals, and buckets; and (b) fish that survived on their own, enduring the exacting perils of evolution, not those that survived with the assistance of our ministrations. If "wild" doesn't satisfy those minimal conditions it is bleached of meaning and no longer marks a useful distinction. Modern ecological notions of an intact ecosystem tend to privilege having all the parts and ignoring whether the parts are natural or artificial, just as they tend to suppress the consequences of having populations of alien organisms mucking up the system. Imagine Greater Yellowstone is like a human body with numerous artificial organs and limbs that is beset by more than 200 tumors. Then decide whether that body is intact. Hard call, I'd say.

In the past several decades these alien trout were joined by other aliens, rendering many of Greater Yellowstone's aquatic ecosystems even more artificial.

Whirling disease, which affects trout, salmon, and grayling, is caused by a parasite that works its way into a fish's nervous system and then attacks cartilage, creating deformities that inhibit feeding and reduce the fish's ability to avoid predators. Whirling disease was first described in Germany in 1903. By 1958 it was in Pennsylvania, probably arriving from Europe in frozen fish. It is now found in most Western states, including all those surrounding Greater Yellowstone. It arrived with shipments of fish from various hatcheries;

by anglers carrying them on their waders and boats; by stream habitat degradation including loss of streamside vegetation from grazing, degradation that favors parasites; by waterfowl and perhaps other birds.

Anglers are upset at the disruption of their fisheries and have suggested several ways to develop resistant hatchery populations, from genetically reengineering the species to importing a resistant strain of rainbows that have been isolated in Germany for the past 150 years. (Brown trout seem relatively immune.) These would, in turn, be used to restock populations of rainbows throughout the American West. I think of this as second-generation artificiality.

If Yellowstone's alien rainbows were the only trout affected by whirling disease, cynics might say that anglers got what they deserved for manipulating trout populations. But whirling disease has infected indigenous cutthroat populations in the Yellowstone River and several tributaries to Yellowstone Lake, including Pelican Creek and Clear Creek. Both are important cutthroat spawning streams.

If whirling disease is a nasty bug, the New Zealand mud snail is a nasty plague. This blandly named little gastropod is a menace worthy of Stephen King's imagination. She—they are all female—reproduces by parthenogenesis (do-it-yourself reproduction, or cloning) and it is prolific. A single mud snail can produce fifty offspring in each reproductive cycle, and it has six cycles a year. That means that a single mud snail can produce, directly and indirectly, more than 300 million identical mud snails in one year.

In the Greater Yellowstone, no known predators or parasites inhibit this catastrophic growth. On the Firehole, mud snails can reach densities of 700,000 or more per square meter. On one stream in Montana they constitute 97 percent of the biomass, virtually eliminating other macroinvertebrates. Populations of mayflies, caddis flies, and stone flies—the trout's primary food—decline. Mud snails pass through a trout's intestine unharmed. They occupy a streambed all the way down to bedrock. They are hard to kill. Scientists predict they will continue to spread throughout Greater Yellowstone's waters. No one knows what to do about this, either, though genetic engineering is again mentioned.

How this has affected the Firehole is much debated by experts more knowledgeable than me. My own *impression* is that there are fewer bugs and the quality of fishing has declined.

Whirling disease and New Zealand mud snails are bad news, but they are only the tip of the alien species iceberg. Alien zooplankton are on their way and the alien zebra mussels are not far behind. The National Park Service spends considerable money each year trying to control some aliens. Both the National Park Service's Strategic Plan and Yellowstone's Master Plan are committed to the reduction and containment—not, it is worth noting, the elimination—of alien species to maintain "natural, environmentally regulated ecosystems." Given the historical trajectory of the Firehole and its inhabitants, what "natural" means here has devolved into "environmentally regulated."

Not all aliens are created equal. No one talks seriously about doing away dandelions or mountain goats. Shall we take arms against a flocks of alien butterflies? We go after knapweed and whirling disease, but there are no plans to eliminate alien trout from Yellowstone.

It is best not to talk about this plain fact. Even to suggest that alien trout should *in principle* be eradicated from national park waters causes normally mild-mannered anglers to express everything from dismay to a desire for your imminent death. So these beautiful, adored intruders from Germany, Scotland, New Zealand, California, and Labrador will continue to duke it out with other aliens and, alas, with the ecosystem's natives. And no one really knows what is going on at the micro level, the most important level of the food chain, the level with the greatest diversity and greatest import. The cumulative consequences of all these battles are not only unpredictable, they are not even contemplated, although in due time they, too, will be subject to regulation in the name of a natural and intact ecosystem.

Decisions about alien species mirror decisions about endangered species. Neither has much to do with conservation science, unfortunately, and much to do with what people like and will fund. How much do we care whether the riffle beetle or the sage sparrow survives?

Craig Thomas, the late Republican senator from Wyoming, explained the majority view succinctly while stumping to reform—I would say eviscerate—the Endangered Species Act. "We should put the emphasis on preserving species that benefit people, are fairly widespread, and have played a role in our development in history," the senator said. Ecological integrity has no place in such a policy. Indeed, it is counter to ecological thought because it suggests, yet again, that what's really important is, well, us.

It is evening. The wind has dropped. Most anglers have left in disgust or retired to dinner. I take one last drive up the Fountain Flats Road before heading home. Halfway to the parking lot I stop to watch a touching scene: a man is teaching his two daughters to cast. They stand in the river on the far side, near the bank. The father hugs one daughter, holding her arm, helping her flex it, seeking that magical *ah-hah* moment when the elements of casting come together. The other daughter is downstream, casting awkwardly, but casting. Unfortunately, she is casting straight down the river, laying her line on the water in a manner such that her fly cannot drift naturally but hangs in the current, creating a wake. This is a classic beginner's mistake. I am both amused and charmed.

Then she catches a big fish that jumps two feet in the air. She screams, her father shouts encouragement, and she stumbles downstream grasping her rod in both hands. The trout is pulling her. I reach for my binoculars.

Swarms of tan caddis hover along the bank. Hydropsyche, X-caddis, Elk Hair Caddis—whatever you wish—they are fairly big and tan. I drive to the end of the road, suit up, and sprint upriver to my favorite spot, though perhaps "sprint" is not the best word to describe an old man running in chest waders.

There is only one other angler on the river, a big fellow with a funky fedora and a silky, graceful cast who over the next hour catches three fish to every one of mine—and I'm doing well by my standards.

By the time I leave it is what I would call dark. The father and his daughters are gone. The women and their chaise lounges are gone. The big fellow, so like the masters I saw here more than forty years ago, still casts gracefully to the bank. I watch him from the parking lot, a shadow against pale rippling water, an acolyte who would no doubt please Father Izaak Walton.

I break down my rod and put the sections into the rod sock and the rod sock into its tube. As I drive south toward the three passes along the Continental Divide, I gnaw on chunks of cold steak. Big drops of rain splash the window. Then, as I gain elevation, snow falls—big, gentle flakes drifting down from the heavens.

3. Modern Wolves

- ▶

The Lamar River rises in the Absaroka Range along the northeastern boundary of Yellowstone National Park and flows northwest to join the Yellowstone River near Tower Junction. All of the river, approximately forty miles in length, and most of its tributaries lie within the park. After converging with Soda Butte Creek just south of Druid Peak, it flows through a broad and fertile basin known as the Lamar Valley. Many visitors judge the Lamar Valley to be the most marvelous place in Yellowstone, largely because of the presence of bison, elk, pronghorn, coyotes, bears, and wolves.

The Lamar has always been admired. Osborne Russell, the most literate of the mountain men, wrote of the Lamar in his *Journal of a Trapper,* an account of his travels between 1834 and 1843: "There is something in the wild romantic scenery of this valley which I cannot nor will I, attempt to describe but the impressions made upon my mind while gazing from a high eminence on the surrounding landscape one evening as the sun was gently gliding behind the western mountains and casting its gigantic shadows across the vale were such as time can never efface from memory."

The valley remains much the same, though the Snake Indians Russell met—"neatly clothed . . . contented and happy"—are gone and a paved highway follows its northern edge. Until recently the valley attracted mainly anglers,

wilderness travelers headed into the backcountry, and tourists curious to enter or leave Yellowstone by a less traveled road. The Lamar
was a good place to see wild animals, but it was not a must-see destination like Old Faithful.

Wolves changed that. Seventy years after being eradicated by
park rangers, the first wolves reintroduced to the Rockies under the
mandate of the Endangered Species Act were released at various locations along the Lamar River. The habitat was perfect and they
flourished. By 2006 their progeny had spread throughout Greater
Yellowstone, providing modern conservation with one of its greatest
success stories. Wolves replaced bears as the prize sighting, and the
Lamar became *the* place to watch wolves, not only in Yellowstone,
but in the world. Now it is definitely a must-see destination and the
mise-en-scene for the phenomenon of wolf watching.

Several decades ago I was devoted to the cause of wolf reintroduction. After they were reintroduced I came to the Lamar to see
them. I saw three. I still remember how pleased I was to see wolves
in Yellowstone again. Since then I've traveled to the Lamar mainly
to fish. But wolf watching in the Lamar has become such a phenomenon that I wanted to return to see the wolves again and the
people who were watching them with such pleasure.

Early June. Dana and I are sitting in the sagebrush on a bench above
the Lamar River with our friend Charlie Craighead and a throng of
wolf watchers. We are delighted to be with Charlie, because we enjoy his company and because he has a knack of seeing more than
most people, and certainly more than we do. He is both a naturalist
and a writer, his most recent book being *The Official Guidebook of
Grand Teton National Park.*

Although he lives in Jackson Hole, Charlie spent a good chunk
of his life in Yellowstone. His father, Frank Craighead, and his un-
cle, John Craighead, through various articles, television specials,
books, and research, did more than anyone else to make grizzly
bears known to Americans. Charlie tagged along, sometimes as a

very junior researcher. In the process he received an education in the natural world rare in its day and nearly impossible now.

Their research convinced the Craigheads that bears and other wildlife needed more habitat than what was preserved in Yellowstone and Grand Teton national parks. They popularized the concept of a greater Yellowstone ecosystem, leading to public and federal acceptance of what was becoming obvious to other, more theoretical branches of science, especially island biogeography.

Thirty-seven other wolf watchers are sitting with us along a sagebrush bench. Perhaps a hundred more occupy other turnouts along the road this pleasant late spring evening, all looking, waiting, and watching. Nothing is happening in this American Serengeti, at least nothing of interest to those who confuse nature with television's adrenaline-pumping nature specials.

Despite the monotony, an undercurrent of latent emotion radiates from the group. In *A Society of Wolves,* park ranger Rick McIntyre notes that in his experience wolf sightings were emotional events: "Some people cried, others embraced family members, and a few hugged the nearest government official."

More accurate names for this evening's assembly might be "wolf lovers," or "wolf groupies," or perhaps even "wolf believers," for they seem faithful followers of a new Order, people waiting to be consecrated by the sight of a beast whose mere existence often rouses in nonbelievers a mixture of hatred or disgust.

Whatever the most suitable name, the audience is varied. Some are locals who, one woman assures me, come here every night; some are tourists driving past and wondering what all the fuss is about; some are pilgrims who have journeyed to spend months near wolves; some are professional photographers and cinematographers working on their portfolios; some belong to commercial wolf-watching classes organized by conservation organizations; some are students working on dissertations; some are park biologists; and a few are park rangers trying to retain a semblance of order in what has become an almost daily spectacle, even in the depths of winter.

Before us stretches the spacious valley, serene under the soft blush of evening light. The remaining patches of snow on the mountains glow a mellow yellow. The river—here a continuum of pools and riffles—is tan from runoff. Except for the highway at our feet, nothing human intrudes on the scene—except people on the sagebrush bench and in the turnouts. It feels archetypal: a tribe sitting on a rise above a plain upon which wander wild beasts, a place not unlike our original mythological Eden, a time before the rat race of modern life. Then, these animals were our prey, our sustenance, and a mirror of our own life and death. Now, perhaps, they are even more laden with meaning.

We screw spotting scopes onto tripods and check settings on binoculars. Dana and I laze in our Crazy Creek chairs—folding contraptions of aluminum, nylon, and foam—and sip tea from a thermos Dana is never without. We glass the animals. Two pronghorn. A coyote studying the pronghorn. Several groups of bison. A lone cow elk. A marsh hawk (which ornithological authorities now insist is a northern harrier) dipping in casual undulations above the sage. But we are not here for these beings, however interesting and beautiful. The show has yet to begin; the key actors remain hidden in the wings.

I am suffering from glass envy. Our old Nikon spotting scope and Zeiss binoculars seem low-rent compared to the glass around us. Charlie has a Leitz scope with an angled viewing prism and a variable power lens plus new Leitz binoculars. Swarkowski spotting scopes—up to $2,000 a whack—are common. Some of the cameras sport lenses as thick as small trees.

Good glass means optical intimacy. Likely the wolves will be so far away we will want to look at them through glass. This feels oddly normal, actually, since most of what we have seen and know about wolves comes from optical images, in photographs and films, on television and computer screens. What most of us know are virtual wolves, as it were. And how many of us want to be close to wolves without intervening glass between us? Not many.

Charlie scans the mountains for grizzlies with his binoculars as casually as most people watch the evening news. He is of medium height, solid, with sandy hair going to gray, a mischievous grin, and twinkling eyes. His manner is that of a man amused by something no one else is aware of yet.

Then, softly, he says, "Grizzly, two o'clock from that patch of snow."

We search with our binoculars, and yes, there's a grizzly, a mere spot to the naked eye, but clearly visible through the 10-power glasses.

Charlie rotates his spotting scope and cranks the magnification up to 60-power. He takes a quick look, smiles, and motions to Dana. She's delighted; she loves watching animals, especially moose and bears, and she adores Charlie—to my slight irritation. I find the grizzly with my Nikon spotting scope, but want to look through Charlie's brighter and more powerful lens. Closer is better, though what counts as closer here is peculiarly modern.

While Dana and I are admiring the grizzly, Charlie announces, softly again, so as not to bother the group, "There's another one." We readjust scopes and binoculars. This one is closer still: a sow with a cinnamon-colored cub.

"Another," he says, with his mischievous smile.

"Really," says Dana, taking the words right out of my mouth. We are having trouble believing we are surrounded by grizzly bears.

We look. Yep, there's another grizzly in a meadow on the lower slopes of Amethyst Mountain, pawing at roots. Its shoulders heave and tug like a dog wrestling a stick from its master. Several people adjust their glass and look.

"Another," Charlie whispers.

The crowd is respectfully silent and quietly amused. This grizzly is on the hill behind and above us, a thousand feet up a ridge at the edge of the forest.

And so it goes. While waiting for the wolves to make their entrance, Charlie locates six grizzly bears. It makes me wonder how many grizzly bears I don't see when I am in the mountains without Charlie. I am not afraid of wolves or mountain lions, but grizzlies are another matter. I prefer to know they are present before we are *really* close, and I prefer to know before they know—idle preferences, however, since the chances of this being the case are low.

Some of the wolf watchers speak a language understood only by the faithful, as in "Last night I saw 21M and 42F." It is as though we have stumbled into a lodge of Masons.

These wolves are numbered. The letter is added to indicate male or female, although it is not always used in speech between those who know the wolves being discussed. They are usually numbered in the order they are captured after being shot from helicopters with anesthetic darts. While tranquilized, they are subjected to blood tests and given antibiotics, vitamins, and usually fitted with a radio collar that can cost up to $2,500. Without being captured and collared there is no way of knowing where the wolves are or how many there are and what they are doing, and this would undermine the goals of wolf management.

Collaring is essential to most scientific studies of wolves. What biologists have learned about wolves and their effect on the ecosystem cannot be overestimated, and there are reasons to believe their presence has already increased biodiversity. It is a tangible instance of the first law of ecology: everything is connected to everything, even things you would not expect, like the connection between wolves and willows.

Nor can the consideration and passion for wolves on the part of park biologists be overestimated, either—it has been well beyond what is required of them. Some speak openly about wolf addiction and needing a fix. More controversially, they suggest that by reintroducing wolves they have reintroduced the "wild," as though that rare quality could be shipped air freight from Canada.

Unfortunately, collaring is also a means of control—a cop collars a criminal; a farmer uses a collar to manage draft animals; a prostitute collars her sadomasochistic john; a parolee wears an ankle collar. A collar entails a power relationship. There is nothing wilder than wolves and more symbolic of wildness. To collar a wolf says a lot about our attitude toward the wild and reminds us of the continuity between the control we mete to animals and the control we mete out to people, of their freedom and our freedom. Technologies ignore species differences. As soon as barbed wire was used to confine animals in a space it was used to confine *people* in a space; ranching became a model for mass control, first of prisoners and then of anyone who opposed state interests. Like us, the Lamar wolves live with regulations, policies, and laws; they inhabit a culture of surveillance, a mixed life of individuality, autonomy, and domination under the constant eye of federal and state managers.

And they are being integrated into our economy. We have a new tourist mecca, a well funded, open-ended science project for federal, state, and academic biologists, and a fresh marketing ploy for conservation foundations. After the wolf is delisted from the Endangered Species Act, trapped and hunted wolves will generate a booming trade in wolf trinkets—wolf hats and coats, stuffed wolf heads, wolf rugs, wolf claw necklaces. In short, wolf reintroduction did not establish wildness in Yellowstone, it created a new phenomenon: modern wolves. I prefer the old-fashioned kind.

Knowing a wolf's number and collar frequency are gateways to knowing an astonishing amount of information about it, rather like knowing a person's Social Security number and computer passwords. A wolf without a number and collar is anonymous: no control, no knowledge. A wolf with a comparatively low number is a celebrity, a wolf worthy of mention, and when the number is mentioned it is assumed you know who the wolf watchers are talking about: as in *What are Brad and Angelina buying now?* Wolf watching in the Lamar has become a branch of celebritology.

Web sites lovingly track wolf activity in the Lamar and elsewhere. You can even take courses on cyber tracking with a handheld computer and a GPS. When a celebrity wolf dies, its death is featured on the Internet and in local newspapers. Its history, lineage, and importance for the wolf recovery effort are spelled out in what is essentially an obituary. The death of ordinary wolves—like the deaths of the rest of us nobodies—is disregarded.

There are also Web sites seething with hostility that provide instructions on how to kill wolves with poison. The preferred poison has accidentally killed a lot of dogs.

---------➤

Several wolf watchers in the audience are communicating with other wolf watchers via radios, rather like cops on a stakeout. One group is stationed across Soda Butte Creek, on a point with a view of the den where the subject of all this attention—the Druid Peak Wolf Pack—live their exceptionally public lives. They must find our attention a tedious bore.

"Any sign?"

"Nothing yet."

The sky turns pink. A lick of breeze troubles the pools in the river. The riffles sing. The crowd is happy, alert, smiling.

Then a sentence surges through the audience like an electric current: "There they are!"

Across the valley, on the flats between the river and the distant line of forest, spread over perhaps two hundred yards, thirteen wolves lope through the sagebrush. Seen individually through the binoculars one might momentarily mistake a single wolf to be a dog out for a casual run with its master. But as a group they are mysterious and ominous: it is something about their number, their sense of mission—and especially their pace, which is steady. It conveys no evidence they might ever tire; it is as unhurried and relentless as fate.

Watching them, the glass between us disappears. I am among the pack in optical intimacy. My mind's eye stretches to be closer. I do not know what "close enough" might mean, but I want to be closer.

Most are gray, a few are darker, perhaps black; it's hard to tell in the fading light. Elk, bison, and pronghorn watch them pass with no visible anxiety. All know what's going on. The pack has a mission, but these peacefully grazing animals are not the targets of that mission and they know this.

No one says a word. We have been silenced by awe.

The wolves lope down the valley and disappear from sight.

People speak excitedly but quietly, the volume appropriate to a church or a bank. "Where did they come from?" "And so suddenly, without warning . . . ?" "Why didn't the other group see them?" "Where are they going?" "Why?"

Like everyone else, we dash for our van like a horde of soccer fans and drive in convoy down the valley. Another crowd tells us where the wolves are. A ranger is waving and yelling, trying to prevent people from parking on the road.

In the dim light we see the pack gathered around a carcass, but it is too late, even with Charlie's sophisticated glass, to observe their behavior. We keep watching anyway, staring at shadows moving among shadows, bound by an ancient force we do not understand.

"What are they feeding on?" Dana asks.

"It's probably an elk. At least I think it's an elk," replies Charlie.

In the Lamar, wolves tend to prey on elk; one study showed that 92 percent of the wolf kills in Yellowstone were elk. Wolf packs will also kill bison. Killing a bison is not easy, even for a wolf pack. They have to learn how to do it. Wolves eat coyotes and cougars, even a grizzly cub when they can. So far they have not killed many mountain sheep, and they are too smart to waste their time chasing pronghorn. But they are not the apex of the food chain, however. Whatever they kill, they have grizzlies to contend with. Grizzlies are dominant and will drive wolves from their kills.

Finally a man who was present when we arrived says, "It's an elk, a cow." We stare into the darkness. Somehow knowing that doesn't make a difference. What we really want to know is deeper. Why are we obsessed with this creature? I have seen many large predators in my life—various bears and mountain lions—but I have never been in awe of them the way I am awed by a wolf pack hunting.

Musing, I realize that it is the overt nature of their predation; the chase in the open, the kill unfolding with all its terror, the visible feeding, the bloody faces. In this way the Lamar seems more like Africa than North America. The clarity of the hunt forces the issue of compassion—for predator and prey, the drama of life and death, the deepest drama of our soul.

Most people I know have compassion for the prey. I like to show them a great photograph by Tom Mangelsen of a cheetah chasing a

Grant's gazelle. The photograph is blurred, capturing well the speed of the chase. The gazelle looks heavy, and the darkness around its eye sockets suggests a death mask. At first glace you feel compassion for the buck. The cheetah, a female, is gaunt, her face less than two feet from the gazelle's haunches. The photograph is known as "The Great Chase." I call it "Life and Death." It is interesting how people's emotions change when you add information. The cheetah has cubs nearby and her energy reserves are taxed by constant nursing—a mother doing her best for her young. Does that make a difference? And then: the gazelle escaped death; it outran the cheetah. Do you feel compassion for the cheetah? Her cubs?

The wolves feeding on this cow elk have pups. Somehow their successful hunt must be balanced with my sorrow for the cow elk. The Lamar, more than any place I know, forces you to work at that balance. And your conclusion will determine more than just what you feel about wolves, it will to an important degree determine what you feel about nature, life, and death. That is quite an achievement for a little valley in Wyoming.

When we leave it's nearly 10:00 p.m. More persistent groups still fill the turnout, staring into darkness, still talking wolf talk in hushed tones.

While driving back to our camp at Slough Creek we discuss the other obvious question: Why, after this nation's tragic unrelenting war against the wolf, did we arrive at this unrelenting love of the wolf? How did some people overcome their cultural conditioning? What changed?

Our war against the wolf has been charted in excruciating detail by biologists, naturalists, and historians, most recently by Jon T. Coleman in his excellent *Vicious: Wolves and Men in America*. We began killing wolves as soon as we landed on the shores of what would become America, the killing did not cease, and our actions went well beyond any reasonable defense of game or stock or people. Wolves were humiliated, mutilated, and tortured, often with what can only be described as glee. The historical record suggests not defense but sadism. There are inexplicable, irrational hatreds hidden in the human soul that are eternally fresh, the blend of fear and ignorance we see in Rwanda, Bosnia, Palestine, and Kashmir. Wolves suffer from the same blend of fear, hatred, and ignorance.

As soon as Yellowstone became a national park the army units administrating it started killing wolves. After the administration of the park was transferred to the newly created National Park Service, park rangers killed wolves. Between 1914 and 1926, rangers killed 136 wolves in Yellowstone. Park rangers also killed mountain lions. Later they killed 229 grizzly bears in five years after they stopped feeding them garbage in front of bleachers. They killed white pelicans. They killed elk because there were "too many"—an unintended consequence of killing wolves and lions and bears. Now the park is killing bison—there are "too many" of them, too. In the winter 2006, with the help of the State of Montana, they killed more than 900 bison.

The reasons for killing seem as endless as the killings. Outside the park, the U.S. Fish and Wildlife Service—the agency charged with reintroducing the wolf to the Northern Rockies—is killing wolves. In Rocky Mountain National Park, the park service has hired professional hunters to kill elk, at night, with silencers and night-scoped equipped rifles. The State of Oregon recently decided to kill 40 percent of its cougars.

One of the anomalies of modern conservation is that institutions created to preserve wildlife spend much of their time and energy killing the beasts they are charged to preserve. And like most anomalies, it is only resolved by a deeper truth: these institutions have replaced evolution, the root process of wildness, with humanly structured systems of value, belief, and control. The salient process now is scientific management, the manipulation of populations according to computer models and politically motivated "target populations."

The federal government has already killed hundreds of wolves— more than 150 in 2006 alone—and the head of the government's wolf-recovery effort, Ed Bangs, says, "If you have 1,000 wolves, and you want 1,000 wolves next year, you have to kill 300 wolves a year."

The older I get, the more scientific management seems to consist simply of killing. It turns out that the population of wolves providing entertainment, knowledge, commodities, and a Swiss cheese of "ecosystem integrity" can only be preserved by the perpetual sacrifice of the "surplus population."

How many wolves were in Yellowstone, or in Greater Yellowstone, no one knows. Ernest Thomas Seton estimated 10,000 to 20,000 wolves roamed Wyoming in the late 1800s—and that was after trappers had been killing them for decades. According to Al Langston of Wyoming Game and Fish, "In 1853 the American Fur Trading Company shipped out 3,000 wolf pelts from posts along the Yellowstone River. By the mid-1860s, these same outposts were shipping out 5,000 to 10,000 wolf pelts a year."

Systematic killing of the wolf began in earnest with two simultaneous and intertwined events: the arrival of the rancher and the decline of the wolves' natural prey due to our slaughter of the once-great herds of bison, elk, and pronghorn. Deprived of their natural prey, wolves turned to livestock; the states responded by placing bounties on their heads. By 1914, the wolf population in Wyoming dwindled to around 1,000. The following year, Congress created a predator control unit of the Biological Survey. It proved all too efficient. Wolves, it turns out, are very easy to kill if you know what you are doing. When the government formally terminated its wolf-eradication program in 1941 few, if any, wolves inhabited our "Wild West." During this entire depressing, shameful history there is not one account of a human being injured by a healthy, wild wolf.

How wolf hate transmogrified into wolf love and the reintroduction of wolves to the West is a story with many heroes. Passage of the Endangered Species Act in 1973 set the stage. Barry Lopez's seminal study, *Of Wolves and Men,* introduced many readers to the wolf and its fate. Farley Mowat's *Never Cry Wolf* (and the movie based on it) forced anyone with an open mind to question the image of the wolf in "Little Red Riding Hood." Biologist David Mech's many publications, based on a lifetime devotion to wolf ecology, provided the backbone to modern wolf science. And a consortium of environmental groups, such as the Defenders of Wildlife and the Wolf Fund, aroused pubic support.

In January 1995, after two decades of scientific studies, public hearings, and 160,000 written comments—the majority supporting wolf reintroduction—the U.S. Fish and Wildlife Service, under the courageous leadership of Mollie Beattie, introduced fourteen wolves from Alberta, Canada, into enclosures along three tributaries of the Lamar River at Crystal Creek, Rose Creek, and Soda Butte Creek. After a period of isolation to allow them to become accustomed to their new home, the wolves were released.

In January 1996, seventeen more wolves, trapped in British Columbia, entered holding pens in Yellowstone. Five of this group, a pair of adults plus three yearlings, became the famous Druid Peak Wolf Pack. Additional reintroductions were carried out in Idaho. Montana had its own incipient population, mainly near the border with Canada.

Wolf reintroduction succeeded beyond anyone's wildest expectations. As of the fall of 2006, the U.S. Fish and Wildlife Service estimates that more than 1,200 wolves now live in the Northern Rockies. The avant-garde arm of the American conservation movement scored a great victory.

Unfortunately, wherever there is an avant-garde, there is a rear guard—the derriere of humanity. No sooner had the wolves been released than it became obvious that wolf hatred was alive and well in America. What was, and is, at issue are *ideas* about wolves. Wolf reintroduction was fundamentally an intellectual battle—and it still is. As Ed Bangs says in his typically wry manner, "Wolves and wolf management have nothing to do with reality."

In April 1995, only a month after the first wolves were released from their pens, the alpha male of the Rose Creek pack, Number Ten, a magnificent, bold, 122-pound fellow nicknamed "The Big Guy," was shot near Red Lodge, Montana, by Chad McKittrick, a local reprobate. McKittrick decapitated Number Ten, skinned him, and stuffed the head and pelt into a plastic garbage bag.

Eventually he was arrested. For many in Montana and Wyoming,

McKittrick was a hero. Locals bought him beer; he signed autographs; he rode in the July 4 parade in Red Lodge, Montana, wearing a pistol on his hip and a T-shirt that said NORTHERN ROCKIES WOLF REDUCTION PROJECT. After being found guilty, the local magistrate gave McKittrick six months in detention and a $10,000 fine.

Fortunately, Ten's mate, Number Nine, and their pups were found by biologists and returned to their original enclosure at Rose Creek. There Number Nine raised the first wolves born in Greater Yellowstone in sixty years. Her descendents constitute a large percentage of the wolves in Greater Yellowstone.

Although ranchers have legitimate concerns about predators, some people just hate wolves, and they are not nice people. Renée Askins, who founded and ran the Wolf Fund, a nonprofit devoted to reintroducing wolves to Yellowstone, received death threats from wolf haters. That was not unusual in the 1980s and 1990s. The head of another nonprofit promoting wolf recovery left Wyoming because of death threats.

One threat came after Renée agreed to give a wolf lecture in Dubois, Wyoming, a ranching and logging community northeast of Jackson Hole. She asked me what she should do. Renée is an uncommonly courageous and tenacious woman who spent years driving around Greater Yellowstone in a dilapidated car, often in the middle of winter, giving lectures supporting wolf recovery. She has a smile that can melt nails. I was very much in love with her at the time and I didn't want her to be intimidated. I replied in my best macho style, "Not to worry, Askins, I'll go with you."

We drove to Dubois in *my* dilapidated car. I left a loaded, sawed-off .12-gauge shotgun in the front seat and walked into the lecture hall armed with a 9 mm semi-automatic, extra magazines, and a snub-nosed .357 magnum in a small-of-the-back holster. Not everyone in the environmental movement is a tree-hugging pacifist. You may wonder why we didn't simply call the police or the sheriff. If you wonder that, you wouldn't understand the answer.

The audience was divided by a wide aisle. On the west side sat members of the environmental community, out to support Renée and wolf reintroduction. To the east were concerned ranchers and wolf haters. I sat down in the middle of them. I was not amused.

After Renée finished her polished and persuasive lecture, she asked for questions. Immediately a huge man in overalls stood and asked "Who pays your salary?"

Renée replied that she didn't have a salary. And this was true: she ran the Wolf Fund on pure passion and intellect. I had nicknamed her "the little engine that could."

Nonplussed, the man said, with considerable pride, "My grandfather killed all the Indians and wolves and grizzlies in this valley and I don't want any woman from back East telling me what to do."

No one said a word. But then, this is Wyoming. He could have said that his grandfather had killed all the Jews in the valley and no one would have said a word.

The man sitting next to me rose and stated that the wolves in British Columbia had devastated the mountain sheep population. What did Renée think about that?

Renée replied she didn't know about the situation in British Columbia, but that since wolves and mountain sheep evolved together, she doubted one would eliminate the other.

The man next to me went on: "I hear they aren't going to be able to hunt deer in Minnesota because of the wolves killing them all."

I turned to him. "That's inane."

He stared at me blankly. "Look," I said, "I'll bet you a hundred dollars hunters killed more than a hundred thousand deer in Minnesota last season."

He sat down and stared at me, cold. I gave him my best smile. It was so quiet you could hear people breathe.

Not much more was said after that. After all, as Ed Bangs said, wolf reintroduction was not about reality, and wolf haters have no interest in facts. We drove home to Jackson Hole, my eyes glued to the rearview mirror.

In 2006, there were 3,000 wolves in Minnesota. The deer population was estimated at over a million and increasing. Deer are so numerous they are considered pests. Hunters killed 200,000 of them.

Over the border in Wisconsin, 45,000 deer were involved in vehicular accidents, five times more than were killed by wolves. As Friedrich von Schiller said, against stupidity even the gods fight in vain.

Nearly twenty years later, in her book, *Shadow Mountain: A Memoir of Wolves, a Woman, and the Wild,* Renée reproduced several of many nasty messages left on the Wolf Fund's answering machine. This one is typical:

"Yeah, as far as I'm concerned you can just fuck all them wolves. Shoot every one of those motherfuckers right between the eyes. Skin their pelt. Sell it. Only thing you can do with 'em. Ain't worth shit. All they fucking do is eat sheep and chase cows. They fucking suck. Just like goddamn coyotes. Just shoot the motherfuckers. Kill every last one of the bitches. Fuck 'em all. And fuck your nonprofit organization. All you're doing is fucking over people and trying to make 'em feel sorry for the bastards they don't know what the fuck they can do. Them wolves are more fucking problems than a guy knows what the fuck to do with. The guy that gets this fucking message can shove it up his ass. If it's a bitch she can suck my dick, all fucking eight inches of it, down her fucking throat."

A decade of living with wolves has not reduced the hyperbole and posturing. In 2003, Robert Fanning, chairman and founder of Friends of the Northern Yellowstone Elk Herd, claimed that "the Yellowstone ecosystem has become a biological desert," that "the largest migrating elk herd on Earth [the northern Yellowstone elk herd, which in 2003 numbered around 9,000 animals] will be completely extinct in three years," and that "entire communities in Montana will vanish because no one spoke up for social justice for the people who were forced to live with wolves."

Like the elimination of deer in Minnesota, none of these predictions were borne out by subsequent events. In 2006, the Yellowstone National Park biologists estimated the northern herd at more than 8,000, substantially fewer than it was when wolves were reintroduced, but research suggests that the main causes for decline are hunting and ongoing drought. Elsewhere, elk populations are booming despite the presence of wolves. Communities bordering Greater

Yellowstone enjoy meteoric growth, and an economist estimated that wolves were worth $35 million to local tourism.

And so it goes. A Wyoming senator proclaimed that if wolves were reintroduced to Wyoming, children would not be safe at school bus stops. Fremont County, Wyoming, "outlawed" wolves and grizzlies. A Wyoming Game and Fish biologist was disciplined by the governor for speaking candidly about wolves at a public forum in Montana. Most deplorably, the Bush administration ran advertisements using the wolf as a symbol for terrorists.

Every human structure is created and maintained by dualism. When we established where wolves should be, we thereby established where they should not be; where they are safe, and where they can be killed with impunity; who can artificially sustain their lives with antibiotics and vitamins, and who can subject them to torture. From the beginning, the structure proposed by wolf reintroduction was a token population managed by killing the "surplus" of reproduction, a model derived from Aldo Leopold's influential text *Game Management*, a model that mimics not the logic of nature, but the logic of a chicken factory.

Leopold said, famously, "To keep every cog and wheel is the first precaution of intelligent tinkering." The wolf was a missing part, whether cog or wheel I do not know. If "part" and "tinkering" sound a bit mechanical, well, they are mechanical, and "tinker" also has regrettable associations with incompetence. Dictionaries define "tinker" as "a mender of metal household utensils," "one who enjoys experimenting with and repairing machine parts," "to manipulate unskillfully," "to fiddle," and "to meddle." This is a surprisingly accurate description of the theory and practice of wildlife management.

Some people who fought for wolf reintroduction didn't want to tinker. My own interests and goals were not scientific but ontological. I wanted the American West to *be* a certain way, a place where populations of beasts could *be* wild and *be* free, not constructed, artificial, and controlled. I believed the American West was one of the last places on Earth where this was possible, and in retrospect I regret we did not wait for natural populations to migrate south from Canada, a process that was already well underway but hindered by the isolation of Greater Yellowstone from similar ecosystems farther north. Without corridors to other ecosystems we resort to artifice.

With being listed as threatened under the Endangered Species Act comes being delisted under the Endangered Species Act, and I fear what will happen when wolves are finally delisted and managed by the State of Wyoming. After a wolf population reaches a "target population" they can be removed from the act's protection. This target population has been exceeded. Idaho, Montana, and Wyoming have submitted management plans to the U.S. Fish and Wildlife Service over the past several years and Idaho's and Montana's were accepted, Wyoming's was rejected because the plan lacked sufficient controls on human-caused wolf mortality. Wyoming Game and Fish biologists had recommended that the wolf be a trophy game animal statewide, but the state legislature ignored their expert advice, licked the feet of the agriculture lobby, and proposed the wolf be given a dual classification. In Yellowstone and Grand Teton national parks, wolves would remain protected. In some areas adjacent to Yellowstone and Grand Teton, wolves would be classified as trophy game animals managed by hunting seasons. In the rest of the state, including other wilderness areas, the wolf would be classified as a predator and as such would not even be protected by the State's anticruelty laws. Wolf haters will be free to do anything they want to a wolf—shoot them, burn them, torture them, you name it. The state legislature and the governor intend to immediately legitimize the slaughter of hundreds of wolves, thereby reducing the population to the absolutely bare minimum required by the federal delisting process.

Thus the price of keeping all the parts of the ecosystem—by reintroduction, public spectacle, aggressive management, and killing—is high, very high. If given a voice these modern wolves might have well chosen to remain in Canada.

September, dawn, Soda Butte Creek. Ranger Rick McIntyre can usually be found along the Lamar highway from around 5:00 a.m. to

8:00 a.m. and 6:00 p.m. to dark. Another ranger told me that Mc-
Intyre has been watching wolves in the Lamar for more than five
hundred days without a break. He has authored two fine books on
wolves. No one knows more about the Druid Peak Wolf Pack. He
stands in the middle of a group of avid wolf watchers, dispensing
information and talking on his radio.

There are nineteen vehicles in the parking lot. Some people sit in
their cars and trucks waiting for the action, their idling engines
tainting the crisp morning air with diesel fumes.

Mist rises from the creek; a small hatch of caddis flutters about in
crazed fashion. The Lamar is golden now, the aspen and cottonwoods, the grasses. The first dusting of snow covers the highest
peaks. The river is low and clear. The elk are fat, their fur a rich, polished tan, their mane a dark chocolate. Bulls are collecting harems,
touting their virility, posturing. Some grasshoppers have survived
the frosts. I find one among the sagebrush, stiff with cold. I warm it
in my hand until I feel its legs begin to move. Then I let it go.

A few people stand about stomping feet to keep warm. The usual
array of high-tech gear glitters in the morning sun. A clique of
wolf-watching regulars talk wolf talk.

"We saw a griz chasing five wolves near the mouth of Crystal
Creek."

"I saw three wolves chase a mountain lion off an elk carcass near
Slough Creek. That lion went up a tree like lightning. The alpha female kept lunging at it, probably eight, ten feet. Never seen a wolf
jump so high."

"There's a sow across from the ranger station on the south side of
the river. In the driftwood along the shore. She chased a cow and
calf. The cow made it, the calf didn't. Cow finally stopped and
looked back. Three times she stopped and looked."

McIntyre is the master of ceremonies for the Druid Peak Wolf
Pack. His job is to educate the public about wolves and he loves his
job. He fields questions on everything—wolf biology, the location
of the various packs, identifying marks of various wolves, their ge-
nealogy, their personal quirks, and their interpersonal quarrels. If

you love wolves, you can happily spend hours listening to him—which is what you do when there are no wolves to watch. This morning there are no wolves to watch.

We drive back and forth to various parking lots looking for action. Several miles up Soda Butte Creek we spot a gawky moose calf running wildly, clearly spooked. Then it lies down in deep grass under some spruce, its ears alert, watching the hill behind us.

Two hours later we return. The calf is still in deep grass, watching the hill. Three men are standing next to their campers in a parking lot, their tripod-mounted cameras pointed at the hapless moose. They tell us his story.

"A cow moose with two calves swam the swollen creek. That calf there in the grass got swept downstream and barely reached shore. The cow and the other calf went up the hill without searching for him."

"She left him and isn't coming back," says another man.

Perhaps, but the calf is doing what it is supposed to do: lay low and wait for Mom to return. Between the mother and her calf lies a road streaming with traffic, and a clutch of humans—including us. But perhaps she has indeed abandoned the weakest of her progeny, a common event in the wild.

The men are bored. They have their pictures of a cute moose calf. What they are waiting for is the kill.

We head to Silvergate, a town just outside the park boundary with a year-round population of 20. We want breakfast at the Log Cabin Café, the closest restaurant to the Lamar and one of our favorites in Greater Yellowstone. Because of covenants in place since 1937, Silvergate retains the ambiance of old Montana. The buildings are wood, either log or siding. No junk shops with rubber tomahawks. An entrepreneur from Atlanta has bought up most of the town and he intends to keep it this way. Unlike nearby Cooke City, there are several fine places to spend the night.

The café is crowded with wolf watchers and their leader, who is still expounding, unaware that some people have heard it before and would prefer to eat in relative silence. As always, I am pleased with the quotations on the menu. Emerson and Muir might be expected, but "Trees are the Earth's Endless Effort to Speak to the Listening Heaven," a line from the Nobel prize–winning Indian poet Rabindranath Tagore? How did the Bengal Renaissance reach Silvergate, Montana?

On the wall is Parks Reese's poster entitled REINTRODUCING THE WOLF, 1995. Against a background of the Lamar Valley, a man shakes hands/paws with a wolf. Behind him is a welcoming procession of elk, ground squirrel, deer, mouse, rabbit, moose, and pronghorn. The rest of the wall space is littered with mounted trophies: mountain sheep, moose, deer, mountain goat, pronghorn, several bear skins, a stuffed rainbow trout. All our complex hodgepodge of relations to the wild are manifest right here in this restaurant: the wild animal as archetype, idea, resource, exotic intruder, prey, commodity, decoration, recreation, and entertainment.

After our meal we check the Lamar for wolves. No wolves.

We drive to the steep cliffs of Barronette Peak to watch mountain goats and immediately spot seven. It's easy: through binoculars, their white coats stand out from the dark surrounding rock.

Like the foreign trout imported into Greater Yellowstone, mountain goats are aliens introduced from the Pacific Northwest to the Beartooth Range by the State of Montana as a sop to the hunting fraternity, the very people who pay the salaries of those who did the importing.

The goats soon spread across the border into Wyoming and Yellowstone National Park. Idaho also imported goats into the western edge of Greater Yellowstone, and that population spread into Wyoming, too, occupying an area slated for wilderness consideration by Congress on the north side of the Snake River. Now Greater Yellowstone supports a thriving population of mountain goats whose habitat is virtually the same as that of the indigenous mountain sheep, a species that is in trouble.

Goats are more aggressive than sheep; one study found that goats displace bighorns five times more often than bighorns displace goats. They can double their population in nine years. They devour mosses and lichens crucial for stabilizing fragile alpine soils, they eat rare alpine plants, they create wallows that fragment or destroy crucial habitat. In short, mountain goats are a self-inflicted ecological mess, a mess that no one will do anything about because, unlike wolves, everyone *likes* mountain goats. And, alas, wolves don't seem interested in eating goats.

We drive back to the Lamar. No wolves. The Soda Butte parking lot is empty save for a lone Winnebago. An elderly couple sits at a card table under an awning, playing cards. We head back toward Silvergate to look at Icebox Canyon.

An hour later we are back at Soda Butte. A few people are about. Three wolves have come and gone, we're told. They are down valley, but no one seems to know where.

After another hour of increasingly frantic driving, we decide to stop, exhausted. Wolf watching is not a fuel-efficient activity. Dana sunbathes on a spot of grass next to Soda Butte Creek while I paint a watercolor of *the* Soda Butte, an odd sinter cone next to the road.

At dusk we are back at the junction. The usual crowd is there, too, but no one has seen a wolf. The disappointment is palpable, as though after having waited all day to see an opera they had been turned away at the door.

As the parking lot empties, ranger Rick McIntyre says, "A slow night."

4. Alpine Tundra: The First Domino

The Beartooth Highway extends sixty-four miles between Cooke City and Red Lodge, both in Montana, although for much of that distance it passes through Wyoming. The middle section of the highway lies atop the Beartooth Plateau, one of many expanses of alpine tundra—Hellroaring, Silver Run, Froze-to-Death, Line Creek—separated by deeply cut glacial valleys. All are part of an uplifted block of Precambrian granite and gneiss, what geologists call a "batholith." This block is the largest mountain mass in Greater Yellowstone and the largest contiguous land mass more than 10,000 feet in the lower forty-eight states, a vast pedestal in the sky where walking is easy and the days are lonely.

At Beartooth Pass, 10,974 feet, the highway becomes the highest road in Wyoming. (The bear's tooth that gives its name to so many features is a pinnacle near Beartooth Mountain that resembles a tooth.) For several miles on either side of the pass it winds above timberline before dropping steeply into a gorge through which flows a lovely stream called Rock Creek. From late spring until midsummer a stunning display of alpine wildflowers borders this section of the highway, and for those willing to walk the plateaus the pageantry can be enjoyed for hundreds of square miles. Each year I make a pilgrimage to these plateaus to look at flowers and walk in the sky, for the sky here is so all-encompassingly spacious that walking seems akin to flying.

Since Charles Kuralt pronounced the Beartooth Highway the most beautiful road in America, the judgment has become commonplace. It is a beautiful drive but its construction, from 1932 to 1936, prevented the area from being included in the Absaroka-Beartooth Wilderness, with its attendant protections, and it was permanently separated from the North Absaroka Wilderness. The resulting fragmentation of habitat was one of the most egregious in the history of Greater Yellowstone.

Recent efforts to give the Wyoming section of the plateau wilderness status floundered in the swamp of Wyoming politics, despite the fact that less than 1 percent of Wyoming is alpine tundra and needs all the protection it can get. Montana representative Pat Williams attempted to have more of the plateau designated federal wilderness during the 1990s, but his efforts failed because such status clashed with the economic interests of Greater Yellowstone's nemesis, the energy industry.

On a positive note, in 2000 the Forest Service designated 20,275 acres along Line Creek Plateau a Research Natural Area. This provided minimal protection for twenty-four rare vascular plant species and several threatened mammals, including the wolf, the grizzly, and one of the rarest of our critters, the lynx. That is likely as much protection as the Beartooth will receive, however much we might wish it to be otherwise, however much the ecosystem needs it to be otherwise.

The highway—a National Scenic Byway since 1989—brought a steady stream of tourism and development to what was, in the 1930s, one of the most remote areas in America. The road is being "improved," which means made safe for Winnebagos—widened, repaved, and, straightened in sections, which will inevitably increase pollution, noise, and accidents with wildlife. For six months each winter the highway is unplowed. Red Lodge and Cooke City are literally dead ends—a fact that both towns would like to change. Year-round access across would help their economies, no doubt, but to keep the road clear would be a Herculean task that would further stress the fragile alpine ecosystem. Many of us prefer the cities remain dead ends. For me, the only downside to visiting the Beartooth is going through Cooke City, a place I'd like to see become a deader end.

Cooke City was named—appropriately, one thinks in retrospect—to honor the robber baron Jay Cooke. In the fall of 1873, Cooke and his railroad went bankrupt, triggering the Panic of 1873 and dragging the American economy into six years of depression, a depression from which Cooke City has yet to recover.

Cooke's sole connection to Cooke City was symptomatic of the speculation that still plagues the town. Cooke invested in a mining venture that never materialized because the miners didn't own the land—it belonged to the Crow Indians—and they had grossly exaggerated its value. The miners anticipated that Cooke would provide the new town with both a railroad and capital to subsidize their dreams. He didn't.

Without a railroad, Cooke City could not economically market its ore. The miners tried to get a railroad—for decades. They sought to lay track across Yellowstone National Park from Gardiner, Montana. They proposed to either cross over or tunnel under the Beartooth Plateau from Red Lodge. They dug their mines deeper in anticipation of finding fortune. They never did.

Cooke City consists of Main Street, lined with business establishments and at each end of which until recently sat wrecked police cars. The Cooke City Store has been here since 1886 and is a National Historical Site. Collarless dogs roam the main street. As one leaves town a sign warns there is no gas for eighty miles. A hundred brave and often drunk souls spend the winter here, seemingly outnumbered by snowmobiles.

Late June. I will not spend the night in Cooke City, though sometimes I stop to eat. There are only two good places to eat in Cooke City. The others vie with a truck stop in Wells, Nevada, for the title of worst meal I've ever had—and that includes the dives I survived in years of traveling through the boondocks of India, Pakistan, Nepal, China, Bhutan, Tibet, Turkey, and Peru. Our destination today, in contrast, is a noble institution. The décor is western funk—pine paneling, red deck chairs, a Harley Davidson logo, and a sign declaring WELCOME BIKERS.

The crowd is a mix of elderly dudes in studded leather, hippies, college kids, a group of trendy, retired folks resting between bouts of watching wolves, a few sullen anglers who evidently didn't know the rivers are still muddy from runoff, and a real cowboy, the rowels on his spurs jingling. Like many establishments in Cooke City, the café is open only in the summer. I ask the cook, a young man with a pigtail dangling beneath his green Mohawk, why they close for the winter. "No heat because there isn't any insulation," he replies.

Dana and I settle in for lunch. Rio growls at the local dogs from the safety of the truck. I'm here for their selection of beer—130 kinds line the back wall, arranged like medals. Most are from Western breweries, small companies in Wyoming, Montana, Oregon, and California that make great beer. They exhibit the bold graphic labels and iconoclastic names characteristic of the species: Moose Drool, Powder Hound, Renegade Red, Scape Goat, Black Widow, Wild Fly, Dead Guy, and Yellow Snow. I select Steelhead Extra Stout because it has the consistency of crankcase oil.

"What do you want, sweetheart?"

"Poppy-seed rum cake—and tea." She never orders anything else here.

Thus fortified, we head for the Beartooth under threatening skies.

From Cooke City the road crosses Colter Pass and descends into the Clarks Fork, a tributary of the Yellowstone River. It's historic country. Colter is John Colter, a member of the Lewis and Clark expedition who left the expedition in July 1806 to return to the mountains with other trappers. The following year he traveled alone, in winter, across the headwaters of the Green, Snake, Madison, and Yellowstone rivers—a circumambulation of much of what is now Greater Yellowstone.

His route remains a matter of speculation but is thought to follow the Bannock Trail. The Bannock were a Plains tribe centered in southern Idaho. After the bison population in their region collapsed (no one knows why), they migrated annually across Yellowstone to hunt bison in the upper Missouri basin. Their preferred route was between Soda Butte Creek and the upper Clarks Fork—what is now called Colter Pass. Since Colter's passage is speculation, and the passage of the Bannock anything but, it seems the very least we could do was name it Bannock Pass. This was unlikely. Colter was and is a local hero—he is certainly one of my heroes. Colter is a common boy's name in these parts, right up there with Shane.

Clark, of course, is Capt. William Clark of Lewis and Clark fame. (Why the plural—"Clarks Fork"—is used instead of the possessive—as in "Clark's Nutcracker"—is another Wyoming mystery.) While descending the Yellowstone River to the Missouri on their return journey, the expedition camped at the tributary's mouth. Clark named the river after himself.

The Clarks Fork, the only river in Wyoming with federally designated "wild and scenic" status, flows through a valley noted for dude ranches and fine fishing before plunging into the Clarks Fork Canyon, the toughest stretch of whitewater in Greater Yellowstone. Like the Beartooth Highway, it is by common assent one of the most beautiful places in the country.

Ernest Hemingway loved the Clarks Fork. In the early 1930s he rented a cabin at the L-Bar-T ranch near the Montana border and fished the river—"the best fishing in the world," he said. One day he and a friend caught forty-nine rainbows and cutthroats in the canyon. In another three-day period, while fishing alone, he took ninety-two trout. Eventually he built his own cabin at the head of Timber Creek. A grizzly broke in each time he went away.

As Hemingway worked on what would become *Death in the Afternoon*, he hunted elk and bighorn sheep near Pilot and Index peaks, he shot grouse on the sagebrush flats, he killed several bears over dead horses used for bait, and he fished obsessively. When he finally left, he feared that the then-proposed Beartooth Highway would ruin the country, the hunting and fishing.

Fishing is still good, especially in the canyon, but native fish populations have suffered the usual depredations. Montana stocked hatchery brook trout in the headwater creeks; Wyoming stocked hatchery-raised brown trout and rainbow trout in the rest of the river. Today the native Yellowstone cutthroats are imperiled. Wyoming has ceased trying to support the remaining wild cut-throats with hatchery stock—which is just as well since hatchery fish reduce the genetic vitality of wild fish. Wild native cutthroats are still found, however.

The river is polluted with copper, cadmium, and silver residues from the mines at Cooke City. Cleanup by the Environmental Protection Agency requires Wyoming's Department of Environmental Quality to establish the Total Maximum Daily Load (TMDL) of metals for the river, a measurement that would help determine its health and resilience. The department couldn't care less. It simply notes that the Clarks Fork is already polluted when it enters Wyoming from Montana, and that it continues to be impaired "for an undetermined distance downstream." The State of Montana doesn't care about the river, either, since it has only two miles of the Clarks Fork. Then, too, in Montana, the river flows through Gallatin National Forest; in Wyoming, it flows through Shoshone National Forest. Who then is ultimately responsible for this National Wild and Scenic River? Nobody. Hemingway's beloved river is a vivid example of why political boundaries inhibit healthy ecosystems.

After descending to 7,000 feet along the Clarks Fork, we climb rapidly onto the Beartooth Plateau. Open forest gives way to glacier-carved lakes and alpine meadows studded with subalpine fir, spruce, and whitebark. Several trails lead into the near-million-acre Absaroka-Beartooth Wilderness, the most visited wilderness in the United States and home of the highest peak in Montana, 12,799-foot Granite Peak, 1,000 feet lower than the highest peaks in the Wind River range and the Tetons but isolated, formidable, and infamous for bad weather. Mountain country doesn't get any better than the Beartooth.

Above Long Lake the road is one of the few places in the country where you can drive for miles above timberline. Here you are up in the sky; indeed, you are often above the clouds. You are not on a peak—there is nothing sufficiently pointed or isolated to be a peak, and the major Beartooth peaks are far away. No, these are plateaus, rolling sweeps of land dotted with rocky outcrops, tarns, incipient creeks, and carpets of flowers, a place with unique ecosystems and natural history.

Most writers refer to this land as alpine tundra, but it is different from Arctic tundra. In *Beartooth Country*, Bob Anderson states the difference succinctly. "In general," he says, "the alpine is a harsher environment; it experiences more wind, less vapor pressure, lower surface soil temperatures, higher ultraviolet radiation, less soil moisture, and greater diurnal temperature fluctuations." Snow covers the soil for much of the year, often limiting plant growth to several weeks. Pollination by insects is less common than at lower elevations. And most of the plateaus are separated from each other by deep canyons, so it is an inherently fragmented habitat.

Alpine tundra is austere. Trees are absent because the amount of photosynthesis essential for large plants requires a certain degree of warmth, and the Beartooth is not warm. Indeed, Greater Yellowstone is the fourth coldest region in the United States, including Alaska. The lowest recorded temperature in Montana is 70 degrees below 0 at Roger's Pass in 1954. The 70-degree reading is colder than any temperature recorded in Europe, including Russia. Montana also holds the world's record for the largest twenty-four-hour temperature change—103 degrees. The mean summer temperature in the Beartooth is around 50 degrees.

And yet despite all this, 530 species of plants make their home on the Beartooth, substantially more than the typical 200–300 species in other regions of mountain tundra. The Beartooth is flush with alpine flora, inexplicably so, and anyone who loves alpine flora feels an obligation to visit and indulge their passion.

The drifts are still ten feet deep along sections of the road. Churning clouds fill the sky. Pasqueflowers—large, elegant, solitary, creamy white and pale lavender—flop back and forth in the wind.

The pasqueflower is a wild crocus and, like many crocus, a herald of spring. Mountain buttercups pierce thin patches of snow and sheets of ice.

Since Dana is new to this country every flower is a surprise.

"Stop," she cries. "What's that?"

Sometimes I know the answer.

The higher we climb toward Beartooth Pass, the harder the wind blows. At the summit we turn west and park at the overlook to admire the mountain scene. The truck shudders in the battering winds. Pebbles ping off the hood. Botanizing seems at best a marginal activity. Like good tourists, we get out for a photo. Dana's parka and pants billow like sails. She buries her hands in her armpits, hugging herself.

"What do you think?" I ask.

"It's like winter and we just finished eight months of winter."

Rio is hiding behind a front tire. I throw her Frisbee. She ignores it.

We turn around and slink off the plateau. Long Lake is laced with whitecaps. As we pass Beartooth Lake, snow begins to fall. We decide that tea and poppy-seed rum cake at the Beartooth Café would be a nice start to the drive back to Jackson Hole.

We return at the end of the first week of July. I believe early July is best for flowers on the plateau, but they can always be found wherever snow is melting, even in September, or later in the north-facing cirques. All summer it will be spring somewhere on the Beartooth.

The temperature at Beartooth Pass is pleasant—in the 50s. The wind is brisk, the sky clear. The flowers are at their peak, though unnoticed at forty-five miles per hour; from the truck the landscape seems a swath of green broken by occasional blurs of yellow.

Most alpine flowers are tiny and often protected behind stones and outcrops or among bunches of grass and sedge. Befriending them requires a walk. We park at 10,500 feet, at a turnout, pack up, and head east into the bogs at the head of a creek. I've planned a circular tour down the creek, over a bumpy ridge into the headwaters of another nascent creek, then back over the ridge to the truck. Four miles at most—a jaunt.

Purists would disapprove. They oppose turnouts—people park and walk around! Walking on tundra can dislodge rocks, disturb soil! A dog may disturb birds nesting on the ground, and where else can they nest? Walking on tundra crushes flowers! Etc. What to do?

These arguments apply to all walking in the mountains, and I am not a sufficiently deep ecologist to forgo walking in the mountains. If people do not walk in the mountains then people will not come to love the mountains, and that is not good, either, for people or for mountains. We take due care.

On the other hand, I do not kid myself. Although in general mountain ecosystems suffer less impact than more habitable locations, no ecosystem is more fragile than alpine tundra. If you kick a rock, five centuries may pass before the area reestablishes itself with the same array of plants. If you remove soil, somewhere between a thousand and ten thousand years will pass before it regenerates. Most species inhabiting alpine tundra are exquisitely precise consequences of microgeography; shift a rock a few inches or casually kick a stone and you produce a difference, the difference between moist, snow-covered habitat and snow-free desiccated habitat.

Worse, each act of destruction must be assessed against the background of our warming climate and the unpredictable ways it will inhibit regeneration. Paleoclimate records indicate that high mountain environments respond to minor climate change. For instance, research in Sweeden suggests that the treeline rises up to 500 feet for every 1 degree C increase in mean summer temperature. Current predictions call for increases of 3 to 5 degrees C over the next century. If this is even approximately true for the Northern Rockies, then most of the alpine tundra in Greater Yellowstone will disappear, slowly replaced by ecosystems that are now at lower elevations, mainly forest.

Alpine areas with more detailed historical records than we have for the Beartooth already show marked changes. The U.S. Geological Survey reports that aerial photography and GIS surveys show krummholz in the Colorado Rockies is expanding vertically at the rate of one meter every twenty-seven years. In the Alps, which are experiencing the warmest weather in 1,250 years, some alpine plants that were common one hundred years ago are now confined to the highest peaks, 90 percent of the glaciers are receding, and the ski industry is worried.

Perhaps the saddest indicator is the decline of the much-beloved American pika, a small member of the rabbit family that inhabits mountain regions. It cannot survive more than six hours in temperatures warmer than about 80 degrees F. Another report from the Geological Survey warns that of the known pika sites in the Great Basin, the pika populations are extinct at 36 percent of them.

Dana must endure this lecture, and I know that she would prefer silence, but I am obsessed and angry even here, where both obsession and anger are stupid.

"No one seems to say much about how global warming will affect mountains," she says. "We hear about the Arctic and Antarctic and the flooding of Florida but we don't hear much about alpine flowers or pikas." Good point. Even Al Gore's film on global warming spends too much time worrying about places far away. We need to know how global warming is going to affect Greater Yellowstone and Cleveland.

We stick to the snowfields as much as possible to reduce impact—which is not to say that snowfields do not register our impact. They do. It's just that we know little about how walking impacts snowfield ecosystems. Few people realize that snowfields harbor a collection of creatures constituting an ecosystem. Everything required for a self-sustaining, self-organizing structure is present: algae, aquatic organisms, spiders, springtails, worms (including the snow worm—small, black, wiggly), and various windborn insects. When the birds feed on the surface of the snow they leave droppings that provide additional nutrients to the snowfield's ecosystem.

A long snowbank makes for easier walking. Rio rolls in the snow, one of her favorite summer pleasures. A group of ravens strut about, pecking, eating I know not what. Delicate pipits run along the ground next to the snow, gleaning. At a distance you could mistake them for shorebirds. Pipits breed here on the tundra and migrate south for the winter, often as far as South America. Of the bird species identified in Greater Yellowstone, approximately one-third migrate out of the United States each winter—yet another indication of the flexible boundary of our stationary map-oriented ecosystems. In most of the areas where these birds overwinter they enjoy no legal protection and are threatened by pesticides, herbicides, hunting, and habitat loss. Again, what happens in Yucatan affects Greater Yellowstone, and what happens in Greater Yellowstone affects Yucatan—and lots of other places. If you get too picky about the boundaries of Greater Yellowstone, you miss the main point.

A flock of black rosy finches sweep past, and that's a treat. They are handsome birds, dark charcoal with a gray head, and on their wings and bellies are slashes of rose madder. They nest in cliffs. The nest of the black rosy-finch has eluded me despite considerable time spent looking for one. The population visiting the summit of the Grand Teton during the summer is rather tame, pecking at your feet, perching beside you on rocks. Here they keep their distance.

Snowfields melt under the intense high-altitude solar radiation of summer and the melt supplies water to the marsh at the head of the creek. These areas of melt are also distinct ecosystems, specific collections of willow, grass, rush, and sedge all interwoven with flowers. I make a feeble attempt to find out if the willows are Barrett willow, a rare plant in Wyoming. I conclude I'm not much good at willow identification. Dana, a gardener at heart, just looks at the flowers, oblivious to my identification anxieties.

Water seeps and gurgles among rocks, clear as gin, a sign of its high oxygen content. There is no silt. The surface of the ground is level and covered with nearly flat rocks, like parquet. Freezing temperatures last night left ice on the fringes of rocks and crusted the mosses. The morning sun melted it some, but fragments still lurk in recesses between rocks and hummocks, gleaming like shards of crystal.

The chief attraction of the marsh is the marsh marigold, a large white flower with a cluster of bright yellow pistils and shiny green basal leaves. Some alpine marshes are littered with them. When you see elk grazing a marsh up here they are usually eating marsh marigolds. Kings crown, a member of the stonecrop family, is also common. It is only five inches high but bursting with tiny flowers, blood red or darker, sometimes almost black. At the edge of the marsh, on drier ground, I find silky phacelia, a spike of purple petals and stamens set off by yellow anthers. It looks like a purple bottle brush, but what a name! A friend of mine wanted to name his daughter Silky Phacelia. And so it goes. We dawdle, looking and pointing, paying too much attention to the flowers and not enough to the bog. Soon our feet are soaked. If you stand in a bog long enough, you sink.

We climb in zigzag fashion through a gentle meadow ridge above us into a rock-strewn area on the other side, which is technically called a fellfield. Beneath us is a boulder field, to the right more boulder fields, stretches of scree and talus, more fellfields From the road, all this terrain looks tediously similar: rocky. But up close the amount and size of rock varies and this variation leads to different plant communities: Meadows are flat or gentle and are at least 50 percent soil. Fellfields are rocky fields that are constantly blown clear of snow where mat plants, mosses, and grasses surround the rocks. Boulder fields are just that. Talus is a field of rocks you could pick up, scree a field of rocks you could throw.

For most Americans such distinctions are of little interest, and only a few appreciate or understand alpine ecology. There exists no standard academic text on the subject. Fortunately we have an excellent introduction, *Song of the Alpine,* by Joyce Gellhorn; a classic of natural history, *Land Above the Trees: A Guide to American Alpine Tundra,* by Ann Zwinger and Beatrice Willard; and numerous guides to alpine flowers. But the public remains stunningly ignorant of alpine ecosystems, and this is unfortunate because as Greater

Yellowstone begins to delaminate, the alpine ecosystems will go first—they are the first domino.

The key to understanding the plants on alpine tundra is ice. Glaciers didn't eat this far back into the granitic block of the plateau because the wind blew off much of the snow and the sun melted the rest each summer. To develop, a glacier requires deep, unmelting snow that will over time compress into ice of a sufficient weight to set it sliding downhill. Nonetheless, the topography here is caused by ice and to a considerably lesser degree by acid from lichen. Both fracture boulders into rocks, rocks into talus, talus into scree, and scree into highly mineralized BB-size gravel nearly devoid of nutrients—it is not soil. Plants develop slowly, often cunningly creating their own soil. For example, moss campion, a low cushion of tiny leaves and flowers supporting a tap root five feet long, accumulates detritus in its leaf mass, thus slowly enriching the gravel and allowing the plant to expand its circumstance.

Around noon the wind freshens. We find shelter in a pile of boulders behind which grows alpine sorrel and penstemon—mountain penstemon, I think. The grass is so tufted and hummocky we have difficulty getting comfortable, but we nestle in, cloistered and warm, the flat rock face above us serving as a reflector. Rio finds an abandoned burrow under an overhang, curls up in the filthy entrance, and falls sleep.

The featherweight mountaineering stove simmers happily. Within minutes we are enjoying tea and crackers. After a long silence, and a second cup of tea, Dana says, "I'd like to spend the night here in the quiet, under the stars."

"We can do that." We are only two miles from the road, an easy walk over a ridge, far enough to eliminate sounds from the highway.

"Are there grizzly here?"

"Probably."

"It's so quiet and peaceful. And it has dimension, like the sea."

As Rockwell Kent said in his Alaskan journal, "The wonder of the wilderness was its tranquility." I wish I had said that first. It grasps the salient point: not just tranquility, but *wonder* at tranquility. Wilderness is a surprise. We were raised on nature films that converted nature into thrilling entertainment; we still expect to find predators lurking everywhere in the wildness, and danger and excitement. But instead we find tranquility. And wonder at it.

Interesting word, "wonder." From Old English *wundrain:* "to be affected with astonishment." Its antonyms name the most pervasive symptoms of modern life: indifference, boredom, ennui. The dictionary strains to explain wonder, mentioning awe, astonishment, marvel, miracle, wizardry, bewilderment (note the "wild" in "bewilderment"). Finally it offers this: "Far superior to anything formerly recognized or foreseen."

Indeed.

We walk south into the sky, a pale, bleached, blue sky near the horizon and, straight up, deep cobalt. I am happy. The farther I can see, the happier I am.

We turn west. Fellfields become boulder fields. Some are round and perched upon one another in a manner suggesting they might topple. Others are rectangular slabs, like sarcophagi. Soon we are hopping instead of walking. Rio wanders among the boulders, finding her own way. She does not like to jump on things that might move. She disappears, reappears, disappears again, doing everything she can to avoid boulders.

The wind is fierce. We are at slightly less than 11,000 feet. The temperature is approaching unpleasant. Dana's slightly pained expression tells me she's thinking of winter again.

We snuggle in the lee of another overhanging rock and peer through our binoculars. Off to the south, two miles away, across the flats leading to Deep Lake, are seventeen elk strung along the twin mounds of Tolman Mountain. Their pelage is still a bit scruffy: spring pelage. Most graze casually, but several lie about, chewing, like cows in a pasture. The northern flanks of the mountain are green beneath a sliver of melting snow bank.

"That's why they are up here—fresh grass."

Through the binoculars the world is all green: mint green beneath the snow fields, gray green in the meadows, bottle green in the bogs and marshes—a bucolic bliss for ungulates.

And then: "What's that?"

The wreck of a car from the thirties or forties, rusted, abandoned smack in the middle of a marsh surrounded by hummocks and rock and seeps. The body has been stripped of parts and dignity. The owner drove into the bog and got bogged down, literally. An early expedition from Red Lodge to Cooke City? A hunting trip gone awry? Early winter?

We traverse into a stiff wind through fields of buttercups and enter a meadow encrusted with tiny flowers. Within a single square foot of turf Dana counts over a dozen species of flowers, not to mention several grasses and sedges. Dana is wiser than I am; she simply enjoys the flowers. I set about figuring out what they all are.

This means I need my flower guides. *Alpine Flower Finder*, by Janet L. Wingate and Loraine Yeatts, is a pamphlet that fits in my shirt pocket. Then, of course, the bible, carefully protected in a ziplock bag: John J. Craighead, Frank C. Craighead Jr., and Ray J. Davis, *A Field Guide to Rocky Mountain Wildflowers*. I also carry *Alpine Wildflowers*, by Dee Strickler, both for the quality photographs and the interesting descriptions. On the shelf at home is the arcane but indispensable *Alpine Flora of the Rocky Mountains*, Vol. 1, *The Middle Rockies*, by W. Richard Scott. Unless you are desperately obsessive, these will do.

To identify flowers one uses a dichotomous key that presents two alternate choices of floral characteristics that facilitate classification and hence identification. Most botanical keys are as user-friendly as computer code (and the logic is the same), but the key in *Alpine Flower Finder* is a treat. However, identifying alpine flowers, especially the tiny ones, is hard. You must master botanical nomenclature; you must know your basal and whorled, stamen and pistil, calyx and palmate.

I carry two lenses. A large, square magnifier, the kind one finds in office supply stores, which has a hole drilled in the handle so you can sling it around your neck; it allows you to see tiny flowers well enough to enjoy their beauty and complexity. A 10-power loupe is required to study the smaller parts of flowers and such minutia as dwarf clover, ice grass, and lichen. Unless you do this fairly often, you find yourself reidentifying alpine plants. At one time I collected alpine plants and pressed them in a small journal used only for that purpose. I don't do that anymore. The little book, always a bit poignant, is now embarrassing and downright sad, and studying it is about as pleasant as studying the photographs of an autopsy.

Since you will be on your elbows most of the time, bring a foam pad or (my choice) a Crazy Creek chair. I carry a needle to separate flower parts. I glued my needle onto a piece of cork from a wine bottle and fashioned it to fit into an old ink pen from which the ink apparatus had been removed. With the needle encased in the pen I can hold it with ease and protect myself from the point when it's in the pack. (When fishing, I use it to tease apart wind-knots in my leader.)

You can also, like Dana, forgo identification and simply enjoy the beauty before you. Do you really need to know that the splendor confronting you is a *Gentianopsis barbellata*? As Holmes said to Watson, the mind is like an attic and it has only so much room. Or as the Dalai Lama said more eloquently: "The objects of knowledge are truly infinite; choose carefully." If, on the other hand, you wish to transcend the blather of politicians and the idiocy of the daily news, then—believe me—an hour on your belly at 10,800 feet with your lenses, needle, and flower books will do the trick.

Besides trying to identify what I don't know, I look for favorites. I find umbrella starwort, a miniscule joy—twenty or thirty of its tiny pinkish flowers could be placed on top of a penny. Pink and white dwarf clover is common. Sedges. Two kinds of phlox. I search for rock jasmine without success.

Dana is getting cold. Too kind to confront me with this fact when I am happy as a clam, she becomes increasingly inquisitive: it's not quite a cross-examination, but pointed.

"Does it smell like jasmine?"

"I don't know. I've never smelled it."

"Never?"

"No."

"Are you sure it's in the Beartooth?"

"Well . . . no."

Left unasked—though it hangs in the air as obvious as a dirigible, is something along the lines of "How long will you, we, continue to search for something rare and hard to find, something that you are not sure exists here, especially when your hands are shaking from the cold and your eyes are watering so badly from the gale that you can't even see through your glasses, much less a loupe?"

It is already late when we strike the abandoned two-track leading south to Deep Lake. By the time we reach the truck the temperature has dropped again and the wind is blowing harder. Dana's pants and parka are billowing again. She's tucked her hands into her armpits. It's time for poppy-seed rum cake.

August. The parking lot for the Line Creek Plateau Trail. This time I am with Rio. Line Creek Plateau is beautiful and loaded with life; it's home to bighorn sheep, mountain goats, sometimes a wolf pack, perhaps an occasional grizzly, and an impressive array of rare plants. I'm not here for those reasons, however. I love wandering above timberline on foot, and this is a good place to indulge such love. It is not usually crowded. A few intrepid mountain bikers use this trail; indeed, it has become something of a classic. But it ends in a steep 3,000-foot drop into Maurice Creek that gives pause to anyone with a modicum of respect for their groin or their knees. I'll walk to the edge of the plateau and return.

The weather feels muggy, even at 10,000 feet, but a breeze out of the southwest cools us. The peaks along the western skyline vanish into billowing clouds. I'm terrified of the thunderstorms on these barren plateaus—I've been struck by ground currents on the Grand Teton. However, I have good gear and thunderstorms pass quickly—generally.

The trail dips to a little lake near the head of Wyoming Creek and then climbs onto the plateau. Two dozen lakes lie upstream. I would usually wander there, but today I seek a longer walk—though not before I savor several bright clumps of bluish purple moss gentian along the lake shore.

Like many writers, I like to walk in empty places because it frees my mind, especially if I am alone. Walking, like breathing, usually does not require your attention. If you are with someone else, your attention goes to them, and you focus on pace. If you are in front, you consider how far behind they are; if you're behind, you attend to keeping up, irritated at going faster than you wish. And nothing is more distracting than human speech. So much of our life is given to communication with others—by body language, facial expression, or language—that we cannot ignore them if present. Often our attention to them is barely conscious, but it is always present.

If you walk alone in empty places your mind and body take care of themselves, like they're on autopilot or cruise control. You do not tire as quickly as when you're walking with other people, and your mind is freed for other matters. You discover your natural pace. Without a trail, your body tends to wander, and your mind wanders, too. Wandering body/mind finds new places. Imagination flourishes, increasing—another one of Turner's Laws—as a cube of the distance from the road.

"Wander" is again from the Old English—*wandrain*, "to move about aimlessly." Thus *wandrain* is delightfully close to *wundrain*, "wonder." It is also related to our "wind." Nor is this connection limited to the West and English. The Japanese poet Bassho begins his travel narrative, *Narrow Road to the Deep North*, with this: "I myself have been tempted for a long time by the cloud-moving wind—filled with a strong desire to wander." I don't know a place in Greater Yellowstone windier than the Beartooth Plateau, a great place to wander in wonder.

We do not often realize the connection between a freed body and freed mind, but when wandering alpine tundra it has the force of fundamental fact. This is not my discovery. In *Land Above the Trees,*

Zwinger and Willard call alpine tundra the "landscape of ultimate freedom." Like all freedom, it's a bit spooky.

Rio stays near, aware of this. She is a herding dog. Her primary concern is my well-being, and I trust her to notice danger before I do. She will do her best to protect me—all sixty pounds of her. She once bit a 300-pound bear in the butt. Her vigilance frees my mind from worry.

When the trail climbs onto the plateau, crossing from Wyoming into Montana, I strike out in an easterly direction, above Line Lake, avoiding the steep drop-off into the various branches of Line Creek. I contour just beneath 10,000 feet, winding around the canyon rim. Occasionally I stop and glass for sheep and goats. Nothing.

Smog fills the Bridger Desert, 4,000 feet beneath me, an arid plain that during an average year receives only half the precipitation of Tucson. Perhaps at no other place in the ecosystem is it so obvious that Greater Yellowstone is an island rising from a dry, thermal sea. The haze blocks the view of the Big Horn range, 125 miles away. Once upon a time I could see the Big Horns from the Beartooth, but I have not seen them for many years. Energy companies have drilled more gas and oil wells in the Bridger Desert than I want to think about; thousands more are planned.

The clouds are building with the heat of the day, beautiful, billowing towers of vapor sucked by low pressure from the Pacific off Mexico. The wind is freshening. Rio is happily sniffing everywhere, doing her best to wag her docked tail and glancing at me with a look that says, "Why don't we do this every day?"

Because I guide the Grand Teton at least once a week during the summer, I am fairly well adjusted to the altitude; on the Grand I sleep even higher than this. Walking at this altitude is easy for me. I think Rio notices it more than I do.

When the terrain becomes too rocky, we traverse higher, onto the crown of the plateau. Often I sit in my Crazy Creek chair, which allows me to write and to paint watercolors on a small board placed across my knees. Rio gets water in a clever collapsible canvas cup.

There is no water here, not a drop, and, of course, no shade. She hides in my shadow, panting.

I pine for one of the Chinese umbrellas I carried around the Himalayas. It was rarely used for rain, often for shade. When I first went to the Hindu Kush, a dry and bleak mountain range, thirty years ago, I didn't understand why people carried umbrellas, an unfortunate lapse of wit since "umbrella" is from "umbra," which means "shade." My companions sat under their portable shade. I sat in the 100-degree sun. I soon acquired a Chinese umbrella with a steel post—the first of many—and I wish I had it now.

I have a goal of sorts: the last knob before the trail descends into Maurice Creek, about six miles from the trailhead. Eventually I rejoin the trail as it passes through a narrow neck several hundred yards wide. The forests begin to climb out of the canyons and close in a bit. After five miles I've dropped only three hundred feet, but the main thing that determines timberline here is wind, not elevation. Forests hover at both edges of the plateau; the trunks of some trees are silver, blasted by gravel and ice. Their tops are ragged. They seem hunkered down, as if hiding. The wind is up now; the day is gray. I feel exposed, both a physical fact and an emotion.

Two Clark's nutcrackers glide across the ridge; their undulating flight and flashes of white are telltale signs. They are no doubt burying whitebark seeds at the edge of this windy ridge. Five Ravens. "Nevermore," I squawk, my customary greeting. I haven't seen another person all day.

No doubt most people would find this a desolate scene, appealing only to addicts of the sublime. Faced with the bleak sands of Cape Cod, Thoreau seconds what he felt on the summit of Katahdin: "My spirits rose in proportion to the outward dreariness." I agree. I love bad weather. There is nothing worse than bald skies and sunny climes.

We turn for home. Squalls roll off the peaks like surf. Thunder rumbles to the north, over Hellroaring Plateau. Clouds of graupel, ashen veils, drift across the Rock River valley. Suddenly they billow over the plateau before me, like debris blown from an explosion. Time for battle gear.

One stuff-sack contains gear I tell every one of my basic climbing classes to always, always, carry in the mountains: gloves, ski hat, sweater, rain gear tops and bottoms. I put on everything I have. I pull the hat down over my log-billed fishing cap. The bill protects my face; the wool hat cushions the impact of hail. I tighten the parka hood over both. I take a compass reading in case I am enveloped in a cloud bank—a disorienting event on tundra.

I sit in the chair with my back to the maelstrom and wait, bending forward over my knees, my pack protecting my neck. Rio, having been through this before, lies in front of me, her head beneath my knees, her body snug against my leg. I shift my body to afford her more protection.

Graupel skitters along the ground to the south. I wonder if there will be hail. Graupel is not hail. Once called "soft hail," graupel starts as an ice crystal that on its descent through a cumulus cloud had supercooled droplets freeze to its surface. Hail, on the other hand, begins as either a raindrop or graupel. Caught in the updraft of a storm cloud, it circulates. As supercooled droplets freeze to it, it grows . . . to the size of golf balls, hardballs, even softballs. Several years ago hail the size of volleyballs fell in Nebraska. In contrast, graupel is relatively harmless stuff, though closely correlated with lightning.

Real wind arrives, like a wall. Had I been standing, I would have been knocked down. I grab Rio's collar. I've seen elk become hysterical from being battered by hail.

The rain is drenching. The graupel hurts, but at least it is graupel, not hail. I wait, ruminating on the impossibility of escape and the wisdom and freedom buried in the impossibility of escape.

A flash of lightning, an incandescent glow, and then the crack of thunder. Rio jerks. I grab a fist of fur along her back with my other hand and hold her tight. Clouds everywhere. The spectrum is muted, color seen through frosted glass.

Suddenly, it is lighter, as if a magic wand erased the gray. The dark cloud that had enveloped us passes off the plateau, off the edge of the island that is Greater Yellowstone, its top dazzling white, its bottom black. Beneath the cloud, yellow light illuminates the drought-brown Bridger Desert, the thermal sea surrounding this higher island.

Sheets of graupel or rain—I cannot tell—hang in the air, shimmering, before they disappear into the light and evaporate, never reaching the ground. Technically this is called "virga," but the word fails to capture the magic and the mystery of it or the trace of sadness. The old Japanese poets knew this as *aware*, the sadness of impermanence, the falling leaves of autumn, the falling virga of the desert. From here it seems the ranchers below must suffer a disappointment of biblical proportion, destined to forever see the moisture that would bring relief but rarely enjoying the reality of its presence.

White balls the size of peas litter the ground. Some of the ridges to the west are white, some not. Like a tornado, a thunderstorm is fickle. The mountains gleam with running water. I stand stiffly and look around. Rio runs in circles, jumps, and shakes herself with glee. We share a feeling of buoyancy, of light wrested from dark, though there is nothing wrong with darkness.

The sun is warming a world that is probably 30 degrees colder than before the storm. I tie the rain gear to the pack to dry. Untied it would blow away and I don't want to move rocks to hold it down—no moving rocks above timberline!

I break out a bar of summer sausage and cut rings for us. Since Rio was a puppy we've always shared all meat. I stare into the lines of clouds that tower above the desert, great anvils and mushrooms that will soon evaporate to nothingness—self-liberating themselves, as the Tibetan Buddhists say.

When I first went into the mountains as a young man more than fifty years ago, I believed that within the clarity of immense space I would glimpse a truth. I've often sought that vision—looking across a sea of metallic ridges in the Hindu Kush, or the numberless dunes of the Taklimakan Desert, or the endless glaciers leading to K2, or the infinite green canopy east of the Andes, or the adamantine snowy plains of Tibet. I believe it now, though it eludes me still.

Most of the hail has melted by the time we resume our wandering, though pieces remain buried in the grass and sedge and along the lees of ridges. By the time we reach the trailhead, toward dusk, the last of the graupel has vanished, each and every one, and the sky is filled with jaunty cotton-candy clouds racing east.

5. The South Fork

After leaving Jackson Hole the Snake River cuts through hard Madison Limestone between the Wyoming Range and the Snake Range mountains, forming a spectacular canyon with famous rapids, and exiting into Grand Valley, where it is joined by two major tributaries, the Greys and the Salt. Grand Valley was a riparian paradise. Not surprisingly, people loved the place. In *Across the Wide Missouri,* Bernard DeVoto says that the Snake River is "nowhere lovelier than in the stretch from the lower end of its first great canyon till it comes entirely out of the mountains."

Like most other paradises along the Snake, Grand Valley was dammed, beneath a place appropriately named Calamity Point, in 1956 by the Army Corps of Engineers. The Palisades Dam inundated twenty-nine miles of Grand Valley including the farms that had occupied the rich soil. Like the Jackson Lake Reservoir, the Palisades Reservoir exists to provide irrigation water for Idaho's farmers. And like the Jackson Lake Reservoir, it is quite a pretty lake when full of water—which is, again, only for a short time during summer. The rest of the year it is the usual collection of mud fats.

What is known in Idaho as the South Fork of the Snake River begins at the outlet of the Palisades Dam. Why the Snake River, which has by this point flowed over one hundred miles from Yellowstone through Jackson Hole, becomes a "fork" when it enters Idaho, particularly when it has three times the volume of the Snake's only other "fork," the Henry's Fork, is one of the many abnormalities one finds in Idaho.

Because the dam controls the flow to the river below, the South Fork is a tailwater fishery. Anglers like tailwater fisheries: no scouring muddy floods from spring runoff, just managed flows of clean water filled with trout: 3,000 trout per mile, according to the Idaho Department of Fish and Game; 4,000–7,000 trout a mile, according to local outfitters—counting is political. People claim 70-fish days and speak in hushed tones of monster fish stacked in pools like logs. That has not been my experience, but the combination of damn good fishing and stunning beauty has made the South Fork one of my favorite places to fish since I came into this country. I usually fish from the bank; at times I've kayaked it and camped. It used to be a lonely place.

The premier section of the river is the Canyon. The trapper Osborne Russell wrote in his *Journal* of 1838 that the river "comes thro. this kanyon for about 12 Mls. where the rock rises 2 or 300 feet forms a bench and ascends gradually to the Mountain which approaches very close on the Nth side and on the South is about 3 or 4 Mls distant and an occasional ravine running from the mountain to the river thro the rock on the Nth side forms convenient places for encamping as the bench and low Spurs are well clothed with bunch grass." As geography, Russell's description cannot be improved upon, though the usual run today from put-in to take-out is twenty-six miles.

Who owns the canyon and its environs is maddeningly complex. A section on the north side of the river is part of Targhee National Forest. Most of the river-bottom land is owned by the Bureau of Land Management. Acreage is purchased and preserved from development by an obscure piece of Congressional legislation—the Land and Water Conservation Fund—which is funded by royalties from oil and gas leases and sales of surplus federal lands. Finally, the Nature Conservancy and various land trusts provide various levels of additional protection.

These multiple efforts share the same rationale: to preserve what the U.S. Fish and Wildlife Service calls "the most important fish and wildlife habitat in the state of Idaho." Indeed, the most extensive riparian and wetland habitats in Greater Yellowstone are in eastern Idaho, on the western edge of the ecosystem. The South Fork, the Henry's Fork of the Snake, the Teton River, the Bear River, and the Blackfoot River are among the most biologically important areas in the ecosystem; they are also among the most degraded and vulnerable. The western edge of Island Yellowstone is crumbling from human development. After the South Fork leaves Greater Yellowstone it becomes the land of, well, just like the Idaho license plate says— "Famous Potatoes."

Most people float the canyon from Conant Valley to the Byington takeout, spending one very long day on the river, or camping one night on Russell's bunch-grass benches, now home to fifteen public campgrounds where, unlike in 1838, permits and portable toilets are de rigueur. The river is often crowded; everyone from trout bums and local meat-fisherman to CEOs and Vice President Cheney will be found there during the summer. I tend to skirt midsummer, preferring late June and autumn, the latter because the cottonwood forests edging the river are in full splendor, the former because of an elegant insect known everywhere in the West as the salmon fly, a fly that drives trout crazy.

Late June. The parking lot at the Conant Valley Boat Access, fourteen miles below the Palisades Dam, is packed with trucks, SUVs, boat trailers, boats, anglers, and guides. There is a line at the boat ramp. Guides mingle and talk shop while clients make one last trip to a real john and rig rods. Talking shop means talking salmonflies: Where are they in the canyon? What was it like yesterday? What were you fishing with?

The object of all this attention is a member of the stonefly family, which, along with mayflies and caddis flies are the reason we fish with flies instead of worms. Most stoneflies are big, but the salmon fly *(Pteronarcys californica)* is the biggest in our part of the world;

most specimens on the South Fork are two to three inches long. Its body color is dull orange, its two sets of wings are amber, and its venation is black and distinct. When one lands on you, and they do, you notice it.

Salmon flies spend the first two to four years of their life as blackish nymphs. They are always available to trout on the bottom of the river, and it is always worthwhile fishing for trout with imitation stonefly nymphs. The sequence of their emergence has been carefully studied. The adult nymphs first change body color—to orange—then they migrate to shore, molt, crawl about, and cling to rocks, grasses, and willows. They mate. Several days later the females fly over the river to deposit their eggs on the water—"the hatch"—before they die. When they are on the water, they are vulnerable to trout, especially since they don't fly well. Often they look like a crashing helicopter. Both their migration to shore and their flight make for mythically good fishing.

"The Hatch" (capitalized) moves upriver at a maddeningly fickle rate. E-mails, cell phones, Web sites, GPSs, and fax machines track its progress. They are now in the Canyon section of the South Fork, miles of legendary trout water. There these peaceful creatures with tiny brains will be hunted by an armada of humans armed with a million dollars' worth of the latest high-tech gear. If this isn't Veblen's conspicuous consumption, I don't know what is. Together we will . . . Well, we'd best wait to see what we will do. A salmon-fly hatch is too capricious to predict.

The day is sunny and warm, and there will be an afternoon breeze—perfect conditions. Bob Schuster and I are being guided today by Boots Allen, the son of the renowned guide Joe Allen. Boots was raised on the Snake River, rowing boats and fishing. He won "Best Guide" for the past two years in the Jackson Hole One-Fly fly-fishing competition, a prestigious event that draws teams from all over the world to the Snake River and whose profits go entirely to benefit the fishery. He is also a consummate tier of flies. There is no better fishing guide in Greater Yellowstone. Bob is an attorney in

Jackson, one of my best friends, and an old friend of Boots. Bob is also my official fishing partner.

Since we are friends we can needle each other, a relief in what can all too readily become a deadly serious pursuit. Boots is getting his doctorate in Sociology from the University of Texas in an eminently practical subject for a fishing guide—Kirgiz migration patterns. Bob and I want him to disregard the degree, forgo the prison of academia, and enter the fishing business.

"So where you gonna teach, Boots? Iowa?"

He ignores us.

"Not many trout in Iowa, Boots. Mississippi? Not many steelhead in Mississippi."

As we slip Boots's spacious Clackacraft driftboat into the current, it veers sharply downstream. The river is running at 10,500 cubic feet per second, normal for this time of year, but that's big, pushy water.

Fluffy, white cottonlike masses the size of golf balls litter the river. Each is embedded with tiny seeds from the cottonwood forest along the river, probably the largest surviving cottonwood forest in the West. Beneath these large, stately trees are red-ozier dogwood, chokecherry, water birch, willows, and various grasses. The banks have been undercut by high water and, in the past, flooding. Along these banks, often shaded by forest, is where the trout lie. On the South Fork you are usually casting to the banks, the closer the better.

Boots has rigged us to cover all the options. Bob casts a Terra-X salmonfly imitation, one of Boots's creations. I'm throwing a repulsive black nymph tied to a big Gamakatsu saltwater hook that looks dangerous.

We are hitting the bank above where Pine Creek enters the river through one of Osborne Russell's "deep ravines." We work hard in the pools around Pine Creek but without success. I don't mind. The sun is up, and the river pours over the long bars of gravel and cobbles, a lullaby of water rushing into narrow runs. We glide over deep emerald green pools of mesmerizing beauty.

In Russell's day, Pine Creek was a major passage from the lower Snake to what is now Teton Valley and Jackson Hole. These days Pine Creek is best known as a prime cutthroat spawning area and is closed to fishing in the spring. There is a fish dam here, as there are on many of the South Fork's tributaries. The dams block access to the spawning waters. Local volunteers hand-net the trout and remove the rainbow and rainbow/cutthroat hybrids that are reducing the genetic purity of the South Fork's native cutthroat population—the Yellowstone cutthroat and the Snake River fine-spotted cutthroat. This enables the cutthroat to proceed to their spawning grounds.

After Yellowstone Lake and the upper Yellowstone River, the South Fork is the most important fishery for the survival of the Yellowstone cutthroat. This fish has virtually disappeared from the Teton River, just to the north, and it is under assault in Yellowstone Lake from alien trout and disease.

Idaho Fish and Game stocked rainbows here during the 1980s. Why, when there were two species of cutthroats? Because anglers like rainbows, which jump like acrobats when hooked. Unfortunately, they spawn at the same time as cutthroats, so the species interbreed, diminishing the genetic purity of the cutthroat. And rainbows appear to be outcompeting the cutthroats. Twenty years ago there were 4,000 cutthroats a mile; in 2002 there were approximately 1,000 each of cutthroats and rainbows. More recently I've heard 1,500 of each—no one really knows. Both species (and the hybrids) are under pressure from the ever-growing number of anglers.

Conservation groups have attempted to have the Yellowstone cutthroat listed as threatened under the Endangered Species Act. Idaho detests the idea since it would place many river systems used for irrigation under the kind of federal restrictions that local voters loath. Farmers are particularly adamant since listing would undoubtedly affect the amount of water available for irrigation, and thus their incomes. Then, too, some political groups pressure state game and fish commissions to manage for maximum fish populations regardless of whether they are native or alien. Conservation organizations like Trout Unlimited disagree. They want to mitigate the effects of the alien rainbow through management and help assure the Yellowstone cutthroat's survival.

As usual, management means killing. The upshot of all this political wrangling is that anglers are now asked to kill rainbows on the South Fork to help save cutthroats. "Keep 'em and eat 'em" has replaced the catch-and-release ethic most modern anglers were raised on. As Trout Unlimited, which gets as much credit as anyone for instilling the catch-and-release ethic, says in a brochure on the South Fork, "Ironically, this ethic, based largely on a commitment to leave resources intact for future generations, may now be the biggest obstacle to protection of a healthy cutthroat fishery." Very, very complicated, this matter of conservation.

This in turn has provoked other layers of fierce resistance. Some anglers, especially guides, want the rainbows in the river because their clients prefer catching them—the "they are beautiful and they jump" argument. Furthermore, with increasing pressure on all trout in the South Fork, anglers don't want to reduce the fish populations on their world-class fly-fishing river for any reason. And finally, many anglers, it must be said, simply don't want to kill fish—or anything else. I am reminded of a friend who said the hardest thing for Peace Corps trainees was learning to kill chickens and guinea pigs. The catch-and-release movement is thus impaled on its own petard: millions of modern fishing folk don't want to be part of the food chain; they just want to have fun, and killing isn't fun. The fly-fishing fraternity is filled with those who are quite happy to catch and release fish all day and then order a dinner of farmed trout for twenty-five dollars at a fine restaurant.

There the issue stands: good ecology versus money and fun.

"Where are the fish, Boots?"

"Where are the salmon flies, Boots?"

The life of a guide is not an easy one. Expectations are nasty things. The more perfect the setup, the greater the disappointment. Boots points out, reasonably, that the other boats aren't catching anything, either. When we pass them, we trade fishing gossip. There is indeed little action.

"Boots, you're absolved."

We bide our time. I'm not perturbed by the lack of action. Perhaps it's the lullaby of water washing over gravel bars, perhaps the negative ions, I don't know. And surely the flies will fly, the fish will feed. We see an occasional salmon fly, but damn few, and the trout have obviously not keyed into feeding on them. Strange, yes, but fishing is a mystery.

Bob lands a small cutthroat. I go into teasing mode.

"Boots, is that a trout or a minnow or something between a trout and a minnow?"

"Hey, it's worth points," Boots says, referring to the point system of the One-Fly competition.

"Boots, I don't want points, I want big fish, the bigger the better. I'm insecure."

Bob is wearing his gentle smile, a smile I most often see when he is fishing.

"Boots," he says, "we suffer from 'big-itis', believe it or not."

Around noon, Bob lands a fat Yellowstone cutthroat, sixteen inches long. As soon as the fish strikes, Boots says it's a Yellowstone cutt; he saw the flash of its golden yellow belly. The two indigenous species are similar, but the spots on the Snake River fine-spotted cutthroat are smaller—thus the name—and the belly tends to be white and pale yellow, not gold. Both are beautiful—the Yellowstone flashy, the fine-spotted elegant. We release it and stop for lunch on a wide, sunny gravel bar surrounded by deep green grasses and great views of the river upstream and down. No mosquitoes, several ospreys and eagles, a pleasant riffle with lots of negative ions streaming our way.

Although guides now commonly prepare haute cuisine lunches served on folding tables with chairs and various other amenities, Boots knows we want exactly the same thing every time we go fishing together: buckets of cold fried chicken, olives, chocolate chip cookies, and soda pop—although we would never dream of eating that way at home. We bake in the sun and look for bugs.

After lunch we walk up a side channel to look for fish. What we find as soon as we leave the gravel bar is riveting. The grasses and bushes are covered with masses of salmon flies. I run my hand through one clump of grass and end up with six silent monsters clinging to my fingers. Midday, sunny, breezy—this is prime time for them to be on the river, but they are not.

"Vexing to the spirit."

"Still copulating?"

"Well, I don't blame them."

Having shucked their nymphal husk, salmon flies spend several days in the light, mate, and die. Why should they hurry just to satisfy the cravings of anglers?

Back on the river, we turn to other offerings: Yellow Sallys and Pale Morning Duns, Chernobyl Ants and Fat Alberts, X-Caddis and Stimulators, Wooly Buggers and Double Bunnies.

"Has anyone written a history of fly names, Boots?"

"Nope. Not that I know of. Good idea for a book, though."

"Sounds to me like writing a telephone book."

We float dry flies into the riffles, we pound the banks with foam attractors, and we dredge the pools with streamers. We pick up a few fish, but it's a strangely slow day on this great river, a reminder of fishing's vicissitudes.

Driving home, Boots asks if we want to try the South Fork again next week.

Bob says, "Why don't we try the Green? What do you think?" Bob likes the Green River as much as he does the South Fork, and a disappointing day always puts you off a river.

"Yeah, the Green will be good now."

We agree we'll let the South Fork rest for a while. That probably means the end of the salmon fly season for us. Next week we'll fish the Green for big browns, and I will try to avoid giving them lectures on natural gas development in the area. Boots will continue to guide the South Fork, though his main efforts will be on his home water, the Snake proper, in Jackson Hole. But I'm not through with the South Fork for the year.

---------->

October. Greg Goodyear and I float his drift boat off its trailer at the Conant Valley launch site. Greg calls Julie's Shuttle Service on his cell phone and tells her where to find the keys and twenty-five bucks; when we reach Byington, probably after dark, his truck and trailer will be waiting for us. As we push off, the swift current grips the bow and we turn downriver. Greg rows as I rig my rod. It's cold. My thermometer reads 54 degrees when I submerge it and 29 degrees when I hold it in the air. No other boats in sight; no sound but water lapping the hull. Strands of mist hover above the river like smoke from a guttered fire. The frost on the cobbles and willows glitters like crushed pearls.

We bob through the first riffles, discussing tactics. During the summer, Greg is a fly-fishing guide. He is also a climber, a skier, a hunter, a woodworker, and for many years the best kayaker in Wyoming. Like most professionals, he is a perfectionist, knowledgeable and expert in everything he turns his attention to. Although I am not a paying client, Greg is definitely the guide. I will defer to him, not only because he is a far better fly-fisherman than I am but because he guides the South Fork. The repetition, intimacy, and constant instruction of guiding create an expertise rarely attained by someone whose livelihood doesn't depend on another person catching fish. Besides, I can't row. He doesn't believe that, but I soon convince him beyond all doubt. He rows, I fish.

Simplicity rules fly-fishing on the South Fork in late autumn. Only two hatches are common, the midge and the *Baetis*, and they won't be about until the air is warmer. Both are tiny: their dry fly imitations start at about the size of a pea and get smaller, usually the smaller the better. The last grasshoppers went with a week of frost. A few Mahogany Duns may linger but are nothing worth concentrating on. This morning a trout's breakfast lives in deep water—thus the big rod and large streamers that mimic small fish.

When it comes to streamers, I don't mess around. I use a nine-and-a-half-foot steelhead rod with a floating fly line and a short, heavy leader. This is not overkill: Idaho's record brown trout was landed in these waters in 1981. The fish was a yard long and weighted 26.4 pounds. That's a serious fish.

The water is dark, so Greg suggests a White Zonker, a minnow imitation. I search my box of streamers and hold up a white tungsten cone-headed, tinsel-wrapped, buggy-eyed concoction with hunched shoulders that reminds me of a vulture. It is not a Zonker. Greg nods: "That'll do." I don't like trout flies with eyes; they remind me of spinning lures, and I agree with a sign I once saw along a Kashmir trout stream that said, "Spinners are Sinners." I'm being guided today, however, so, a White Vulture—with a barbless hook, of course.

Greg holds the boat steady at the edge of deep water along the northern bank while I cast. I let the streamer sink and drift into the depths, mending line, then retrieve, stripping in line.

"Be more aggressive with the stripping," Greg suggests. I give him my best gnarly stare: I'm not accustomed to being asked to be more aggressive about anything.

I stand in the bow, my thighs wedged between the braces built into the front deck, and I cast. Cast, cast, cast. Nothing.

The mist burns off with a stiff breeze; the boat shudders; I feel colder. We are fine, though, dressed nearly identically in felt-soled chest waders, layers of polypropylene, and ski hats.

We decide to change to an Olive Wool-Headed Sculpin pattern created by Mike Lawson, a legendary guide who often fishes these waters. A sculpin is a small, ugly, bottom-dwelling fish, but they are quite a meal compared to a fly.

More casts. The rod's guides are clogged with ice, and more ice from the stripped-in line coats my bare fingers. I fiddle with the guides, I suck my fingers.

"Aren't your fingers cold?"

"No. It's one of the few advantages of spending your life climbing mountains." I can tell Greg is a wee bit impressed, and he is a very hard man to impress.

Greg holds the boat where he wants it in the current, rowing slightly, patiently. He has spent years of his life in currents and can ride eddies and seams the way a fine horseman can ride a horse: a touch here, a slight lean with the body there—effortless.

I cast to the bank and retrieve, more rapidly, moving my rod back and forth sideways to create more variety of movement.

Bang. I hook a good fish. Soon Greg is netting a sixteen-inch female brown trout. We admire her beauty briefly and slip her into the pool. She darts instantly into the depths, a flash of lightning into darkness.

"Nice fish."

There aren't that many brown trout here—their numbers increase as you go downriver. All anglers like browns; they adapt to a wide variety of habitats and temperature extremes, and they are smart and beautiful. Fortunately, browns spawn in the fall and hence do not hybridize with cutthroats. That browns are just another alien invader of the ecosystem is ignored by everyone—state, feds, anglers, and public alike.

As the day warms a bit I switch to a lighter rod with a floating line and an A.K. Best pattern of a Blue-Winged Olive, Best being one of the most innovative fly tiers in the West. It is one of those patterns that are so perfect it gives you confidence. I can imagine one mounted and framed.

Like any craftsman, you've got to believe in your tools. Perhaps a third of the allure of fly-fishing lies with the beauty of its tools. Another third lies in the beauty of the landscape where trout and their cousins—salmon, steelhead, and char—live. What's left? The beauty of the fish. If they were not so beautiful I would not inconvenience them so. I cannot imagine going to all this trouble for a sculpin. Take a look at James Prosek's *Trout of the World* and you will see what I mean. The trout of Corsica, Armenia, Iceland, Mongolia, France, Japan; of the Caspian and Aral seas, of Spain and Bosnia and Morocco, and those of many other countries—all are among the most beautiful creatures on earth. If we did not fish, we would not see them, and if we did not see them, we would not care about them. For good reason, anglers are the leaders in fishery conservation.

Greg suggests I switch to a dropper rig: a large, high-floating fly trailing a small nymph pattern on about eighteen inches of tippet. I watch as Greg ties a large red thing onto my leader.

"What do you call that?" I ask.

"I call it The Red-Winged Thing," he says without a hint of a smile. He has mastered the deadpan brand of cowboy cool.

The Red-Winged Thing is constructed of several layers of foam, red tinsel, and rubber legs. It's ugly as sin but floats higher than a cork. The dropper is a small Zebra Midge—if you can figure out what that might mean.

You don't cast a dropper rig; you lob it as best you can, aiming with the floater as the dropper swings merrily around like an electron about an atom.

Droppers work—perhaps too well, I sometimes think. Immediately I pick up a nice rainbow beneath a gravel bar. Then I miss several strikes.

"This ain't their first rodeo," Greg drawls, playing cowboy again. He grew up in Amherst, Massachusetts, so he has to work at it.

The canyon cliffs close in to the south, mostly gray, volcanic rock with ledges upon which grow cedar and conifers. Further south is a major highway and the Caribou National Forest—a reminder that there were once woodland caribou here. They are the most endangered animals in the forty-eight states; there are just forty-one left in northern Idaho, and that population would be extinct without the transplantation of caribou from Canada. There is no adequate recovery plan in place and no one talks of reintroducing them to Greater Yellowstone.

The river seems wild this time of year—seeming wildness is often seasonal in Greater Yellowstone. There are deer, elk, moose, black bears, mountain lions. We see beaver and immature bald eagles. Several areas along the river are officially off-limits in an effort to protect the bald eagle population. Currently there are thirteen bald eagle nesting areas along the river, which account for a third of the bald eagles in Greater Yellowstone and half the bald eagles in Idaho. That is a stunning figure and a judgment of what the rest of Idaho—a state that prides itself on its rivers—must be like. Here we are at the western edge of Island Yellowstone; a few more miles down river the wildlife situation becomes grim.

At present the eagle population is stable, but this seemingly wild place is in fact a narrow fragile corridor through developed land that lacks long-term protection. Above us on the north side of the river is the Canyon Rim Trail, open to hikers, mountain bikers, motorcycles, and ATVs; on the south are farms, a highway, and clusters of trophy homes. And both development and the rate of development are increasing. The entire region begs for more preservation.

Fortunately, we are still alone on the river. The late season insulates us, as does our being on the river in the middle of the week.

I catch another rainbow. Then three more. That bothers me.

"Where are the cutts?" I like catching natives; I couldn't care less if rainbows jump higher.

"They're here."

Near Lufkin Bottom I pick up two cutts on a small Adams parachute pattern that I claim I can see better than my favored A. K. Best pattern. Greg really gets the credit, though. My eyesight is not what it used to be, my reflexes have slowed—the usual excuses. Greg sees the strikes coming with remarkable acuity.

"Go! Go! Go!" he yells, his voice rising with excitement.

I console myself with the thought that he is nearly thirty years younger than I am. I start catching cutts.

A dirt road now borders the north side of the river, providing access from the town of Heise. Burns Creek enters the river from the north through another of Russell's "deep ravines." Like Pine Creek, Burns Creek provides important cutthroat spawning habitat. Across the river is Fisher Bottom, home of the writer Vardis Fisher, whose novel *Mountain Man* became Robert Redford's movie *Jeremiah Johnson*. I mention this factoid to Greg.

He replies, "A lucky writer, I'd say, tucked into a corner of this canyon fifty years ago."

Because of the road, this is where I usually fish from the shore. The best spots always (of course) seem to be on the other side. I want to go where I haven't been, so we drift toward high cliffs fringed with conifers.

I pound the banks. No luck. We drift for a while without fishing, enjoying the splendor.

Midafternoon, the south bank: we are plying a seam under a canopy of cottonwood and chokecherry. The water is dappled gold and emerald green, with lines of silver and pewter streaming beneath the forest. Boulders and smaller rocks lie several feet beneath the surface. Multiple cutthroats are sipping *Baetis*. They feed with the insistent repetition of a metronome. Greg holds the boat in the current. I cast a frail 6X leader—the merest glimmer of a line—and a tiny Parachute Adams.

Sip, sip. Sip, sip.

No strikes. It's maddening. Then I miss one: struck too soon. The fly is perfect; the fish are feeding. It's my fault, no doubt about it. A steady upstream breeze is spoiling havoc with my feather-light offering; it's hard to follow my fly in the fractured colors reflecting off the surface—more excuses.

Sip, sip.

Greg is about to jump out of his skin. We both are. Fly-fishing doesn't get any better than this.

"Below the end of the log. Eighteen inches. No, sixteen inches. You're too low. Higher. Higher. That's it, that's it. Go! Go! Go!"

Bang.

"Put more pressure on him."

"It's a 6X tippet."

"Don't worry about the tippet. It's stronger than you think."

"Nice fish."

I take over the oars, doing my best to keep the boat where it belongs while Greg takes his turn. He casts with startling elegance, particularly since he is using my rod, not his own. He lands two cutts before my efforts at the oars fail and we crash into a gravel bar with a nasty grating sound. The drift boat stops dead.

"Sorry," I mutter.

"Don't worry about the bottom; Clackacraft insures it for life."
We get out and float the boat clear.

A distant whine informs us of a motorboat, our first of the day. It
rounds the bend below us, its dull gray bow raised like a swimming
animal. The sound shatters our stillness, like a chain saw in a closet.
It grinds by us, we bob over its wake, it disappears upriver and finally, after several minutes, the racket fades.

"I hate it, I hate it, I hate it forever. The very least Dick Cheney
could do for his favorite trout river is get rid of the goddamn jet
boats."

Greg smiles his wan smile—he's used to them. I can't fathom
why they are still allowed on this river. A jet boat ruins what fishing
is about. And they smell like hell.

"Craven meat fisherman, I suppose, using worms and spinners?"

"Yeah, they used to be the bad guys, now they're the good guys—
killing rainbows, doing more to help the cutthroats survive than you
are by releasing them," Greg offers.

"It appears my hypocrisy knows no bounds."

My own catch-and-release tendencies have been in flux for decades. Now I am inclined to return native trout and kill all the
alien—rainbows, browns, brookies, and lake trout. That's a princi-
pled position, I assure myself. But today I don't kill anything and
that is becoming my norm. Why?

The truth is a mishmash of ambivalence and indecision surrounding the issue of compassion—compassion for the individual,
compassion for the species, compassion for the ecosystem. How are
they to be weighed? I only know that as I've gotten older it's become
harder to kill anything, even for compelling reasons. To kill for the
cause of fishery management is to become enmeshed in the very artificial management policies I find so distasteful. It is killing for an
idea, and that, I think, is always a mistake.

I feel that I ought as a resident of the ecosystem and a part of the
food chain to take a responsible role in that food chain, to kill wild
native fish and eat them. Now I put the wild native fish back and eat
the others—sometimes. Once the fish and the ecosystem are no

longer wild, clarity fades. One thing I've learned from traveling around the ecosystem is how complicated the matter of its preservation has become. And it is likely to become even more complicated.

When John Varley retired recently from the Yellowstone Center for Resources after thirty years in Yellowstone National Park he said, "I think the paradigm we've managed for in the past fifty years will have to change in the next fifty years because of climate change, invasive species, and a host of other issues. . . . The cause of pristine wildness was a great one to pursue, but if the Arctic melts, even the Alaska parks won't be immune from massive change." Since the South Fork sits at the edge of island Yellowstone, it and its fish will be one of the first places affected by such massive change. The thought makes me appreciate every trip here.

The breeze we've been fighting all day was the harbinger of changing weather. A low line of leaden clouds brings blowing rain. We don rain parkas. For the first time I put on gloves. Realizing we never stopped for lunch, we devour two sandwiches each and wash them down with sweet, hot, milky tea from my thermos.

I squint into the storm, now blowing sleet, now rain. We are barely moving. Both drift boats and rafts sit high enough above the water to catch winds that thwart progress. Greg begins to row downriver.

"Bummer, dude."

"Yeah, bummer," he says, minus the cowboy humor. After my pathetic performance there is no question of me rowing into the wind.

We pass two white drift boats beached on a gravel bar. One guide and client are fishing a side channel; the other group appears to be breaking camp. They have a fire going; an elderly couple stands close in a puddle of water, staring into the flames, hoods up.

"Imagine the conversation," I snicker. " 'Honey, I told you we should have gone to Maui.' "

The mood has changed. Wind blows clouds of copper leaves from the cottonwoods; they litter the dry swales like hordes of old coins. The landscape is subdued: tan and gray cobble bars, yellow ochre grasses, dull orange trees, Venetian red willows, charcoal skies, umber shadows beneath cliffs, conifer forests all but hidden in a jade gloom.

"Great weather for browns," I comment.

Greg nods, and rows.

I change to the steelhead rod and cast the Wool-Headed Sculpin toward the bank. Cast, strip, cast.

"Lets try the other side of the river," says Greg, oblivious to his labors. "There is a good run beneath a steep bank."

Bang. Another nice brown. Then another. The wind drops, the dark clouds fade to an ashen sky.

I try rowing again (I'm a bit better without the wind) while Greg chucks streamers at the undercut bank and picks up two browns in as many casts.

These steeply cut banks are intrinsic to the structure of the South Fork. The river sees some dauntingly high water, and floods are considered the area's primary natural hazard. The river is flowing at about 3,000 cubic feet per second—normal for this time of year. But in early summer 1997 the South Fork flooded, cresting at 43,500 cubic feet per second. The flood damaged 300 homes and caused $50 million in damage. The federal government provided flood relief. Few were brave enough to say the flood was the best thing that could have happened to the South Fork, even though these forests are formally known as "floodplain cottonwood forests"—and, again, it's worth repeating, probably the last great cottonwood forest in the West.

Although residents are loath to admit it, floods are essential for the health of the South Fork's ecosystems, and the levees built to protect houses are detrimental to their health. Cottonwood forests require flooding to reproduce; silt and sandbanks are the home of young cottonwoods. And it's good for the fishing. Research has shown that unconfined streams produced seven to eight times as many trout as confined streams.

But floods aren't so good for proposed housing developments on the riverfront. The number of structures along the South Fork has nearly doubled in twenty years and many of them are in the 100-year floodplain. The Army Corps of Engineers has permitted the construction of rip-rap levies that stabilize the front yards of expensive trophy homes. This "solves" one problem and creates others—problems for both private and public lands.

The levees restrain the river to deep channels instead of spreading over the floodplain in multiple channels. This in turn increases the force of the river, thus further increasing the potential of destruction downriver. Has any of this slowed real-estate development? Of course not.

The South Fork is like a priceless jewel in a cheap setting. If we are not very careful, we'll lose it. The economic value of the river—in terms of landscape, loss of recreation, loss of income to the local communities—is millions of dollars every year. No doubt in the future the American taxpayer will be asked to spend million of dollars to "rehabilitate" this channelized river to protect it from destroying the very landscape that led everyone to build homes here in the first place.

The Army Corps of Engineers is constructing $54 million worth of such rehabilitation right now along the levees in Jackson Hole. Both history and the law of unintended consequences suggest their efforts will have further detrimental effects on both the landscape and its ecology. Thus we circle the drain, wondering how we got into this mess.

It is dark. I'm still casting, so weary I'm making a mess of things.

"Want to stop now?" Greg asks.

"I thought you'd never ask." A hard man, that Greg Goodyear.

I break down my rods in their tubes and tuck reels into their pockets in my boat bag. The ship is in order. Greg rows into darkness, knowing exactly where he is going, feeling the currents and seams rather than seeing them. The great river surges through roots that hang from the banks like spiders. The oarlocks groan; the night smells of plowed earth; the Canyon section of the river and its wildness are gone.

In the dark, the architecture of the boat ramp at Byington is like a scene from *Star Wars*. I drink the last bit of tea from my ancient Stanley thermos and set it on the ground while we strap the boat to the trailer. In the darkness, I forget the thermos, my companion on many fine trips. I pray the person who finds it loves the South Fork, and that old thermos spends its next life in a fine drift boat floating through sparking riffles, with a man or woman chasing native cutts beside healthy cottonwood forests filled with eagles and moose and all the other noble critters.

6. The Wyoming Range

The dirt road from Big Piney, Wyoming, to the Snider Basin Guard Station at the southern end of the Wyoming Range follows, in a general way, the Lander Cutoff portion of the Oregon Trail. Except for occasional historical markers and graves, many pitifully small, one would not know that the road follows America's first Federal Highway, or that in 1857 alone 13,000 pioneers passed through these sagebrush-covered hills seeking more bucolic lands further west. Dusty, lonely, and monotonous, it is a road that induces either sleep or conversation.

Maria Newcomb is driving; I'm riding shotgun. Her father, Rod Newcomb, lounges in the backseat, alternately napping or asking succinct questions in his dry manner. Rod and I intend to walk the southern half of Wyoming's namesake range from Snider Basin for approximately forty miles north to where a road traverses the range at McDougal Gap. Maria has agreed to drop us off, thus the long, isolated drive. We're discussing whitebark pines, my favorite tree and the subject of Maria's recently completed master's thesis from the School of Forestry at the University of Montana. Whitebark pines will be an integral element of the jaunt we are about to undertake, because most of our route lies between 8,000 feet and timberline—whitebark pine country in Greater Yellowstone.

Whitebark pine, *Pinus albicaulis*, sometimes called "stone pine," is circumboreal, with subspecies ranging from the Alps through the Carpathians to the Urals and on across Siberia to Japan, Korea, and North America. It inhabits only mountain ecosystems, always in symbiotic relation with a member of the corvid family. The two are so interdependent some botanists call the whitebark a "bird pine." In Greater Yellowstone the corvid is called the "Clark's nutcracker" (*Nucifraga columbiana*).

The Wyoming Range is the southernmost limit of the whitebark pine in the Rocky Mountains. Whitebark pine forest covers more than half a million acres of Greater Yellowstone; it defines, ecologically and aesthetically, the upper subalpine regions of the ecosystem. The tree thrives in conditions we associate with high mountains: steep slopes with poor soil regularly exposed to winds that often reach hurricane force. It is what ecologists call a "keystone mutualist"—a keystone being the stone at the top of an arch that keeps the other stones in the arch from collapsing. Every keystone species is essential to diversity in its ecosystem.

Whitebark pine literally builds ecosystems—including a big chunk of Greater Yellowstone. If the population of a keystone species declines, the effects cascade throughout the ecosystem and alter virtually everything, from mammal populations to insect distributions, floral disease, and fire regimes. Thus the whitebark is like a fulcrum whose balance vitally affects the health of our ecosystem. And like every balance it has a tipping point beyond which it does not recover.

Unfortunately, whitebark pine has been decimated throughout the northern Rockies by white pine blister rust (an exotic parasite from Eurasia accidentally introduced in Vancouver, British Columbia, in 1910), the pine bark beetle, and a warming climate that, literally, eliminates its habitat. Montana has already lost over half its whitebark pine forest, and whitebark pines are virtually gone from Glacier National Park.

Maria knows, feels, and expresses all of this in her modest way. She has conducted whitebark surveys as part of her research, though not here, so she asks Rod and me to look for sick whitebark.

The Snider Basin Guard Station, a cluster of vacant white

buildings on a bench above South Piney Creek, is quiet as a church. One sign advises that they can be rented during the summer, another warns of hantavirus in the buildings—which no doubt shrinks the number of people considering residence. I consider this to be an example of Forest Service humor.

We park at a cattle guard and unload our gear. Rod strolls off to look at the buildings while Maria and I conclude our whitebark conversation. Suddenly—I would say out of nowhere but we are nowhere—an SUV appears with the sheriff of Sublette County at the wheel. The window slides down with the usual electric hum and the Sheriff points at Rod.

"Is he with you?"

"Yep. What's up?"

"Oh nothin'. Just lookin' for illegals."

The window slides up, and without a further glance or wave the sheriff cruises down the road toward Big Piney.

Rod and I shoulder our packs, groaning like beasts of burden. Maria waves good-bye. As her little Honda fades into the distance, we sink into the silence and walk west along a muddy two-track that ascends steadily through sagebrush and meadow toward the forest above. Although it is beautiful weather in mid-July, we won't see another person for five days.

The Wyoming Range extends from the headwaters of La Barge Creek, South Piney Creek, and the Greys River north to the junction of the Hoback and Snake rivers, near Jackson Hole. Its 700,000 acres is part of the largest roadless area in Wyoming. Of all the ranges in Greater Yellowstone, it is among the least known and the least visited—at least during the summer. It is undoubtedly the least seen. The only place you notice its imposing length is from U.S. 191 and 189, two highways in the Upper Green River Basin. Even then, the mountains fail to impress because the jagged ramparts of the Wind River Range, to the east, and the spectacular Gros Ventre Range, to the north, capture your attention.

In winter, however, snowmobiles incessantly ply the 353 miles of the Wyoming Range Snowmobile Trail, injecting the local economies with much-needed income. According to one survey, the range ranks among the ten best snowmobiling sites in the country. I believe it. Come January, their telltale tracks score the pristine peaks with graffiti and their grinding cacophony fills the now-silent valleys like a symphony of jackhammers.

Unlike Greater Yellowstone's famous granitic ranges—the Tetons, Wind Rivers, and Beartooth—the Wyoming Range consists of layers of sedimentary deposits: limestone, shale, sandstone, clay, and conglomerate, all cracked, shattered, buckled, and upended by faulting. It is part of the 5,000-mile tract of rock extending from Alaska to Mexico known as the Overthrust Belt. Sadly for those who love the American West, the Overthrust Belt contains immense deposits of coal, oil, natural gas, and coal-bed methane, which the energy industry is developing with scant, if any, consideration of its pernicious effects on the health of Greater Yellowstone.

The mountains of the Wyoming Range are generally rounded, though in some places long-gone glaciers carved steep cirques and lines of cliffs. Eminently walkable ridges link the summits. Its vast meadows are rich and wet, emerald green, and teeming with wildlife. The northern slopes are covered by dense forest. Flowers bloom in an abundance not exceeded anywhere in the ecosystem.

Our traverse of the range will follow a route the federal government has designated "The Wyoming Range National Recreation Trail"—"national recreation trail" being a designation that recognizes "exemplary trails of local and regional significance." On our topographic maps it appears as "The Wyoming Range Trail."

One would think such a fancy name would mean trail signs replete with directions and mileage, but we see none. The only guidebook for the range is charmingly vague about our route, so much so I didn't read it carefully or bring it along. We have the guidebook's recommended topographic maps; we have a compass; between us we have nearly a hundred years of experience in the mountains. Surely this is sufficient.

We feel no need to stay close together. The only sound is the soft thump of my boots in dust. We pass a dilapidated cabin, a memorial plaque, a boarded-up hunting camp. Lupine, yarrow, and wild buck-wheat are abundant. So are moose droppings. Half the moose in Wyoming live in these mountains. A great blue heron cruises above the willows, then gracefully folds its wings and drops to a sandbar along South Piney Creek.

The forest brings welcome shade. We rest at the edge of an open field filled with horsemint and mats of bright green moss through which flow seeps and rills that trickle across the trail. Beneath us, the creek meanders through thickets of willow—prime moose habitat. The streambed appears paved with yellow, gold, and bronze rocks the color of old cave paintings. Scattered among the willows are patches of fresh grass studded with vermilion paintbrush. The only sounds are the wind in the trees, the gurgle of the creek—mountain sounds.

Finally we find a Wyoming Range Trail sign with directions to Cheese Pass. We dig out our maps. The Wyoming Peak quadrangle shows our trail leading off the map to the west; it appears to reap-pear on that map just short of Cheese Pass. The gap is a mere three-sixteenths of an inch, a measly dent. Unfortunately, the quadrangle to the west, Poison Meadows, was not on the list of maps the guidebook recommended as essential for the trip. Hmmmm . . . Certainly nothing important could happen in that tiny gap, could it? I fail to look at the opposite flap of my map—which clearly shows the Wyoming Range Trail reappearing from the west. Hmmmm . . .

An obvious shortcut leads from where we are up the North Fork of South Piney Creek to the east side of Cheese Pass. I believe in shortcuts. We fold the map and head north. Alas, at precisely the middle of that tiny indentation on the unrecommended but all-too-essential Poison Meadows quadrangle, the Wyoming Range Trail turns north along the slopes west of Cheese Pass. What appears to be the case is not—it's a different trail altogether that "reappears" on the Wyoming Peak quadrangle. We have embarked upon our first, say, exploration.

We climb steeply for two miles up an increasingly slim trail, stopping occasionally to admire the creek. Avalanche paths line the mountain slopes. The vegetation in the tracks is different from the surrounding forest, a difference that increases floral diversity. Additional diversity is distributed vertically: the higher slopes subject to annual avalanches contain short flexible plants and shrubs; those lower down that endure occasional slides contain larger shrubs and small trees. The avalanche paths terminate in a patchwork of tangled trees, the debris of large avalanches that slide every fifty or one hundred years. Occasionally a particular tree has survived, standing nobly in open terrain.

"Why has that lone fir survived?" I ask.

Rod, who founded the American Avalanche Institute in 1974 and who knows as much about avalanches as anyone on the planet (he was awarded the American Avalanche Association's Professional's Honorary Membership Award in 2004) drops his customary reticence to discourse on his favorite subject, though he remains laconic.

"No one knows why a particular tree is spared. The forces are very complex and can't be predicted."

"Why do avalanches stop where they do?"

"The force of an avalanche dissipates as gravity decreases with the angle. The big ones come to rest at about ten degrees."

Rod is sixty-nine, of medium height, rail thin, and clean shaven, with trimmed gray hair. He is utterly intransigent about his principles, which is why his manner often reminds me of Gary Cooper in *High Noon*. His pack looks half his size, perhaps a bit more. We've guided together in the Tetons for twenty-five years and enjoyed several memorable adventures, including one involving my willful disregard of maps.

We leave the creek, now only a brook, and climb a steep ridge, eventually reaching high meadows and stands of whitebark pine. I smell elk. Before I can say anything, Rod says "I smell elk." We sit down, get out the binoculars, and wait.

Four herds of elk summer in the Wyoming Range, a total of roughly 10,000 elk, or one out of ten elk in the state. It is also home to the largest population of mule deer in the state, 50,000 animals, or, again, one out of ten in the state. An acquaintance of mine who obsessively hunts for trophy bucks says the range is the best place in Wyoming to find a record rack. There is no better big-game habitat in Greater Yellowstone. No wonder that 12,000 hunters received licenses to hunt here in 2004.

We glass the area but see nothing. They are bedded down in the forest this time of day, probably watching us. Nonetheless, for the rest of the day I smell elk.

The trail forks into ever-smaller branches, some of which peter out in meadows. Something is amiss, but I don't care and Rod kindly chooses not to mention our previous map adventure. We choose a promising game trail solely on the grounds that it leads through a stand of whitebark pine forest. Unfortunately, we find it is filled with dead and dying trees.

Whitebark pine has suffered at our hands for nearly a century now, though it has only recently affected Greater Yellowstone. We logged it for the cheapest and most shoddy chipboard, cutting 600-year old trees for a logging industry that in Greater Yellowstone was at times subsidized by the American taxpayer to the tune of twenty-seven dollars a tree. We suppressed fires, giving the subalpine fir an artificial advantage in its competition with whitebark and abetting the spread of the pine bark beetle. We warmed the climate, which will soon force the species higher as it seeks cooler temperatures, even though in many places, like here, there are no higher places for it to go. Warmer temperatures increased pine bark beetle populations to plague levels. We introduced white pine blister rust. So, to be blunt, the plight of the whitebark pine is our fault.

We reach a shallow saddle from which we can see Mount Darby and Fish Creek Mountain to the east. The smell of elk is still intense, but now we glass for bighorn sheep. Both mountains harbor small populations of sheep transplanted from other herds in an attempt to repopulate these mountains. The Wyoming Range was once famous for mountain sheep and sheep hunting. Teddy Roosevelt hunted here; Roosevelt Meadows, farther north, is named for his camp. The last native bighorn were shot in the 1960s. The forty or so mountain sheep still in the range—artificially reintroduced in the 1980s—are just hanging on, and their ability to connect with other mountain sheep populations in Greater Yellowstone is at best tenuous.

We don't see any sheep.

Although this relic mountain sheep population is distressing, such losses and reintroductions are common. In the American West, mountain sheep numbers are only a fraction of what they were before Europeans arrived. Ironically, Wyoming had to import mountain sheep from Oregon to bolster its residual population. The director of Wyoming Game and Fish, Terry Cleveland, once boasted, "This is what wildlife conservation is all about." But no, this is what wildlife conservation in Wyoming has been reduced to by a century of federal and state folly, a combination of ignorance and mismanagement in the face of remorseless pressure from sheep ranchers.

"What got them?" asks Rod.

"Domestic sheep that spread disease to their wild cousins. Habitat loss. Too much hunting. Acid rain that affects mineral content in soil and water, which in turn some believe affects a lamb's bone development. As usual, the causes are cumulative in a way we don't understand. When the tree line rises with global warming, they'll be gone. Mountain sheep won't live in forest."

As recently as 1965, at least 345,000 sheep grazed the Wyoming Range and the Salt River Range, just to the west. Despite the Forest Service studies demonstrating the destructiveness of sheep in mountain habitat—destructive to both flora and fauna—they still graze this range, albeit in limited numbers. The only good thing domestic sheep grazing in these ranges ever produced was an excellent book, C. L. Rawlins's *Broken Country*.

"With mountain-sheep-hunting permits going for as much as three hundred thousand dollars a whack at lotteries in Montana, one would think that the profit motive would replace domestic sheep with wild sheep," I continue, warming to one of my favorite rants.

But this ignores the Jurassic mind-set of Wyoming politics. When a professor at the University of Wyoming Law School wrote a book critically assessing the environmental impacts of grazing on federal lands in the West, a state senator threatened to end funding for the Law School. So much for free speech.

It's late. Our "trail" has disintegrated into a web of traces we can no longer honestly pretend are trails. They lead off the saddle in all directions. We're a mile from anything that the map indicates is a trail, and it is not the Wyoming Range National Recreation Trail.

We work west, bushwhacking now, until we gain a buttercup-covered knoll at 10,200 feet beneath a minor peak sheltering a relic snowfield. Melting snow provides water for dinner and tea.

Game trails crisscross the red sandstone scree above us. A cow elk wanders out of the forest, takes our measure, and begins grazing flowers and sedges only twenty yards from us, quite indifferent to two old men sipping tea. Wouldn't happen in hunting season—they know what's going on.

The sky is still clear; no clouds or wind all day. "Perfect weather," says Rod—his only comment for the evening.

We sleep in starlight, doing our best to avoid the mosquitoes and flies. Rod has a head net; I apply liberal doses of 100 percent DEET—to no avail. DEET doesn't stop the buzzing. It is warm and damp, too warm for a sleeping bag, even at this altitude. I'm either too hot or too exposed and paranoid about it. The buzzing keeps me awake well after Rod is sound asleep. Finally, late, a stiff breeze rustles the firs, the temperature drops, and the bugs leave.

We rise early, eager to find the trail. We can see where it is; the problem is getting there. Before us lies a north-facing slope of thick forest tangled with deadfall and dense underbrush—a healthy old-growth forest.

We thrash down and across, trying to retain as much altitude as possible. Finally the gradient lessens and we stumble on traces of an ancient path next to a rock wall apparently built by sheepherders to keep flocks together at a tricky passage. Or was it perhaps Indians driving game? We don't know. Fresh elk sign everywhere. Elk hunters have the highest success rate in the Wyoming Range of any area in the state, and you couldn't hunt in prettier country.

In the shaded forest are heartleaf arnica, Canada violet, woodland strawberry, and a small white draba I can't identify, though I suspect it to be the boreal draba, a critically rare species in Wyoming and a species of special concern.

Thick forest is perfect habitat for Canada lynx and their main prey, snowshoe hares. Even though I know my chance of seeing even lynx sign is virtually zero, I look for tracks in the bogs. A lynx is a big cat weighing up to forty pounds, with tufted ears and big furry paws, a beast worthy of myth and my favorite critter in the ecosystem, even though I've never seen one.

This is probably the best lynx habitat in the Greater Yellowstone ecosystem. During the winter of 1971–72 trappers caught eighteen lynx in the Wyoming Range. Then the numbers declined—no one knows for certain how much, or when. The lynx, along with the fisher and the least weasel, is among the most endangered mammals in Greater Yellowstone. In 2000, it was listed as threatened under the Endangered Species Act. This created the usual committees and rounds of research to establish how the listing would affect use of federal lands. A group of scientists developed a reasonable plan to help the lynx, but the Forest Service, acutely sensitive to political pressure, gutted it in favor of logging, mining, grazing, and recreational interests.

At the time of its listing, researchers found only four sets of lynx tracks in the Wyoming range. In 2001 they found no sign of lynx. The listing may have come too late. John Squires, a biologist at the Rocky Mountain Research Station in Missoula, Montana, says, "It appears that lynx in the Wyoming Range are either in the process of going out, or have gone out. We don't know why."

Well, we may not *know* why, but several damn fine conjectures are staring us in the face. Logging leaves clear-cuts instead of dense forests; clear-cuts reduce cover for a myriad of small mammals and birds—red squirrels, voles, grouse—increasing their exposure to all predators, thus reducing the number available to lynx. Snowmobiles pack thousands of miles of lynx-friendly powder snow into hard trails coyotes can then use to penetrate deep into the mountains where the same snow historically limited their presence. Since coyotes feed on the lynx's primary food sources the lynx's food supply declines further. The last two lynx tracked via radio collar by Wyoming state biologists starved to death.

Last winter a group of biologists made a concerted effort to find signs of lynx in the Wyoming Range. They found nothing. Records of lynx elsewhere in Greater Yellowstone remain rare, and the federal government refuses to consider the range critical habitat for lynx recovery efforts—an absurdity that reflects political pressure to keep the mountains open to energy development. Until the lynx population is restored, the ecosystem will not be intact. So we have, yet again, another line in the sand: If we can't save the remains of the southernmost natural lynx population in one of the least visited, remote, and biologically rich chunks of lynx habitat in Greater Yellowstone, then where?

More game trails. We follow one when we can, lose it, find another, and keep going. Soon we reach a fork of Fish Creek, a stream that flows from Cheese Pass, and after an easy ford scramble a short distance to a real trail. The mosquitoes are gone, but we notice that no amount of DEET will repel a small yellow fly. We eat lunch on a ridge sufficiently exposed to catch a breeze that helps keep the flies at bay. For some reason they are feeding on Rod and ignoring me.

We walk north through open cirques backed by red and yellow sedimentary cliffs dotted with snowfields. In the meadows the trail simply disappears into shoulder-high wildflowers. We climb onto the tops of big boulders to search for it. More bushwhacking. A long, particularly miserable bushwhack takes us down into Middle Piney Creek through miles of horsemint and avalanche debris. The little yellow flies are worse when we lose altitude. Rod is covered with welts, many of which are bleeding. The trail has disappeared again. Then, about the time I was sure Rod would mention the consequences of my past disinterest in maps, we hit two intersecting trails marked by an ancient, broken post. I pick it up and lo!—the chevron emblem of the Wyoming Range National Recreational Trail. It was lying facedown in the dirt.

The trail doesn't improve much because of its official designation. There are few markers: sometimes a cairn, sometimes a sharp pole stuck in a pile of rocks. The map tells us where the trail is supposed to be, or was, and at times we glimpse sections of it in the distance. It's not really a problem. All maps are imaginary abstractions, schemata that simplify what lies before your eyes, and it's pleasing to use those eyes, and your mind, instead of tramping someone else's designated rut. In his book *Small Is Beautiful,* the economist E. F. Schumacher puts it perfectly: "A man who uses an imaginary map, thinking that it is a true one, is likely to be worse off than someone with no map at all; for he will fail to inquire whenever he can, to observe every detail on his way, and to search continuously with all his senses and all his intelligence for indications of where he should go." Our path, trail or not, contours at about 10,000 feet—the loveliest altitude in the ecosystem. Just above us is timberline, around us uncluttered views of distant mountains.

In the late afternoon we ascend to a long, flat bench above 10,000 feet with a view down canyon to Middle Piney Lake and its empty campground. Above us is Wyoming Peak, 11,378 feet, the highest mountain in the range. It is not much of a climb—a walk, in fact— up a pyramid of rubble. Regrettably, the Forest Service has left the remains of an old fire lookout on the summit. I have no desire to climb to the summit.

Stunted, dead whitebark line the ridge above us. A group of their gray skeletons fool me: I think they are mountain sheep lying down. My enthusiasm fools Rod, too. The binoculars prove me wrong.

Camp is beneath the east face of Wyoming Peak, among patches of gooseberry and wild currant. They are a fateful contribution to the whitebark's destiny, for the gooseberry and the wild currant are members of the genus *Ribes,* which hosts the spores of the white pine blister rust. Winds blow the fungus onto the pines; after a year or so of infection, the pines release other wind-borne spores that can infect *Ribes* for hundreds of miles. No one has the slightest idea what to do about it, though fortunately a few trees seem resistant and there are plans to reforest areas in the Northern Rockies that lose trees to the rust. However, replanting 500,000 acres at high altitudes would require a massive agriculture operation that might well be worse than simply losing the whitebark. Nor would it protect the whitebark from the pine bark beetle or from a warmer climate. Like the plight of the cutthroat trout, the tragedy surrounding the whitebark pine symbolizes for me the depth of our muddle: another Humpty Dumpty Deal again, another spiderweb to repair with our fingers.

A rivulet draining a snow bank near the summit of the peak is sluicing mud and rocks down a gully on the east face and enlarging an alluvial fan at the bottom. Rod goes over to watch the action. All aspects of the mountain world interest him to a degree uncommon even among mountain guides. I sketch and work on my journal.

Toward dusk three bull elk, their racks still dressed in velvet, stroll onto a sunlit ridge to the east. We glass them with the interest of hunters, though we have not hunted elk in years. The world grows still beneath us. As the light fades from the sagebrush sea below us, a violet umbra rises above the Wind River Range, miles to the east, signaling rest.

Dawn arrives slowly, subtly, a mere tinge of pink. After a while a sliver of sun creeps over the rim of the earth, flooding the peaks above us in a burst of golden light. The whitebark-lined ridge above us soon glows, revealing four cow elk feeding on fresh grass. We watch them through binoculars as we drink tea in silence. Silence—the universal refuge and our inviolable asylum, wrote Thoreau; the only voice of God, said Melville.

The morning's first task is clear: a gentle hill of dark shale leads to a saddle between Wyoming Peak and Peak 10,720, slightly to the northeast. The hill is furrowed with domestic sheep trails and the dirt bike ruts we've been following since Middle Piney—quite illegal here. Wild, silent, and empty these mountains, but sadly, criminally, scarred.

In the morning chill, minus the ubiquitous yellow flies, we enjoy a pleasant, invigorating climb. The saddle at the top is covered with mats of white and pale lavender phlox. Craighead, Craighead, and Davis's *A Field Guide to Rocky Mountain Wildflowers* informs us that this phlox blooms "when young red squirrels first start climbing about."

I pray there are lots of them, for the red squirrel is another piece of the Greater Yellowstone's fate. Whitebark pine cones never fall. Red squirrels gnaw them off the tree and bury them in their middens. In the autumn, grizzly bears seek out the middens and stuff themselves with the fat- and protein-filled seeds. These nuts are larger than other conifer seeds in the ecosystem and are 30 to 50 percent fat. Research suggests that whitebark pine seeds provide a quarter to two-thirds of a grizzly's net digested energy. It is the caloric source that allows them to hibernate through the winter.

The dirt-bike tracks rip straight through the mats of phlox. What to do about illegal dirt bikers? Dirt bikers do not stop to identify themselves. Darth Vader helmets hide their faces so well you would not recognize your mother; duct tape covers their license plates, so photographing them is useless. Using a cell phone to call authorities usually results in yawns. The days of rangers patrolling the wilderness like Aragorn are nearly over—that's why the Snider Basin Guard Station is abandoned and the sheriff drives a SUV and looks for illegals. From the looks of the cairns, posts, and signs—indeed, the trail itself—no one has patrolled this section of the Wyoming Range National Recreation Trail for ages.

Beneath the steep cliffs of Mount Coffin, at the top of Straight Creek, sits a lovely cirque with two tarns. From them flows a brook, winding through bands of bench rock and bordered by the most extensive array of Lewis monkey flowers I've ever seen. Named for Capt. Meriwether Lewis, this magenta flower with its yellow throat patches is kitschy in its extravagance. Even though our day has barely begun, we lie with our heads propped against our packs for a half an hour, unwilling to leave.

"Elk heaven," says Rod.

"I could spend the rest of the summer right here," I muse. "No need to move."

A long gentle traverse winds beneath hillsides badly degraded by sheet erosion. If domestic sheep are not moved frequently, they eat everything down to exposed soil, like locusts. Raindrops dislodge particles and remove layers of soil. Unless it is replanted, more rain produces more loss and a positive feedback loop is created that is difficult to reverse. The Wyoming Range was hammered by sheep grazing. One Forest Service report says some areas lost four and a half feet of topsoil. Equally important, domestic sheep eat whitebark seedlings, preventing reforestation. Even though grazing is no longer permitted in this part of the range (though it is permitted farther north), the results of a hundred years of sheep abuse remain obvious.

Lake Creek is surrounded by moist meadows filled with deep purple silky phacelia, white bog orchids, and pink elephant's heads—all rutted and churned by yet more dirt-bike tracks. The stalks of elephant heads are appealing, a spike of little flowers each shaped—exactly, one wants to say—like an elephant's head, replete with trunk. There is no other flower like it in the Rockies. But moistness means bugs, the price, it seems, of July in the Rockies. Rod keeps going. I rant to myself about bikers while trying not to step on flowers—an impossible ambition.

By lunchtime we have climbed into another cirque, this one blocked by a menacing cornice. Seeking a bit of shade, we lunch in a spindly grove of whitebark, serenaded by the raucous squawks of Clark's nutcrackers. This jay is the means chosen by evolution to reproduce whitebark pine in Greater Yellowstone. The nutcracker harvests the seeds from the cone, stores them in a special pouch under its tongue, and flies (up to eighteen miles!) to cache them along windswept ridges. Nutcrackers are industrious: it has been estimated that each caches tens of thousands of seeds every year. Many seeds are not recovered, even though the nutcracker's ability to find its seeds under snow is astonishing. The seeds not consumed are washed away, become lodged, germinate. The species reproduces.

Pines, nutcrackers, squirrels, grizzlies—a delicate web spun by evolution, a web so vulnerable to our invasive abuse.

Above us, a narrow rocky trail leads to the crest of the range. We stare at the cornice. "In a heavy snow year we'd be kicking steps here," says Rod.

Soon we are at it, cranking up to an open ridge, at 10,600 feet. The view is marvelous. We scramble to the top of a gravel bump from which we can see mountain ranges in what my compass tells me is a 340-degree arc. We both know our ranges fairly well, but there are many in the distance—some well into Idaho—we cannot name.

The crest is broad, nearly flat, and covered with what I take to be limestone gravel. Whatever it is, fierce winds have so striated the gravel into channels that it looks like the surface of a sand dune. It is inherently windy here: in the autumn of 2002, winds atop the Wyoming Range were clocked at 114 miles an hour. Wind desiccates, but small flowers are everywhere, spaced evenly, as though planted by a machine. There simply isn't enough moisture for them to clump. I recognize alpine fairy duster and the yellow paintbrush. Another is a yellow member of the parsley family, I can tell that much from the smell—a smell so pungent that grizzlies locate the roots in the spring before the flower appears. *Lomatium graveolens*. Well named, I would say.

Another yellow flower has pods on the stems beneath its tiny petals: a bladderpod, Payson's Bladderpod, I think, another rare species. Many of the flowers here are restricted to limestone strata; sometimes they are limited to particular ranges of limestone strata, and I have never seen these in the granitic ranges I usually frequent.

Again we are hesitant to leave. That's the problem with backpacking—you always have a goal to reach that precludes idleness, the measured idleness requisite to intimacy with the natural world.

Of all forms of walking, ridge walking is best. We strike north through an endless sky, flowers, residual cornices, and lines of krummholz streaming up the slopes from the Greys River valley, the glaciated basin that separates us from the Salt River Range.

"The entire Greys River should have Wild and Scenic status, all fifty-six miles of it," I say. "We have only twenty miles of Wild and Scenic-protected river in all of Wyoming. But if the feds protected it, the protection will put a hole in their plans for energy development."

I've been fishing the Greys for forty years, so I'm a bit narrow-minded about potential gas wells in one of the least developed areas in Wyoming.

Rod says nothing. He's looking at the slopes of the Salt River Range: they are clear-cut as far as the eye can see.

The wind is so fierce Rod removes his visor. I seek protection in the lee of krummholz when I can. A piece of baling wire rolls across my path. Later I pass the remains of a saddle blanket. This country once saw more traffic. Finally we pass the last dip on the crest and see Box Canyon Lake nestled in a broad saddle beneath us. A major trail crosses the range here. A trail sign says: SNIDER BASIN GUARD STATION, 20 MILES (though a good deal longer the way we came); SHEEP CREEK ROAD—MC DOUGAL GAP)—18 MILES. The mosquitoes and flies are bad. We keep going, seeking higher ground.

We go up and down for the rest of the afternoon, in a mellow fashion, though mostly without the benefit of a trail. It has disappeared again, buried in flowers.

Rod spots another herd of elk just as the sun sinks over the crest. In a whitebark grove at the top of a tributary of Roaring Fork Creek are the remains of an old sheepherder's camp. The trees are chopped—one into the shape of a chair. Limbs are hacked off. Railroad spikes have been driven in close intervals for twenty feet up one noble old trunk. Horseshoes protrude from several other trunks, presumably placed as tie-down points for tarps or stock. Tin cans, rubbish.

"Trolls," I mutter. Whenever I judge tolerance is making headway in my soul, I think of sheepherders and understand the Inquisition.

Nonetheless, we camp. We watch more elk, talk shop, and listen to coyotes. Well before dark we are in our sleeping bags, searching for rest.

Sometime in the middle of the night, several elk run through our camp, awaking us with their sharp barks of surprise. A herd must have wandered into us, unaware. I have trouble returning to sleep. I'm fairly trusting of the wilderness, but when you are nearly trampled by elk you begin to obsess about other beings that go bump in the night. I admit I do worry a bit about grizzlies.

Reports of grizzly-bear sightings in the Wyoming Range have increased recently, but it was only in 2002 that an official agency confirmed the presence of one. Sorry to say, it was a dead grizzly. On August 11, a houndsman with his dogs accompanied a U.S. Department of Agriculture trapper to Deadman Mountain, roughly in the center of the range, to look for a bear that had killed ten sheep. The dogs cornered an adult bear. When the bear charged, the houndsman shot it at close range, unaware that it was a grizzly.

At present no other grizzlies are known to inhabit the Wyoming Range, even though it is superb habitat for them. Dr. Chris Servheen, who has led the federal effort to recover grizzly populations in the Northern Rockies, says that "the Wyoming Range is the next place where grizzly bears in the Yellowstone ecosystem will go as the population continues to increase and expand." But Wyoming's Grizzly Bear Management Plan did not allow the grizzlies to live here when they were delisted from protection under the Endangered Species Act. The stated reason is that there would be too many conflicts with people; the real reason, yet again, is that there might be too many conflicts with energy development.

The next morning we work our way north at 10,000 feet along the western edge of North Piney Creek and finally climb to the top of Marten Creek, an expansive divide. At a water break, Rod studies a boulder field to our east.

"More elk?" I ask.

"No."

Then several minutes later, softly: "Well I'll be darned. That may be a rock glacier."

I am ashamed to admit I've never heard of a rock glacier. Later I study hazard maps produced by the Wyoming Geological Survey. It is not a rock glacier. This quadrangle—Mount Schidler—shows a landslide off Peak 10,896. Indeed, I would guess that approximately 20 percent of the entire quadrangle consists of landslides—another hint of how dynamic Greater Yellowstone remains.

Our trail is hidden by flowers again, but I can see where it eventually cuts through a cliff band onto a high plateau. I wander in the general direction, enjoying the easy terrain, the flowers. Rod takes his own path; we both enjoy solitude.

The climb is short and steep. On top we rest and study the five-mile-long hogback of Triple Peak, which fills the view to the northeast. Triple's three summits—the highest being 11,127 feet—dominates the central Wyoming Range. Fellow Exum mountain guide Tom Turiano, in his *Select Peaks of Greater Yellowstone,* says it offers "several superb glisse routes on all flanks," especially in the spring when the dry, cold air keeps the corn snow in perfect condition. Rod, who still skies hard, studies it assiduously, as an owl might study a mouse.

Down again. We don't want to leave the alpine zone and its views, but the trail plunges into the forests of upper Cottonwood Creek. Another sheepherder camp features four .22-250 casings driven into a whitebark trunk. There were once a lot of .22-250s in this country, a fast, flat-shooting round perfect for coyotes and deer, though it was used on everything, including moose. Available in the lever-action Savage 99 rifle, it made a fine saddle gun.

Climbing out of the woods we lose the trail again in a little meadow at the bottom of another avalanche path. Up? Down? I guess wrong, and we end up on a ridiculously steep hillside of grassy hummocks, dense with lupine and sticky geraniums.

"Wouldn't it be ironic if two old guides fell to their death on grass?" I remark. Rod's lips curve ever so slightly into a smile—someone who didn't know him would miss it.

Soon we are bushwhacking through more prime lynx habitat. We thrash for a half mile, gradually losing elevation, until we cross a small stream. Since the trail ascends this stream somewhere above us, all we have to do is follow it. But the going is vicious, so we traverse out into a big meadow, seeking easier ground. After several hundred yards through fields of flowers, we find a grove of subalpine fir. The grass nearby is matted with elk beds and littered with droppings. A rill gurgles unseen beneath the flowers. Bushed, we call it a day. The bugs are bad, our dinner hurried.

A roll of distant thunder to the south makes me put up the tent. Rod prefers to lay his sleeping bag in a tangle of dense fir. A light mist of rain begins to fall as day turns to dusk, then darkness and a steady drizzle. Elk are near: I can smell them again. Occasionally I hear them running in the dark when they smell us. I wish to hell I had hunted elk here when I was younger. All good citizens of Wyoming are interested in elk. Legend has it that when someone from Wyoming reaches the Pearly Gates, Saint Peter asks only one question: "Get your elk?"

The last day is the best. A short bushwhack takes us to the trail again and we quickly regain the crest of the range. For the next two miles a barely visible path snakes along a narrow, grassy, rolling rim above 10,000 feet. No, nothing trumps walking ridges. We cruise, keeping enough distance between us to enhance our solitude.

The pass between Cottonwood Creek and Sheep Creek should be one of the most stunning of the many beautiful passes in the range. But it is not. Domestic sheep trails line the slopes, about a shoulder width apart. We've seen sheep damage before, especially above 10,000 feet, but this is the worst. Subalpine ecosystems simply don't recover from this amount of sheep damage.

I keep moving out of disgust. It is a 1,600-foot descent down Sheep Creek to McDougal Gap—and Rod's truck. The descent is gorgeous; the flowers are shoulder high again. At the truck we gorge on food and down water. We had been out of both. Rod nurses dozens of yellow fly bites. Then we head down Cottonwood Creek for the restaurant at Daniel Junction. Entering the sagebrush again, I feel the absence of alpine flowers and it occurs to me that the best thing we could do for the Wyoming Range is to convert the Wyoming Range National Recreation Trail into a National Wildflower Trail.

But this is not to be. The myriad problems already faced by these lovely mountains are about to be dwarfed by more serious tribulations attending the development of oil, natural gas, and coal-bed methane resources. Since the range is neither a national park nor a wilderness area, it is devoid of substantive protection, even though two-thirds of it is a roadless region crucial to Yellowstone's health and integrity. A bill to protect the Wyoming Range from energy development has been introduced in the Senate, but whether or not it will pass, and to what degree it will provide protection, remains to be seen.

In the summer of 2004, the supervisor of Bridger-Teton National Forest announced, without the customary public comment period, that the Forest Service would auction leases for oil and gas development on 175,000 acres of the Wyoming Range, including 92,000 acres of pristine roadless areas. When local citizens, business leaders, environmental groups, hunting and fishing organizations, Wyoming governor Dave Freudenthal, and Wyoming senator Craig Thomas protested, the Forest Service's Intermountain Regional office decided to withhold leasing until further study of public concerns. In April 2005, the Forest Service announced a new leasing plan of 44,600 acres. This is in addition to a 31,000-acre development by the Bureau of Land Management along South Piney Creek, near the Snider Basin Guard Station where we began our trip, and another 150,000 acres already leased to oil and gas companies in the northern section of the range.

More leases followed, and there is no reason to believe the federal agencies will not try to lease more land in the future. Their strategy is to nibble, nibble, until so much integrity and beauty is lost that no one cares about the vestiges that remain. Fortunately, though, in July 2006 the Interior Board of Land Appeals issued an injunction that halted additional leasing in the Wyoming Range until the BLM updates its environmental assessment—more than a decade old—of the damage to the area that is expected from energy development. During that time the lynx had been listed, the mule-deer population had dropped to half of what the State of Wyoming wanted it to be, and there was increasing concern of the status of the Colorado River's cutthroat populations. The administration ignored these developments and aggressively promoted leasing. Wyoming's sole representative, Barbara Cubin, a stooge of the energy industry, even tried to speed up the leasing process.

Oil and gas and coal-bed methane "development" entails extensive industrial sprawl. Adjacent development in the upper Green River Basin has reached a density of forty well pads per square mile, and there are plans to increase density even more. In some areas no place is more than a quarter of a mile from a road.

And the wells are only the tip of the catastrophic fragmentation of habitat, as any examination of such development in other parts of Wyoming, New Mexico, or Colorado will vividly demonstrate. The wells are embedded in a matrix of roads, pipelines, scars from burying pipelines, power lines, waste pits, seeping toxic sediments, compressor stations the size of factories, pumps, lights, security fencing, weeds, noxious gases, dead springs, dry creeks, empty aquifers, lots of dead animals, and incessant traffic. Air is polluted, water is polluted, land is polluted, sky is polluted. But the Bureau of Land Management, which controls leases on land not under the control of the Forest Service, has had the gall to suggest that this execrable pit of environmental devastation might become a tourist attraction that would compensate local economies for the loss of recreational income.

And yet public officials—even some environmentalists—speak of "appropriate development." This is a malignant conceit. There can be no "appropriate" industrial development in an intact ecosystem. There can be no "appropriate" industrial development in the most important wildlife region in the American West. All such talk is shuck and jive, smoke and mirrors, bait and switch. The end result is fragmentation, and for an intact ecosystem fragmentation is the death of a thousand cuts. The energy corporations say they will restore the abused land. What a joke. Ask the State of Montana if corporations restore abused land. Besides, doing so would be like repairing a spiderweb with your fingers, and we are not that smart or capable.

The current administration has assigned a high priority to energy development; it has ordered federal agencies to expedite oil and gas projects. I would like to be optimistic about the Wyoming Range, but I am not; there is simply too much money involved. The federal government, the state, local communities, and corporations are making billions of dollars in profits, and the industrialization will probably last for a century. People will accept snowmobiling the grid of new roads. I fear hunters will become habituated to stalking elk and deer among gas wells and pipelines. And in a final, fatal irony, hikers and riders traveling the Wyoming Range National Recreation Trail will wind through seventy-five miles of engineered blight that makes a mockery of what the federal government deems the "multiple use" of Wyoming's once-beautiful public lands.

7. The Deep Winds

-->

The Wind River Range—usually shortened to "the Winds" in conversation—extends for 110 miles along the Continental Divide from Union Pass to South Pass. Like the Wyoming Range, it is a peninsular extension of the core ecosystem and a corridor to similar habitat hundreds of miles away. Together they mark the southern limits of Greater Yellowstone. Both ranges descend into the Red Desert and other high basins stretching to Colorado, fundamentally different ecosystems that nonetheless provide crucial havens for Greater Yellowstone wildlife. Elk, deer, and antelope that summer in both ranges, and as far north as Jackson Hole, migrate out of the ecosystem into these desert areas during winter seeking food, a reminder that nature is not organized according to the lines on our maps.

The Winds are the highest and most consistently rugged section of the island we call Greater Yellowstone, as well as the most heavily glaciated region in the contiguous states. The rock is mostly granitic: gneiss in the north, granite in the south. The gneiss is among the oldest rock on the surface of the planet—3.4 billion years old. Climbers judge the granite to be as fine as any climbing rock in the world. Gannet Peak, 13,804 feet, only thirty-four feet higher than the Grand Teton, crowns the range and is the highest summit in Wyoming. Most of it is protected in wilderness areas—the Bridger, the Fitzpatrick, and the Popo Agie—729,000 acres often surrounded by roadless lands and uninhabited sections of the Wind River Indian Reservation. As wilderness, it's one of our nation's crown jewels.

To the west of the main peaks, above the Green River Valley, stretches a terrace I call the "western terrace," ranging in elevation from roughly 9,500 to 10,500 feet. Subsidiary peaks, hills, and hillocks rise from the terrace; innumerable lakes, tarns, pools, ponds, marshes, and bogs mark its surface; and they are all connected by rills and brooks and creeks. Glaciers carved the features on the terrace, and to drive up onto it is to travel through glacial history. Indeed, two of the names used to identify glacial episodes in the Rockies—Bull Lake and Pinedale—derive from geologist Eliot Blackwelder's fieldwork in the Wind River Range in 1915. The best place to see the moraines formed during the Pinedale glaciation is, not surprisingly, around the town of Pinedale, particularly the road leading from the town to a trailhead at Elkhart Park, well up on the western terrace and the most popular access to the northern Winds.

I first drove up this road forty-seven years ago and I have returned many times. I'm back again with Joe Kelsey. Joe is driving. In the back is Toby, a big, gentle, handsome golden retriever with massive feet who has climbed four Wind River peaks of more than 13,000 feet and many more lower summits. Toby is a genuine climbing dog, the fifth generation of golden retrievers to accompany Joe since he first traveled the range in 1969.

Joe is sixty-four years old, tall, lanky, strong in the manner you would expect of a former hockey player at Cornell and gifted in the manner you would expect of a person trained in chemistry and physics. He has a shock of white hair and a moustache to match. We are old friends and fellow mountain guides, but we haven't made a trip together without clients since we climbed the Northwest Face of Half Dome, in Yosemite, in 1970. I enjoy Joe's erudition, sharp wit, and blunt style. Lately I've developed a habit of calling the Winds "the Windy Rivers." Joe gives me a cold look and says: "I've always thought that rather cutesy." I'm looking forward to spending time with him in these mountains, his mountains, his true home.

Joe's 250 trips into the Winds over the past thirty-four years ranged from day-long hikes to several weeks. He loves the place and has written two books about it, including the standard guidebook, *The Wind River Mountains.* Most guidebooks are pedestrian affairs, a hodgepodge of lists and mileages linked by wretched prose, but *The Wind River Mountains* is a gift to everyone who enters the Winds, a guidebook that in grace and scope and authority has few rivals in North America.

Despite all those trips, he has never been where we're headed, Upper Alpine Lake, a remote source of Bull Lake Creek on the eastern side of the range in the Fitzpatrick Wilderness. Joe calls it "the wild heart of the Winds."

We plan a weeklong, circular walk of about fifty miles. A week might seem a bit too long for that distance, but some of our route lacks trails, there will be third-class climbing and steep snow, and the miles are, I remind myself, Wind River miles. Besides, we're too old to be lugging sixty-pound packs through the mountains, and we are too wise to hurry. As the samurais say, "only the weak are in a hurry."

It is late summer. The dense stands of aspen above Fremont Lake are still green; only a few trees are starting to turn—harbingers of autumn. Their leaves, cadmium yellow and orange, complement beautifully the deep blues of the lake. We talk climber's talk, gossip about friends, and catch up on our lives the way friends do on drives.

The Elkhart Park parking lot is half full. Forty years ago it would have been virtually empty this time of year, too late for summer tourists, too early for hunting season.

As soon as Joe opens the back door of his station wagon Toby leaps out, eager for the mountains. We drag our packs out of the car; they are too heavy by far. Mine is worse—binoculars, camera, and painting gear—my crutches. Joe is a minimalist by comparison. Toby isn't too keen about his pack, either. No comments. We've all spent a good portion of our lives carrying big packs in the mountains. We simply get on with it—two hours to our first rest stop.

The trail is crowded. We pass pack llamas and pack horses, people with dogs, people alone. Dogs with packs seem to outnumber people with packs. There is much tail wagging and butt sniffing. We greet friends from Jackson Hole and talk for a moment while standing with our packs on. Four portly, suffering Easterners explain they are on a fishing expedition to Island Lake, twelve miles in. Privately, we doubt they will make it, but we offer encouragement. On a level, open stretch of trail, a man dialing a cell phone runs into Joe. Without apology, he careens on, head cocked to the phone, eyes to the ground, less attentive than a stone.

"At least the dogs pay attention!" I exclaim.

The forest is open, a mixture of subalpine fir, lodgepole, and whitebark pine with a few flowers in between. The delicate, delicious, and charmingly named grouse whortleberry, a member of the blueberry family, covers much of the ground. Favored by everything from birds to bears, most of their berries are gone now. We snack on what remains, and later, among the talus by the lakes, on tart, seedy raspberries and gooseberries.

Hiking the terrace at 10,000 feet provides continual surprise. The trail dips and turns so often you can't predict what's coming—which is nice. The 7½-minute topographical map for this area, "Bridger Lakes, Wyoming," represents roughly 6½ by 8½ miles and shows 753 separate bodies of water. Joe says this quadrangle is not unusual. Other quadrangles show even more, and most of them contain trout. Since coverage of the Wind River Range requires forty-one 7½-minute quadrangles, that's a lot of fishing.

Seventy percent of the Wind River lakes that are more than 9,000 feet have low alkalinity levels, hence they are particularly vulnerable to the consequences of oil, gas, and coal-bed methane development upwind in the Green River Basin and Wyoming Range, which will disgorge a cocktail of toxic fumes into the air twenty-four hours a day for the next fifty to hundred years. The Wind River Range and its three crown jewels of America's wilderness system have the misfortune to be immediately downwind. Air-quality standards already are being violated with only 600 wells in operation—and with 10,000 more planned, pollution can only get worse.

The impending industrial nightmare seems far away this pleasant

September morning. The lakes and ponds we pass are often bordered by steep cliffs and boulder fields, through which scamper chipmunks and picas. The little bleats of the latter are the only sound we hear besides the creak of packs and our panting. Mountains appear from behind hills and then disappear behind hills, like ghosts. Of one minor mound of gneiss, Mount Baldy, Joe remarks, in his offhanded manner: "From its summit you can see more than seventy of the guidebook's 246 peaks."

We stop at Seneca Lake. The sun is gone, and the temperature is plummeting. We boil water for tea and dinner. Since Toby is along, we do not hang our food to discourage bears. This, of course, is apostasy. Official policy requires food to be hung at least ten feet aboveground and ten feet out from the tree trunk. But consider: In thirty-five years in these mountains Joe has never had a problem with bears as long as a dog—or better, dogs—were along. Outfitters I know say the same thing: bears won't come into a camp with dogs.

Official policy discourages dogs in the wilderness on the grounds that bears will charge dogs, and when the dogs retreat to their master for help, the bears come, too. This sounds reasonable, but I can find scant scientific evidence for it—only one instance in the authoritative reference for such matters, Stephen Herrero's *Bear Attacks*, and another on the west side of the Tetons in the fall of 2006. And there is considerable anecdotal evidence to the contrary. Even the head of the government's grizzly study team spends his fall in the mountains hunting with his dogs. We trust Toby.

At dusk I walk down to the lake. Everything is still. Suddenly, above the dark shafts of bottle green water, tiny silver circles appear, in unison, illuminated by the pale sky. Trout are rising to the evening hatch, sipping as delicately as a Victorian lady sips her tea. I sit and watch them until I hear only an occasional splash in the dark.

As we lie in the darkness of our tent, with Toby on watch outside, Joe instructs me in a little Wind River history, a subject on which he has no peer.

As is often the case in Greater Yellowstone, famous historical figures turn up in obscure places. On August 13, 1842, Lt. John C.

Rio in the snow at the cabin.
Credit: Jack Turner

Anglers, Firehole River,
Yellowstone National Park.

Credit: Steve Kobylski

Wolves and Ravens.

Credit: Tom Mangelsen

Beartooth Plateaus.

Credit: Jack Turner

Boots Allen and Bob Schuster on
the South Fork of the Snake River.

Credit: Tom Mangelsen

Inviting Ridges, Wyoming Range.

Credit: Jack Turner

Joe Kelsey and Toby, Alpine Lakes, Wind River Range.

Credit: Jack Turner

Square Top Mountain
and Green River Lake.
Credit: Joe Kelsey

Angler on Flat Creek.
Credit: Steve Kobylski

Lake with the Grand Teton in the distance, Northern Teton Range.

Credit: Jack Turner

Trumpeter Swan.

Credit: Tom Mangelsen

Bison in Winter, Yellowstone National Park.

Credit: Tom Mangelsen

Fremont, who would become a California senator and the first Republican candidate for president, passed Seneca Lake with an illustrious band of mountain men, led by Kit Carson, on their way to climb what is now known as Fremont Peak. Fremont did not like climbing mountains. From the top, he wrote: "A stillness the most profound and a terrible solitude forced themselves constantly on the mind as the great features of the place."

"Did Fremont name the peak after himself?" I ask. This was a common practice then.

"No. Fremont named only two things that I know of: the Golden Gate and Island Lake."

We are up early and off to Island Lake. From its southern shore, at 10,346 feet, is one of the finest views in Wyoming. To the north is Titcomb Basin, encircled with stunning peaks: American Legion Peak, Twin Peaks, Skyline Peak, The Sphinx, Mount Woodrow Wilson, Miriam Peak, Doublet Peak, Mount Helen, Mount Sacagawea, Fremont Peak, and Jackson Peak. I comment on the absence of the old sign identifying Island Lake.

"The Forest Service decided not to erect signs giving lakes names, not to allow more peaks to be named, and to remove mileage from trail signs," says Joe.

These changes are intended to enhance the wilderness experience, but they will take some time to implement. Since guidebooks to the Winds provide mileage data, and lakes are named on all government and private topographic maps, this seems to me a rather feeble offering to wilderness, things the Forest Service can do without offending energy or agriculture interests. Now if they would remove all the signs, cease maintaining all the trails, destroy all the maps of wilderness areas . . .

On a narrow but sandy beach, Toby and I take a dip in the lake, me stark naked, edging slowly deeper, Toby blithely swimming in circles. Joe takes pictures of us and promises no one will ever catch him in water that cold. I threaten him about the pictures.

A bit farther, just below the terminal moraine at the bottom of Titcomb Basin, we turn onto the trail for Indian Basin and Indian

Pass. The Forest Service sign says six miles to Indian Pass. The topographic map says 2.8 miles. Joe says three miles. Perhaps it is just as well the Forest Service leaves mileage off their signs.

Wind River veterans speak of a "Kelsey mile"—a distance subtly determined. A Kelsey mile is derived from experience and Joe has traveled the trail before us many times. A map is an abstraction, a representation of three dimensions reduced to two dimensions, like a painting of a landscape. The reduction in scale induces error. Ups and downs, twists and turns, gnarly talus and sliding scree, the corrugated and the muddy—all elude the abstraction. A Kelsey mile includes them. The result is a charming mixture of subjective and objective. I trust Joe: three miles.

We cross a stream, which would clearly be impassible in early summer, and climb to a string of unnamed lakes at 11,000 feet beneath lofty peaks. The lakes meander among slabs of gneiss topped by numerous boulders; it is a landscape without trees, barren and beautiful, austere as the moon, a landscape for ascetics. The trail has become a footpath. On the slabs are occasional cairns, lonely sentinels.

To the southeast, lit by the setting sun, is Ellingwood Peak, 13,052 feet. We call it "Ellingwood" because it was first climbed by Albert Ellingwood, an eminent mountaineer who made the first ascent, solo, in 1926. Unfortunately, when a popular mayor of Pinedale named Harrower died, locals worked to change the official name of the peak to Harrower. They succeeded; government topographic maps show "Harrower." To honor Ellingwood—and to protest political vanity, Earthwalk maps and Joe's guidebook use both: "Ellingwood" with "Harrower" in parenthesis. No small matter, this naming in the wilderness.

Joe believes that the north arête on Ellingwood is "the best middle-fifth-class climb in Wyoming." Perhaps not everyone agrees. One party took so long they were benighted on the descent and burned their copy of *The Wind River Mountains* to keep warm. Five pages at a time worked best, they said. Joe is unruffled: "Best use of my book I've ever heard of!"

Whatever the case, the arête glows like an ember above dark rock walls veiled with the advancing fragments of a thunderstorm.

I set up the tent in the lee of a garage-sized boulder to escape the wind. Joe's stove is not doing well and needs all the help it can get. He fiddles with the valves and joints to little avail; it still takes an age to boil a quart of water.

After dinner we wander about separately to find comfortable rocks to lean against and watch the storm. Light rain, gentle, almost mist. We are subdued. Indian Pass, tomorrow's first stretch, is 12,120 feet. The next stretch is a bit more than a mile across Knife Point Glacier. The third is Alpine Lakes Pass, also 12,120 feet. Our final leg will be the descent to Upper Alpine Lake. No trails after Indian Pass. We would just as soon not do all that in a storm.

Early the next morning a lone hiker from California passes while we are having breakfast. He's laboring under a big pack, but he is thirty years our junior and looks strong. He, too, is headed for Upper Alpine Lake, "on a walk in the wilderness," he says. We talk weather. The morning wind is shredding the night's gloomy cloud cover. We wish him luck. He disappears up the trail, a pilgrim on a quest.

The climb to the pass is pleasant, but the pass itself is a bit grim. For some unknown reason, the rock slabs suggest a quarry, and the view that greets us is dreadful: the once-magnificent Knife Point Glacier is a corpse. We sit, we stare in disbelief, we grumble. Beneath us is rubble, areas of black muck packed with cobbles, and raw ice laced with hundreds of rivulets—the consequences of deglaciation. It smells like a reef at low tide, a fecund stench altogether contrary to the crisp mountain air we've been enjoying.

When I reached this point in 1972, the glacier spread before my feet. I simply walked onto it straightaway. The last time Joe was here, in 1997, he descended hundreds of feet before putting on his crampons. Researchers suggest that the glacier shrank 850 feet in length in the past twenty years and lost 300 feet in thickness since it was photographed in 1922.

We walk, or rather slide, stumble, slip, hop, and walk down,

down, down. We curse. Toby curses, too. I was raised in a Marine Corps town by a Marine. I know how to curse paragraphs of curses, epic curses. Joe, accustomed to me speaking to clients in a guide's calm professional politeness, is shocked.

"The %$#@*& who don't believe in global warming should be buried up to their &^@*# necks in this slop for the rest of their %$&$@# days to ruminate on their %*&@# stupidity. . . ."

Finally we stop, as tired from anger as from effort. We back up to boulders and roll off our packs. We snack while Toby slakes his thirst in the icy troughs. Above us is 500 feet of steep rubble and scree. Joe curses again, this time about an annoyance more immediate than the planet becoming uninhabitable. It was hard snow when he was last here. "That," he points out, "is the only reason we're hauling our damn crampons for fifty miles." He ascended this pass on his way to the officially unnamed peak east of the pass he calls "Bete Noire"—but he did not descend from the pass to Upper Alpine Lake.

Nothing to do but go at it: step up, slide down, step up, slide down. We each choose our own path and pace, struggling in silence with heads down, penitents for humankind and its foolishness.

On the top of the pass, sitting on a rock, in shorts, running shoes, a fanny pack, and a skimpy sports bra, is a lovely young woman. She is talking to the Californian with the big pack. He looks as flummoxed as we are.

"Where did you come from?" I ask.

She is with a group camped at Lower Alpine Lake, she replies. She ran up to the pass for a look.

I try to be pleasant, friendly. I fail. I succeed in not saying anything to Joe about the wild heart of the Winds. She and the Californian scamper off south, chatting in the manner of those newly in love. Perhaps our pilgrim found his Grail after all.

We descend to Upper Alpine Lake and camp on the only flat spot around—a short day, but we are in no hurry to rush past the place we came to see. Tea takes forever. The stove is even fussier. Everything here *looks* cold; it's like camping in a freezer. When the tea gets colder faster in your cup than it gets hotter on the stove, you know you are in the mountains. We again go to our own selected places to mull over the world and be alone.

Morning. Upper Alpine Lake, situated at 11,335 feet, is deep indigo blue, arctic, and empty; it is too high and cold for trout, though there are probably diatoms and other tiny critters present. It is still as a mirror and reflects the surrounding terrain flawlessly on its surface.

"Rock and ice and sky and Allah," I remark, quoting my old Muslim companions in the Hindu Kush. The stillness and simplicity are like the mind in repose. The desert and the high mountains crystallize a truth about the cosmos our biotic world obscures—we are obsessed with life, the universe is not. Life came from the sea; the great religious traditions came from deserts and mountains. At Upper Alpine Lake, on a chilly, still September morning, sipping cold tea, one gets a glimpse of why.

The lake is surrounded by extensive boulder fields to the west and cliffs to the east. We head east—anything is better than boulder fields with a heavy pack. Soon we are climbing over boulders the size of VWs and scrambling along ledges. Toby is not pleased. Neither are my knees.

We reach cliffs that require either swimming in the lake or negotiating thin ledges. While the ledges would not be a problem for climbers, they are too narrow for Toby. The packs come off and Joe climbs up the face, searching for an easier way. I remain on the lower ledge. Soon I can't see him, and Toby, scrambling up hard terrain between us trying to keep track of his companions, can't see either of us. He howls a cry of such despair I think he has fallen and is injured.

But no. "Tow-bee," sings Joe. Soon Toby joins him, above, and they walk along wet grass below which nasty, downsloping, wet slabs drop precipitously a hundred feet into the dark lake. We all traverse until the distance between us diminishes to a steep slot only fifteen feet long but devoid of security.

Joe urges Toby toward me. He starts down, his huge paws testing for footholds on the tiny slippery holds. He stops. I start to ask how much Toby weighs but decide knowing would not be a positive addition to our situation or my mood. Toby glares at me with the look I've often given my climbing partners, the "What possible chain of events in my life led me to this point" look. Then he starts down again, panting, straight for me, assuming in trusty-dog fashion that I'm braced to stop him if he slips.

"Good dog!"

"Good boy, Toby!"

He keeps coming.

"What a good dog!"

He passes me without a murmur of gratitude. At the bottom there is much cheering and patting. "Good dog!" And it is true: Toby is a good dog, a great dog, all heart.

We agree that there is no easy way around Upper Alpine Lake.

We glissade down a rare patch of snow at the outlet and continue along a creek down to Middle Alpine Lake. Where it meets the lake the creek is paved with black lichen—covered stones, like cobblestone on a street. I hopscotch across through clouds of Callibaetis mayflies trying to rest on dry rocks.

"This would be difficult to cross in early summer," Joe says—he is given to understatement. "You'd have to climb steep snow to bypass it." He is thinking of revisions for the next edition of his guidebook.

Middle Alpine Lake is paler than the upper lake—cobalt blue—because of the increased concentration of glacial powder in the water, a substance known as "rock flour." Altitude is down to 10,988 feet, low enough for willows. Their pale lemon yellow is a welcome addition to the bleak landscape, like tulips in a winter window.

The western shore is strewn with till and talus and boulders. Avoiding fields of larger boulders, for the sake of Toby and for the sake of our knees, is not simple, but we work at it. I'm spooked by boulder fields; they are not without their dangers.

In early August 1998, a shifting boulder trapped the leg of a lone hiker east of here, a minister on his own journey into the wilderness.

Searchers didn't find his body until October. It took him more than a week to die. Like Scott on his retreat from the South Pole, this man of God maintained his diary to the end, a show of character and faith that his death cannot tarnish.

The sheer walls above us are unimaginatively named "the Brown Cliffs." The south face of Eagle Pinnacle, certainly one of the finest unclimbed faces in the Winds, rises above the lake. Joe studies it carefully. He has climbed more than 200 routes in the Winds, twenty-one of them first ascents, and I have no reason to believe he is finished.

This is remote country. Until 1991, the Geological Survey topographic map for this area incorrectly identified the relationships between the Alpine Lakes and their drainages. Climbers, including Joe, noticed the discrepancies but Joe, at least, didn't tell the Survey about it or about another he found on another quadrangle.

"I would not report a mistake on a map," he says. "I take a mistake on a map to be a celebration of wildness—better than an unnamed peak, up there with Thoreau's wild apples."

To our west, waterfalls and cascades from hanging glaciers tumble off the edge of the Continental Divide, feeding the lakes. The glaciers are smaller than indicated on the map, remnants that will soon be gone. "Glacierettes," Joe calls them. I think he's being clever, riffing on "ranchette," but it's an accepted geological term.

"If we keep pumping gases into the atmosphere, all our glaciers will be glacierettes. Future humanoids won't need the distinction."

"And that," Joe sighs, "will be the true end of the Pleistocene."

We pass a low mountain named "the Fortress" and head overland to Lower Alpine Lake. The lake is turquoise blue from even more glacial silt in the water than the lake above it. There is a way around to the southwest—the obvious route, but it is farther around than following the eastern shore. So—fools for trouble—we head east again.

At first it's a pleasant hilly walk, then it "cliffs out," as they say in bushwhacking lingo. Exfoliated slabs slope steeply toward the lake. The last one goes *into* the lake. I head off for a closer look—perhaps it is shallow enough to wade? No. I keep searching.

Joe scouts the slabs above. Toby, always a paragon of responsibility, tries to keep track of both of us again, running back and forth.

Finally, Joe disappears up a crack system and when Toby returns for me, I've gone around a corner. He yowls in full basso profundo, a cry worthy of the Hound of the Baskervilles.

Joe yells back with his distinctive call: "Tooow-bee!"

The yowling continues. Thinking that Toby has surely fallen this time, I scramble upward, yelling. Soon we are all yowling and yelling with no one seeing anyone else. Then, there he is . . . happy dog!

We set off together to find a way though the cliffs—which is not a trivial matter. After several false leads I discover a steep slab running far above us. I yell to Joe. He climbs down and takes Toby's pack. Together we climb and traverse until the angle lessens and we pass trees, the first we've seen in two days, clumps of mountain juniper. Lots of elk droppings dot the ground. The sun is pleasantly warm; the last of my water is pleasantly cool. Clouds play around the peaks to the south.

"Over there," Joe says, pointing, "is the most remote place in the Wind Rivers, 14.87 miles from the nearest road." Yes, two decimal points. He's written a computer program that generates such things.

The most remote place from a road in the contiguous states is thought to be in the Thorofare, just south of the Yellowstone park boundary in the Teton Wilderness, a distance of somewhere between twenty-two to thirty-five miles, depending on whom you believe. It is easy to reach. You can ride a horse down the east side of Yellowstone Lake, up the Yellowstone River, and thence up Thorofare Creek. It is remote by measurement, let us say.

Although Joe's point is a shorter distance from the road, it's far more difficult to reach. There are few maintained roads and fewer maintained trails on the Wind River Indian Reservation east of here, and an awkward permit system—all of which keep the traveler away more effectively than any institutional wilderness designation. Joe's point is psychologically and physically remote. I'm sure that when you get there—he's not sure anyone ever has—it would *feel* remote.

Humans usually go where governments want for them to go; it is a matter of "build it and they will come." Build paved roads and they will come in Winnebagos. Build graded dirt roads and they will come in cars. Build lousy dirt roads and they will come in 4×4s, on ATVs, and dirt bikes. Build trails and they will come on mountain bikes and snowmobiles and horses and llamas. Build paths and they will hike. But if you build nothing, very few will come, which is as it should be in wilderness. The future of wilderness simply depends on not providing access. So does good wildlife habitat. Big game populations need big wilderness, too, and for the same reasons we do—health and sanity. Our failure to preserve the large chunks of habitat needed for intact ecosystems is simply a failure to impede access.

This is not elitism: Winnebagos, 4×4 trucks, ATVs, snowmobiles, and dirt bikes cost lots of money. No, roadless, trailless wilderness is democratic and egalitarian. At my age, I doubt that I will pass this way again. That's fine. I gladly bequeath it to those with the grit to haul their butts this far into the mountains. After all, this country was founded on the principle of individual initiative and enterprise, so why not require them for wilderness access?

The outlet of Lower Alpine Lake spills through an array of chutes carved into the gneiss slabs by abrasive glacial water. The chutes gurgle now; in early summer they roar. I would stop here to paint, but the stream disappears into a narrow gulch filled with a motley collection of boulders, dense scrub, and thick timber. We must find a camp and the gulch is not promising.

We traverse into more open country, level and rocky, gritty and spare with occasional glacial boulders and patches of krummholz. The trees reveal weather; they are flagged to the east, the direction of the prevailing winds. One whitebark grows tight in the lee of a boulder where there is more moisture and protection. The wind has pruned the top and sides of the tree flush with the boulder's protective haven, leaving its outermost limbs a fuzz of dead twigs and fusing rock and tree into a wild harmony no bonsai can equal.

Since we are climbers, we head for slabs whenever we can. Sticky rubber soles on our boots allow us to climb down easily. One slab leads downward for hundreds of feet. At the bottom are fields of flowers, the first flowers we've seen since Indian Basin. There are harebells, a yellow composite neither of us can name, and a fine collection of *Mimulus lewisii,* a spectacular magenta monkey flower that always brightens an alpine scene.

More tired than we care to admit, we camp in a boggy field of grass tussocks by a pond northwest of Camp Lake. Curled in fetal positions, all three of us nap until rain awakens us. We do our best to ignore it. Eventually I set up the tent while Joe gets serious about dinner. We eat in silence. Drizzle cools the food.

Clouds cloak the highest mountains to the northeast. Lonely places, those mountains. Of all the mountaineers I know, few have climbed them, and they usually climbed solo. Our mood is somber. It looks like snow and we are two passes and three days from the warmth and the security of home.

The evening is lightened by Joe's discourse on what I call "socialized mountaineering"—my description of the Sierra Peaks Section of the Sierra Club. We have friends who are hard-core members. I am at turns amused or appalled by its intensive institutionalization, the management committees and archives, the obsession with order, merit, and, especially, lists—lists of who has done what and in what order and when and how fast and how many times. There is even a list of designated "worthy" peaks, and some of our friends won't go near an officially "unworthy" peak. Best, there is a soul with the deliciously medieval title "Keeper of the List."

"Muir would pee his pants if he could see his heritage!" I howl.

With that charming thought, a hard day ends, with graupel clattering on the tent and Toby's wheezing, lip-flapping snores.

In the morning we follow a faint path west and climb a remnant trail built by sheepherders to bring their flocks onto the grassy moors above the forks of the Bull Lake drainage. The trail hasn't been used for years; it isn't maintained by the Forest Service; it doesn't appear on Geological Survey topographic maps. My Earthwalk Press map of the northern Winds shows a faint line that ends at Camp Lake.

An old bridge spanning the outlet at Camp Lake has collapsed into the creek, its logs white with age, like bones. We hop rocks. Joe doesn't need to point out yet again that earlier in the year this crossing would be difficult if not impossible. Especially for sheep, I think; thus the bridge. Few realize that the most difficult challenge of mountain travel in real wilderness is crossing creeks and rivers. It follows that the quickest way to enhance a wilderness is to remove bridges.

On the talus fields above the lake herders shoved aside rocks and cunningly fitted small stones into gaps between them, creating the semblance of a real trail. They were persistent, those sheepherders, I'll give them that. Joe knows a lot about sheepherders in this part of Wyoming. He speaks of them with the delightful disdain a Baptist minister reserves for the machinations of the Devil. In the old days 160,000 sheep munched this part of the Winds, and the land has never recovered.

After the talus, the trail reverts to path, sometimes visible, sometimes not. In thick meadows, we lose it entirely and then we find it again. Wet willows soak my pants and boots. It's drizzling, a cold drizzle driven by a harsh wind. We meander about, searching.

Ramps of gneiss glittering with mica and schist lead upward toward the divide. The path is marked by cairns, crumbled and mossy, like ruins. We climb slowly, enjoying the leisure of another short day while appraising the dark clouds pouring over the pass. At a cold and barren tarn we stop to change into polypro and full rain gear. We are chagrined to discover we are dressed identically, like twins.

Then up again, into the clouds, and on through light, blowing rain, blowing right in our faces—of course. Visibility is down but the path is clear. We drift apart, preferring to be alone. The mood is solemn, the colors pretty. Wetness enhances the tundra's colors, a palette of tan, yellow, mustard, gold, apricot, coral, vermilion, and malachite green. Perhaps the result is not equal to the glory of our eastern forests, but it's not without its own autumnal beauty.

The divide is gentle, a broad plane of tundra crossed by a narrow winding path, perfect for walking. Walking a true path is always pleasant. A trail is constructed with a purpose, usually by beings that will not use it, but a path comes into existence because beings want to walk that path. It is their way. Their walking makes the path. The path was not there before their walking; if they cease walking, the path will disappear. Hence a path belongs to the geography of allusion, a trail does not. One fine cairn reminds me of a poem by Santoka:

> *This is the stone,*
> *drenched with rain,*
> *that marks the way.*

On the other side of the divide the path drops into a deep and narrow valley. Beneath us are whitebark pine forests, rushing streams, and steep cliffs streaked with running water. Clark's nutcrackers hop about on the highest limbs of the pines and squawk. In the distance, three lakes follow each other like jewels on a string: Upper Golden Lake, Louise Lake, and Golden Lake.

The lakes are golden not because of their color—they are rich indigo in this light—but because of golden trout. Goldens are another alien species in Greater Yellowstone, this time from California's southern High Sierra. They arrived in Wyoming by boxcar in 1929.

Goldens are extravagantly colorful and no two are alike, each being a distinct combination of yellow, green, gold, and vermilion—lovely aliens.

Nowadays nearly a hundred lakes in the Winds are home to golden trout. The world's record, 11¼ pounds, was taken from Cook Lake, north of here, in 1948. Since golden trout can hybridize with rainbows and cutthroats, they have. Hence most of the trout populations in the Winds are hybridized, a genetic stew, really, though that doesn't stop anglers from packing into the Winds to catch a "wild golden trout."

More goldens inhabit the Winds than inhabit their native Sierra waters despite an aggressive campaign by the State of California to poison *their* alien fish—mostly brook trout—to protect *their* native fish—goldens. It's all very complicated. Contrary to the demands of ecological integrity, Wyoming Game and Fish is trying hard to establish pure stocks of golden trout in isolated Wind River lakes to keep Wind River anglers happy, and, more reasonable, to provide a reservoir of pure brood stock should disease whip out the depleted island population in their native rivers in California. So our faraway wilderness becomes a refuge for alien fish. Very complicated.

Barely visible in the misty distance are the highlands around Hay Pass, its crest faintly white under a fresh dusting of snow. We camp early again—it is barely afternoon—in a grove of whitebark pine, a grove that each year becomes more sacred as the plague of blister rust and pine beetles advance into the Winds and the climate warms. Someone camped here before us, probably sheep herders; there are the usual broken-off limbs, nails, and an old tin can.

Chickadees flit about the limbs of the pines, singing their song. It is usually transcribed as *chickadee dee dee* or *fee-bee*, often with more syllables, but because of their sociability and cheeky confidence I always think of it as *see-me, see-me.* They are among the most trusting of birds. At home they land on my hand as I fill the feeder. Chickadees weigh less than half an ounce. I cannot comprehend how they so cheerfully endure Wyoming winters.

Both blackcapped and mountain chickadees are common in Greater Yellowstone. To distinguish them you study the head. The mountain chickadee has a black cap with a white eyebrow, or supercilium. The blackcapped chickadee's cap is solid black. They are gleaning insects and larvae among the needles and branches. *See-me, see-me.*

During a break late in the afternoon, I sit against a rock and coax form from a blank journal page with a pencil and brush. When it rains, I put the journal under my parka and wait, watching the clouds. When the rain stops, I continue. I sit against the rock until dark. When I return I find the pale lavender tent glowing from Joe's headlamp. He's reading Annie Proulx's *Close Range: Wyoming Stories.* Toby, stretched across my side of the tent, ignores my arrival. I push him to the middle of the tent; he bench-presses against Joe with his powerful legs, pushing me to the side with his back and groans at my presumption.

We turn our headlamps off and discuss the trajectories of our lives and those of old climbing friends. Some became alpine Horatio Algers, found religion, married, had children, accumulated capital and fame, devoted themselves to various hobbies, and led exemplary American lives. An astonishingly high percentage became multimillionaires. Others remained deviant, not in the criminal sense, but at variance from the norm, either dissolute or eccentric. Many died young, in the mountains. Some went mad. Most migrated into ordinary middle-class lives, mired in Thoreau's quiet desperation. We repeat their stories, mixed with our own, as though massaging a crystal ball, trying to understand the trajectory of our own lives, lives that fall somewhere in between. Slowly, without noticing, we fall silent. Darkness reigns. Toby snores, rain patters, we sleep.

Late in the night I awake to hail rattling the tent. I zip closed the door, wondering if we will finally get snow. We are twenty Wind River miles and another high pass from a road. I stare into darkness and listen to the wind in the pines beyond the hail until they merge in harmony.

Another wet and gloomy morning. The chickadees are silent. Between broken clouds we can see fresh snow above 11,000 feet. Our pass for the day—Fall Creek Pass (which isn't named on most maps)—is hidden behind a ridge, up a broad valley to the southwest of Upper Golden Lake. We pack and leave, anxious to be on our way.

At the point where we leave Upper Golden Lake we find a tent erected square in the middle of the trail. A man unzips the door and peers out, still in his sleeping bag, a disheveled fellow with matted beard and tangled hair. He's so delighted to see us I wonder how long he's been out. We exchange a few words about the weather and leave, bushwhacking toward our pass, about two miles away.

"If I were to make a movie about the Winds, Central Casting would choose him as the archetypal Winds freak," Joe says.

We don't have much room to talk; we've both spent too much

time alone in these mountains and so have many of our friends—what Herman Melville called "isolatoes."

One of those friends, Ray White, travels the Winds for weeks with his handsome Alpine and Toggenburg goats. They weigh up to 190 pounds, can carry forty-five pounds, and live for fifteen years. Whitey, as he is called, loves his goats as most people love their dogs. I think of him as an alpine flâneur.

"Whitey is oblivious to trails," says Joe. "He wanders along at goat pace, going wherever they want to go, a man just looking at the world."

"Haven't you met someone seasoned in the Way of Ease," Yungchia begins his "Song of Realizing the Way," "a person with nothing to do and nothing to master . . . ?" That, for me, is an attainment.

We climb for an hour and then rest beside an unnamed lake at timberline. Most of the other lakes and peaks nearby aren't named either, which is a nice change. The peaks are buried in cloud. The wind has stilled. No ripples crease the silvered surface of the lake. The only birds are flocks of water pipits, skittering along the ground looking for insects. The pipit, like the chickadee, seems forever cheerful. One naturalist observed them riding chunks of ice through the rapids, then flying upstream together to repeat their performance. They effortlessly rise in unison as we pass, groaning under our packs, our eyes to the ground.

Fall Creek Pass—the Continental Divide—is a stroll, though at 11,320 feet, a hypoxic stroll. We rest and enjoy the bright stonecrop and lichen at our feet. But detail is subordinate to an overwhelming sense of space. No one thing is particularly spectacular, merely the grandeur and gravitas of space, the landscape of a Gregorian chant.

Beneath us is Timico Lake, dark and still. When the clouds part we see the Green River Basin. A band of haze hems the horizon—a harbinger of the industrial smog to come. A retired physicist and amateur astronomer who lives there has tracked air quality in the basin for years. His galaxies are fading. The peaks surrounding the valley are no longer sharply etched into the sky. The Forest Service and the Park Service track air quality, too. So does the BLM. We used to have the clearest skies in the country, but no more. The BLM's own analysis of gas development on thirty million acres in the Northern Rockies suggested that it will affect air quality in a dozen national parks, and in some places fail to meet air-quality standards. It will create acid rain that could—read "will"—harm fish and wildlife.

The Park Service, the Forest Service, the Environmental Protection Agency, and a slew of environmental groups have complained to the BLM—to no avail. The State of Wyoming did not want the BLM to adopt measures reducing pollution from gas development, and energy-industry lobbyists set to reworking the rules protecting visibility in national parks. The governor of Wyoming argued that federal visibility guidelines should be withdrawn. Why? As everyone knows, the answer is clear: Follow the money. And to add insult to injury, the federal government has decided to allow the State of Wyoming to seed clouds over the Wind River wilderness areas to artificially increase snowfall that will in turn increase the amount of water available to farmers and ranchers. Ah yes, that lash of federal servitude the State likes to complain about. In reality, national environmental laws and values are constantly flaunted or ignored to privilege economic development.

Above the haze rises the Wyoming Range, seventy-five miles away. I pick out Snider Basin, Wyoming Peak, and McDougal Gap. The fifty-mile traverse I made with Rod Newcomb is at this distance reduced to a few bumps.

The clouds close, the wind rises, sleet stings my face.

The descent to Timico Lake is glorious, my favorite hours of our trip. There is no path now, only open tundra. Walking is easy, the grade moderate. The rain is actually blowing moist clouds. They dissolve, re-form, and dissolve again, like thoughts, like life. The lake lies beneath us like a sapphire encased in a filigree of dull gold. I slow down. I don't want this to end. Joe and Toby disappear, which is fine.

Just as I reach the lake, a shaft of sunlight illuminates a sandy beach upon which Toby rolls, feet in the air, wiggling, scratching his back. I dump my pack and more or less fall down next to Joe. I break out a Snickers bar. We do not say much; we watch Toby and the play of light on the shallow, now turquoise, water.

A path follows the lakeshore. Soon we reach an actual trail. We are on the western terrace again, the shallow Winds, as it were, the standard undulating walk past a myriad of ponds and lakes surrounded by forest. We stop at Chain Lakes, at just less than 10,000 feet, and prepare for what looks like a grim night of storm. We've seen no one since the friendly isolato.

Joe's stove has ceased cooperating. Sullen, dark clouds fill the sky to the north and west, layered masses of pearly grays and charcoals, ragged and blown. Thunder booms, lightning illuminates the sky. More rain. We hastily down our meals and batten the hatches, fully expecting a blizzard.

But there is no blizzard. The morning is cold. Joe's stove simmers, barely, so we forgo breakfast for various emergency bars and lukewarm tea. The sky remains dark. Searching for our route I discover that we are at the intersection of four topographic maps, one of which we don't have along. Joe calls this "Murphy's Law of Topographic Maps."

We indulge in a friendly squabble about "tarn," a word that like many of our mountain words, along with "wilderness," has its roots in northern European languages. The sticking point is whether a tarn must be carved by a glacier. *The Oxford English Dictionary* is mute on that point, I claim, giving simply, "A small mountain lake, having no significant tributaries." Joe thinks it must be carved by a glacier because it is in a cirque. And so we go at each other. We both love tarns. I especially like the little ones that are as black as ink.

The weather is lousy, the parking lot at Elkhart Park beckons: twelve Kelsey miles along the terrace. We head for home.

We pass several groups of fishermen on their way into lakes. Another *isolato* is camped under a tarp by Pole Creek, his rod standing against a tree, ready, his sleeping bag drying over a limb.

"How did you do?" I ask.

"Brookies, nothing but brookies. All small."

"I hope you ate every one of them. They don't belong here; they belong in Labrador." I explain to him my Greater Yellowstone Fishing Regulations: "Be nice to native cutthroats; put them back gently, with love. Eat all other trout—browns, rainbows, goldens, brookies, lake trout—preferably in large numbers, all year. Greater Yellowstone needs all the help it can get. Please do your part."

He smiles a wan smile. It sounds like a reasonable policy, but I can't follow it, either.

I stumble along, nursing knees. Joe waits for me patiently, without comment, his pack resting on a rock. He is buried in the final pages of *Close Range*. Unfortunately for Toby, we pass no dogs. The sky remains ominous, layered with the grays that in this part of the country herald winter.

The parking lot at Elkhart Park is nearly empty. People must feel what's coming, even if they aren't watching the Weather Channel. Two days later a storm dumps a foot of snow in the Winds at 9,000 feet, considerably more on our passes. A traverse through the deep Winds along the Alpine Lakes would now be, as climbers like to say, interesting.

8. Green River Lakes

----------------------------------➤

September. The general rush and hysteria and crowding that attends summer in Jackson Hole is over. Dana and I need a respite from people and Rio needs a vacation from dog life in a national park. Where to go? Dana wants to visit the Green River Lakes because it involves boats and water and a chance at solitude. I want to go because I've been going there for forty-seven years and never regretted a minute of it. We strap a canoe on the truck and head southeast for a three-day trip.

For those versed in the history of western exploration, the drive from Jackson Hole to the Green River Lakes is a delight. The route follows the Snake River to the southern end of Jackson Hole, then ascends the Hoback River, named for the Kentucky mountain man John Hoback, through a canyon of the same name, a canyon that in any other part of the country would be a national park. Alas, it will never receive the protection it deserves. Land has already been leased to energy companies for development, exploratory wells are being drilled, and if history is a guide, rapid, intense industrial development will follow.

The route then crosses a pass between the Gros Ventre and Wyoming ranges, descends into the high steppe of Upper Green River Basin between the Wyoming and Wind River mountains, and ascends the Green to two marvelously secluded bodies of water that are among the most beloved lakes in Wyoming.

In his classic history of the fur trade, *Across the Wide Missouri,* Bernard DeVoto calls the Upper Green River Basin the heart and nerve center of the mountain-fur-trade country. All the famous mountain men and explorers traveled here and many left their names on its features: John Colter, Jim Bridger, Kit Carson, William Ashley, John Fremont, Jedediah Smith, William Sublette, John Hoback, and Thomas Fitzpatrick. No place in Greater Yellowstone is richer in history. But that has not saved it from development.

"The feds would probably allow drilling in Gettysburg if there was oil or gas to be exploited," I say to no one in particular. "Where is our sense of pride and patriotism?"

There are several historical signs along the drive and I often stop to read them, even though I've read them many times before. And besides, Rio gets to sniff the posts. My favorite is the following, posted by the Sublette County Historical Society:

This nearby canyon was a way through the mountains. Its game and Indian trails were followed by the white men. On September 26, 1811, the Astor Party, with William Price Hunt, 61 people and 118 horses entered the canyon here, making their way westward to the Pacific Ocean.

The three legendary trappers, Hoback, Reznor and Robinson, guided the party. These were the first white men to pass this way. From this time on the stream and the canyon became known as The Hoback.

On October 10, 1812, Robert Stuart of the Astor Firm and his 6 companions camped here on their way to St. Louis from Fort Astoria [at the mouth of the Columbia River in present-day Oregon] with the message of the failure of Fort Astoria.

On Sunday, August 23, 1835, Jim Bridger's and Kit Carson's brigade of trappers and Indians and the Reverend Samuel Parker bound northward from the rendezvous on the Green River camped in this area. This basin was known then as Jackson's Little Hole. The Reverend Parker was delivering a sermon to the

Motley [*sic*] group when buffalo appeared. The congregation left
for the hunt without staying for the benediction. This was the
first protestant services held in the Rocky Mountains.

Another sign notes that the Astor Party of 1811 was traveling to
the Pacific from Montreal via St. Louis, a detail that always leaves
me with a sense of the dimension of time and space in those days,
properties we believe are in some sense models of Newtonian stabil-
ity and invariance, and which we also note, in blind contradiction,
are vanishing.

The signs conveniently fail to mention that if buffalo (I prefer to
call them "bison") wandered Sublette County today they would still
be shot—bison are no longer allowed in Sublette County because
ranchers fear bison will transmit brucellosis to their cattle, a much
disputed claim I have little patience with, since cattle originally gave
the disease to bison. Karma kickback. As ye sow, so shall ye reap.

When we reach the Green River at Warren Bridge—named for
the old trestle bridge that remains, parallel to its modern, uglier
kin—we turn north for lunch at one of the many primitive BLM
campgrounds along the river. We are in no hurry. I, in particular, like
to linger here. The spot we choose is bordered by yellowing willows,
sparse groves of aspen, and an occasional conifer. The ground is littered with sticks for Rio to fetch from the river.

I used to camp here when I hunted antelope and grouse. I would
sleep in the back of my truck, cook on the tailgate, and if the hunting was bleak, I would fish those green pools. They are still there,
beautiful pools among rock gardens of glacial boulders.

The Green River flows from glacial waters draining Gannet
Peak, the highest summit in the Wyoming, to its junction with the
Colorado River southwest of Moab, Utah. The Crow Indians knew
the river as the Seedskeedee, their name for sage grouse, a large,
stately, delicious bird famous for its extravagant courtship displays.
Because the Green River eventually reached Mexico, the mountain
men named it the Spanish River; but since the Mexicans called it
the Rio Verde it became, finally, the Green.

The Upper Green River Basin begins when the river crosses a line drawn between the southern tips of the Wind River Mountains and the Wyoming Range. At that point it is roughly 100 miles wide. As it follows the river north it narrows like a funnel until, pinched between mountains, its path turns abruptly east and south to the Green River Lakes.

Ecologically, the Basin is rolling sagebrush plain roughly 7,000–8,000 feet in elevation, broken by deep lakes and numerous streams flowing from the surrounding mountain ranges—an unusual combination of barren steppe, diverse aquatic environments, and lush riparian habitat. It is the largest publicly owned winter range in the Greater Yellowstone Ecosystem, the abode of 100,000 big-game animals, including the country's largest herd of mule deer and the site of a prehistoric migration route for the pronghorn in Grand Teton National Park and the Gros Ventre Range, farther north. The blue-ribbon-trout streams and many lakes offer the usual collection of alien trout species (and alien Kokanee salmon, courtesy of Wyoming Game and Fish) plus remnant populations of Colorado cutthroat trout, a gorgeous critter that has lost 95 percent of its habitat.

For the past century, the Basin has also been home to a vibrant ranching community and is a bastion of Western tradition. More recently it has become the center of what the energy industry and the federal government consider among the most valuable deposits of natural gas in North America: approximately fifteen trillion cubic feet, plus major deposits of oil, oil shale, and coal-bed methane.

Current plans for energy development will transform the Upper Green River Basin into a miasma of development that will devastate the legendary home of the mountain men. The area survived ranching, though it altered its ecology for the worse, but neither its beauty nor its ecological integrity will survive industrialization. All of which graphically illustrates why the Upper Green River Basin is ground zero in the battle to preserve Greater Yellowstone. All the dramatis personae are in place. On one side are the federal government and the energy industry; on the other are virtually every major environmental organization and a collection of locals—including ranchers, labor leaders, outfitters, hunters, anglers, and wealthy Republicans who don't want their backyards converted into an industrial park. On the fence in between is the State of Wyoming, trying to have its cake and eat it too.

I first came into the Upper Green River country in the summer of 1960. A friend and I found summer jobs in Pinedale working for a geophysical exploration company named GSI (now Paulson/GSI). I worked on a survey crew, hustled seismic jugs on the oblique triangle of empty land between the towns of Pinedale, Big Piney, and Farson, land that was dotted with features that evoked the American West—Gobblers Knob, Alkali Creek, and Stud Horse Butte. We commonly saw herds of pronghorn and wild horses; we didn't see any people save our crew for three months.

The emptiness and grandeur captivated my imagination, obliterating human presence. I ignored the rare water tank, the odd cow, the fortified shack in which we stored our explosives, the miles of track we cut through the sagebrush with D-8 Cats, the trucks we drove, the holes we drilled and blasted. To me the place was about space and air and freedom. Never did it occur to me that my labors to collect seismic information would one day alter this spacious land into one of the most densely developed areas in the state.

In 1960, Pinedale was a genuine Western town surrounded by real working ranches and boys my age that caught and broke wild horses. There was a theater, known as the "showhole," that showed a movie every Saturday night and served as a focus for occasional grim fights between sheepherders, oil-field workers, and ranch hands, all big, hard men who seriously hurt one another.

There was also the softer side of the Old West. One evening in a combination restaurant and bar I watched a woman feed coins into a jukebox and dance in turn with each of her two teenage sons. She wore a gay paisley dress; her boys wore cowboy shirts, stovepipe Wrangler jeans, and scuffed boots. Their hair gleamed with pomade. Each son danced with his arms stiff, as far from his mother as he could possibly get, and stared at the ceiling or longingly through the door to the bar where his father stood drinking beer with his friends.

On our one day a week off we fished the lakes and streams around Pinedale and caught so many trout we gave them to the proprietor of the Camp o'the Pines Motel, a woman whose husband had left her and appreciated having fresh fish for her kids. I also visited the Grand Teton and Yellowstone national parks for the first time, went to climbing school (where I still guide in the summers), and caught my first Snake River fine-spotted cutthroat trout in a little creek that is Rio's favorite place to fetch sticks. I was eighteen years old in 1960 and typically impressionable. That summer defined my life.

Eventually we sought adventure to offset the grimly hard work. We drove a Jeep pickup truck up the rutted dirt road to the Green River Lakes and stared in disbelief, as budding climbers always do, at the looming mass of Squaretop Mountain. The retreat, through deep mud after a numbing thunderstorm, seemed to take forever, but then in 1960 I was young and I believed I had forever and the land would never change.

The past forty-seven years have been an annihilating verdict on the values and traditions of old Western life. Aided by multibillion-dollar subsidies from Congress, energy development became lucrative. Wyoming's budget went from a $127 million shortfall to over a billion-dollar surplus. Wealthy folks from the East, Texas, and California bought many of the old ranches, and Sublette County—named for the mountain man Bill Sublette and home to the Museum of the Mountain Man—sank into the modern pit of irony, replete with Ivy League cowboys, Hummers, and log mansions that parodied the humble log cabins of old. Worker shacks and trailers materialized across the sagebrush flats, bringing all the social ills of a boom-and-bust economy. Pinedale's original citizens and their traditions became as endangered as the spotted owl, while modernity rendered their ways of life and work increasingly gratuitous.

And like all threatened people, the locals became somewhat paranoid and defensive. In 2002 the county commissioners passed a resolution stating that wolves and grizzly bears were "economically and socially unacceptable species in Sublette County," a resolution that said more about its citizens than it said about wolves and grizzlies.

So ... Wyoming has another energy boom—there have been many. And when the boom collapses—all booms throughout history eventually go bust—the resources and traditions that could have sustained the state for centuries will be gone. Who will want to vacation in a Superfund site? As a recent article in *Audubon* magazine put it, "Wyoming is ground zero for the Bush energy policy. Everything that is not high mountains in Wyoming is becoming a major gas field." This is not hyperbole.

Fancy PR workers for the energy companies say the land will be restored. Really? Corporations will pay for restoration? Ask Montana whether corporations pay for their environmental messes, even when they are legally required to do so. The federal government? Sure, like New Orleans.

When people ask what Wyoming should do with those billions of dollars in mineral royalties left over in the budget, I say: Invest them. Future generations in this state are going to need more than billions to clean up their wasteland.

The highway crosses sagebrush flats before descending to Daniel Junction, then rises to another sagebrush mesa—the Mesa—above the valley of the New Fork River, a fiord of what has been called the West's "sagebrush sea" into the island of Greater Yellowstone.

"We take sagebrush for granted," I remark. "If I told you that sagebrush is threatened you would think me a fool."

It has taken a while for Dana to appreciate sagebrush steppe—it's rather different from her former home on the north shore of Kauai.

Yep. My wife looks at me like I'm a fool. She's driven from California to Jackson Hole through 1,000 miles of sagebrush, and like everyone who has made that drive she thinks we have plenty of sagebrush.

But like winter forage habitat for ungulates, the preservation of sagebrush was not a concern for those who set aside national parks and wilderness areas, and only 3 percent is protected. The U.S. Geological Survey estimates that 50 percent of the West's sagebrush has been lost and what remains is fragmented by roads, power lines, pipelines, fences, plowing, grazing . . . the list is long.

Since nearly three-quarters of sagebrush habitat is on public land, it can be protected, but we are not only failing to protect it, we continue to destroy it at a rate of thousands of acres a day.

This is nothing new: Rachel Carson mentioned the plight of sagebrush in *Silent Spring,* published in 1962: "One of the most tragic examples of our unthinking bludgeoning of the landscape is to be seen in the sagebrush lands of the West," she wrote. Nothing has changed. In most people's minds, sagebrush ecosystems are relegated to the boring flats you drive through on the way to someplace more interesting. Mark Twain called sagebrush a "distinguished failure."

The destruction of the sagebrush ecosystem has been a holocaust for sage-dependent species—sage grouse, sagebrush lizard, sage thrasher, sage sparrow, sagebrush vole—and a new Eden for exotics, especially alien weeds. The worst, cheatgrass (an immigrant from Russia), now covers more land than sagebrush. It's inedible, wildfire prone, and the affected land is difficult and expensive to reseed with desirable native plants—including, of course, sagebrush. Another Humpty Dumpty Deal.

No bird species depends more on sagebrush than the sage grouse, which flourished throughout the sagebrush steppe that was once a dominant landscape in sixteen Western states. With the loss and degradation of its habitat, sage grouse disappeared from Arizona, British Columbia, Kansas, Nebraska, New Mexico, and Oklahoma. Distribution of the species has declined at least 50 percent, and abundance has dropped 90 percent. Wyoming has the most remaining sage grouse of any state, but Wyoming leks (sage grouse breeding areas) have decreased 50 percent in the last forty years. The Upper Green River Basin is the largest chunk of sage grouse habitat in the state, another ground zero for conservation efforts.

What is the status of sage-grouse populations here? As usual, none of the interested parties agree about the numbers—counting is political—but no one denies that this basin is one of the species' remaining strongholds and that it is suffering plenty. One study suggests that the 1,200 or so sage grouse that live around the Jonah and Pinedale Anticline gas fields will be gone in twenty years. The governor, worried sick that Endangered Species listing will radically curtail energy development, has called for a Sagebrush Grouse Summit. Nor is it just the grouse that are a problem. The mule deer population has already declined 46 percent in the area around the Pinedale Anticline field. They are supposed to be protected in the winter by limits on drilling, but the limits are a farce. The energy companies can request exemptions and the BLM grants damn near every one of their requests.

In December 2003, twenty conservation groups petitioned the U.S. Fish and Wildlife Service to list the sage grouse as either threatened or endangered under the Endangered Species Act. Environmental organizations had previously petitioned to list subspecies of grouse but were rejected. Finally, in one of those spineless acts that confirm the political elasticity of scientific classification, the Service lumped the subspecies into a single category, thereby instantly reducing the rarity of each. The government has tried the same stunt with salmon and steelhead. Whether the stunt works— as science or politics—remains for the courts to decide.

Needless to say, no one but environmentalists are charmed by the possibility of an ESA listing. Severe restrictions would be placed on everything from motorized recreation to natural gas development. Like mule deer and pronghorn, sage grouse don't like drilling rigs, roads, noise, traffic, or power lines, and their population declines in proportion to development, which is increasing in both area and density despite the Bureau of Land Management's former agreements that were intended to force the energy companies to do otherwise. The BLM has never been noted for its sagacity, and given its fawning submission to the energy industry the sage grouse will simply be crowded out despite the usual "study groups," further research, even more further research, and nominal efforts at mitigation. Quite like the tobacco industry: by the time they finally admit the consequences of their actions it will be too late for their victims and the profits will have been distributed and hidden by creative accounting. Corporate lawyers and strategists know that for a fact; they depend on that fact.

I always stop at Cora, a tiny town just off the highway with a general store and post office. We don't stop for food or mail but to see the double dovetail corners on the small cabins bordering a corral. We park without difficulty—ours is the only car in town—and look at several fine examples.

"Someone knew what they were doing," Dana says.

"Yes they did. Hard to imagine work like that now. I heard it was a man from Kentucky just passing through. Lot of good men from Kentucky."

Dana laughs. She knows my mother's family came over the Cumberland Gap to Kentucky with the Boones and the Crocketts, and she knows I'm still quite proud of the fact.

To the east of the valley long finger-shaped lakes drain the western slopes of the mountains through narrow gorges, which open into deep lakes carved by glaciers. Above it all rise the major peaks of the Winds—Helen, Sacagawea, Fremont, and Gannet, the highest peak in Wyoming. Hay fields surround the New Fork River, level fields that were once sagebrush, now a camel-tan from the autumn harvest. Groves of narrow-leaf cottonwoods follow the river; they are turning gold. Like the Green, the New Fork is a superb trout stream.

North of Black Butte the valley narrows, the Green River rejoins the road, and we reach the boundary of Bridger-Teton National Forest. North of here the valley lies between two important wilderness areas, the Gros Ventre Wilderness to the west, and the Bridger Wilderness to the east. On each side, between the wilderness and the road, lies a maze of decrepit forest roads leading to old clear-cut forest leases. The valley itself is leased to ranchers running cow/calf operations. Grizzlies are present and often killed, both legally and illegally. It is one of the most essential wildlife corridors in Greater Yellowstone: wolf packs, pronghorn, and elk still use it to travel to crucial winter forage in the Green River Basin. It is also, alas, the most vulnerable corridor in the ecosystem.

Regrettably, this narrow valley is also at risk to industrialization by energy companies, though for the moment it is safe. On March 7, 2003, the Forest Service supervisor for Bridger-Teton, Kniffy Hamilton, courageously declined to open 376,000 acres, from the forest boundary here north over the Continental Divide and west along Hoback River, to oil and gas drilling. To open these lands to development would drive a wedge into Greater Yellowstone, severing the Wind River Range and the Green River Basin from the main body of the ecosystem and radically reducing the size of the "island." Hamilton concluded that industrial development in this area—an area larger than Grand Teton National Park—would "compromise the area's character." No kidding. To think otherwise you would have to be brain dead.

Predictably, the energy industry charged that her decision was "irresponsible."

Unfortunately, her decision was temporary. It will be reconsidered in the future, and with the country's increasing dependence on oil and gas, no one knows what that future decision might be. The drive to the Green River Lakes is a reminder that wilderness is protected, other Forest Service land is not. Saving Greater Yellowstone from fragmentation requires saving all the parts. An intact ecosystem, like a body, requires a functioning unity of many parts, not just some. Lose too many parts and "saving" is meaningless. When I ask the emergency room doctor to save my wife, I don't want him to return with her chin and liver.

It is forty-five miles to the campground, most of it over a dirt road that is vastly improved from the road I traveled forty-five years ago. It is, however, deeply rutted from RVs beating their way out from the Green River Lakes Campground after the first autumn storms. Some of the willow beds along the river are muted purple; the water is clear, its surface dimpled with feeding trout. We stop at my favorite holes to look—no time to fish—and watch two ospreys ply their trade over the river. Dana spots three moose—her favorite mammal—all cows.

At Wagon Creek the river begins its 180-degree turn east and back south. The hills are closer now, the ridges lined with groves of cadmium yellow aspen. In the distance is Three Waters Mountain, a peak whose summit drains into the Mississippi, the Columbia, and the Colorado. Beyond are immense flats of alpine tundra along the Continental Divide.

With all this open sagebrush, and the tundra above, one might conclude this was easy country for rambling. You would be wrong. Between the sage flats and the tundra flats are steep, glacier-carved walls and jumbles of scree, talus, and boulders interspersed with dense forest filled with deadfall—the worst bushwhacking I've ever seen, and justly infamous.

As we turn south along the curve of the hook, we pass a reach of uncharacteristically still water. Above two lakes and three to four miles of willow meadows, a narrow precipitous gorge leads into the mountains.

We drive through the campground to a sandy beach at the south end of Green River Lake. I want to show Dana where what would become forty years of travels by canoe and kayak began long ago on a sunny afternoon when I saw sitting on the beach, her bow gently bobbing over lapping waves, the most beautiful canoe I'd ever seen, so beautiful it converted me instantly to canoeing—something I had never done. I knew I had to find a canoe exactly like the one before me. It was a Chestnut the Prospector model, built of cedar, oak, and canvas in Fredericton, New Brunswick. She was seventeen feet long with a thirty-seven-inch beam, and was painted a pale lime green. Several years passed before I managed to get one, but when I did, it lead to memorable adventures in New Brunswick, Colorado, and, finally, the Northwest Territories.

The owner of this beautiful craft was heading for the Upper Green River Lake. He explained that the two lakes are connected by a mile of stream which can be lined during the summer by walking up the bank or wading with ropes attached to the bow and stern to steer and haul the canoe. Depending on the depth of the water, this was either mildly exhausting or pure hell, usually the latter. If the water level is high, you fight the current; if it is low, you drag your laden boat through and over rock gardens. The reward was a less-visited lake and access to a yet higher section of the river, really a stream, which could also be lined if the water was sufficiently deep and one was sufficiently patient. This took you to the slopes beneath Squaretop. From there day hikes led into the spectacular mountain valleys, all of them rewarding. He did it every summer, he said. He was quite convincing. The seed planted, I did the trip twice during the next few years, once in a canoe and once in a kayak. I regret I haven't done it every year since.

The campground was at one time large and well appointed; in the summer it was often filled with RVs and trailers. Sadly, most of the trees have been cut down because pine bark beetles infected the lodgepole pine, and the deadwood was a fire hazard. But if the campground is a blight, the beauty of the lake remains unmarred.

There are only two other groups camping with us—both hunters, it appears. A nearby parking lot marks the beginning of the Highline Trail, the main north/south thoroughfare for the Wind River Range. The wilderness boundary circles the sides and southern portion of the lake, so it lacks protection. A ranger cabin, occupied during the summer months, stands abandoned. It looks and feels like the end of one world and the beginning of another, and it is.

After setting up camp we cross the campground to the deserted beach again. The view is stunning. On the left are long white cliffs of dolomite and limestone deposited 300–450 million years ago. Dead ahead, above the surface of the deep blue lake, stands Squaretop, a monolith of gneiss in the shape of a tree stump, 11,695 feet high. Its imposing walls are home to a dozen or so climbs, some scrambles, some formidable. To the right is Big Sheep Mountain (well-named, I hear), its summit marked by a radically tilted, layered sequence of sandstone, shale, limestone, and dolomite. The bands are so well defined they seem etched by a master engraver.

As Joe Kelsey notes in *The Wind River Mountains,* "There are no peaks in this area, only flats of varying breadths." We are traveling at the bottom of a cleft carved by a glacier from a vast plateau. These "peaks" are the remnant of the plateau; the rest has been washed all the way to the Pacific.

Morning finds us back at the beach beside an utterly still lake that mirrors broken cloud cover. We load the canoe, a borrowed, thoroughly modern boat, graceless and devoid of charm, but constructed of indestructible polyethylene that, given the late date and eight years of drought, will be appropriate for the rocky channel.

I push us off the beach and clean my boot in the lake before settling into the canoe. We paddle beneath the steep, luscious banks along the western shore. Dana is happy; she loves boats and water. Rio is not happy; she hates boats, though she loves water. Given her druthers she would swim, but I judge it's a bit cold for that this time of year. She cowers among the gear bags, soaked from fetching sticks out of the lake, ears down.

We paddle lazily, staying in the lee of the cliffs to avoid a breeze that scallops the surface of the water. At the base of the cliff are deep pools fed by waterfalls that the dry summer has reduced to ribbons. The two miles to the inlet pass in silence and peace.

After an hour, we stop at another sandy beach to stretch our legs and just enjoy a beach, which is not a common feature in Greater Yellowstone. The sun has come out. Dana settles into the ever-present Crazy Creek chair and soaks up rays, happy as a wanderer arriving home. I throw more sticks into the lake for Rio; she is lovingly irrepressible and numbingly insatiable. But it's all a diversion: we must contend with the channel.

The channel between the two lakes is bordered for most of its length with grasses and sedge that earlier in the season display an impressive array of flowers. Now, except for a few harebells, the flowers are gone. What in the summer was a muddy swamp is now a dry, parched swale of browns and ochres. The runnels where high water still coursed late in the season are surrounded with thickets of golden willows, intricate as filigree.

As we approach the south end of Green River Lake, Dana says, "Smoke!"

It's coming off a slope up Clear Creek, a stream that descends from the east. As we draw closer we can see flames. No one is fighting it since wilderness policy allows wildfires to burn when they don't threaten human structures. This one is burning up a narrow defile that leads to miles of rocky tundra, so it will be left to smolder, eventually benefiting many wild beings.

Glaciers recede during periods of warming, leaving a barrier of rocks to mark the point of recession. The barriers, called "moraines," create lakes. One hundred years ago, Clear Creek flowed straight into Green River Lake. Now it enters the river channel a thousand feet above the lake. Porcupine Creek enters near the same point from the west. Their alluvia, together with the remains of smaller moraines, created the delta between the two lakes—upper and lower. Slowly, both lakes are filling.

With a warming climate, the glaciers feeding the lakes will disappear, the runoff will diminish, and the land between the two lakes will increase. Eventually the ice will return, glaciers will re-form, new gorges will be carved, the glaciers will retreat, and new lakes will form. The cycle will endure. In nature, cycles win and stasis loses, regardless of how much we prefer the way things are.

I've brought hip waders for the grimmer sections. When the water level is deep enough to float the canoe, I walk along the shore, usually on a grassy trail smashed flat by anglers. If I am sufficiently cunning, I can guide the canoe with little effort. Then the river broadens, leaving it too shallow to float anything but a leaf. I wade out onto the algae-covered cobbles and pull, slipping on the rocks and cursing.

Other sections are shallow riffles with a fine rock bottom, easier to walk on but still too shallow for our canoe's draft. Occasionally larger boulders dot the channel, some sufficiently submerged to go unnoticed until the canoe grinds to a halt. I pull, Dana pushes, Rio barks. Even though the difference in elevation between the two lakes is trivial—only seven feet—in low water this one mile takes on the proportions of an epic. The afternoon passes in anything but silence and peace. The polyethylene hull sticks to the rocks, I curse and mutter.

"OK, I admit it. We would trash a wood-and-canvas canoe like the Prospector here this time of year."

The outlet of the upper lake is dotted with more boulders and the telltale rings of rising trout. Our picturesque campsite is at the end of a peninsula where the river bored through the moraine. The site is ancient, and like most old campsites it's a bit worn: the trees are scarred by limbs hacked off for fires. But the vista is so lovely, I forgive the perpetrators. Beauty has overwhelmed their sins.

Beyond, the lake glows a milky turquoise under a molten sky. Although it is five miles distant, Squaretop dominates the scene. Halfway down the shoreline a small white wall tent and three horses suggest the presence of elk hunters, though hunting season hasn't started yet so they must be scouting. The elk here will winter in the Green River Basin, migrating when the autumn snow is too deep for them to graze the meadows in these high mountains. Until then this country offers great elk hunting.

Shortly after we arrive, the hunters leave and we are again blessed with solitude. With perfect timing the elk begin to bugle.

The lake is turquoise because glacial silt tints the water. Current, wind, and waves keep the particles dispersed. It's pretty, similar to many lakes in the Canadian Rockies, but the silt diminishes the quantity of aquatic flora and fauna, so it harbors fewer fish than the lower lake. Yet it functions to filter the river, allowing the lower lake to remain clear and its fish to flourish.

Given the difficulty in the channel we abandon plans for lining the river above the upper lake. It's too late now, but the upper river is easier than the channel; because it is split into braids and oxbows, some still backwaters can be paddled. Instead, we end a difficult morning and laze about. Despite my friend Kelsey's beliefs about dogs and bears, I'm a bit paranoid. Grizzlies now occupy the northern end of the Winds. I hang our food in a tree, doing the usual balancing act with food bags, bags of rocks, a ski pole, and a hank of carefully stacked rope perched on the top of the bag of rocks.

Dana finds another beach upon which to meditate and read and study the panorama. I catch a few fish among the boulders at the outlet. The afternoon passes. The vista is so perfect we are not inclined to hike; it is enough to sit and look.

This country is new to Dana, and I enjoy explaining terminology that is strange to anyone new to these mountains. "Moraine," "alluvial fan," "gneiss," "glacial polish." There is a sense in which you do not see the country unless you possess a pertinent vocabulary. "Visit" and "vision" are related words. John Stilgoe, in his elegant *Shallow Water Dictionary: A Grounding in Estuary English*, says, "Landscape—or seascape—that lacks vocabulary cannot be seen, cannot be accurately, usefully visited." I agree.

At first this striking claim is counterintuitive, but on reflection both obvious and penetrating. Without vocabulary the world is like a gestalt drawing we see and yet do not see until—there it is!—the old woman's face appears, the duck, the rabbit. To usefully visit is to notice and attend to differences and distinctions, to discriminate the smoothness of a cobble polished by tumbling and a slab polished by a passing glacier.

Distinctions are pleasing to me; I find pleasure in knowing and saying *dipper, arête, tarn,* and I love the mnemonic ditties that naturalists use to remember difference. The needles of the *firs* are *flat,* their boughs *furry.* The needles of the *spruce* are *square,* the boughs *sticky. Rushes* are *round. Sedges* have *edges.*

And like all writers, I like tropes. I tell my mountaineering students: "Granite and gneiss contain roughly the same ingredients. But with granite it's like putting the ingredients in a Cuisinart for an hour: a homogenous blend. With gneiss it's like putting the ingredients in a wooden bowl and stirring a few times with a spoon: you end up with all these beautiful bands of unmixed quartzite." Or: "A glacier is nothing but a big piece of sandpaper. Frozen water is a mineral, a mineral filled with bits of abrasive rock it has gouged off the mountain's walls. A thousand feet of it weighs a zillion tons. Gravity sends it downhill, grinding a U-shaped valley for 100,000 years. When it hits the valley floor, it's like a big sandpaper fist: it punches and grinds a hole. When the glacier melts, the runoff from snow and the meltwater from the remaining glacier run down the valley and fill the hole—a lake."

Similarly, Dana tells me about humpback whales, dolphins, the native flowers of Hawaii, the constitution and variety of leis, and the words for different kinds of lava—my favorite is *a'a*. She tells me about the monk seal that accompanied her on walks along the beach. But most often she talks about humpback whales. She has been close to whales off the coast of Maui many times but never touched them. She thought it would be rude.

We sit on the beach facing Squaretop, now shrouded in clouds, drink hot toddies, and meditate until well after dark. Then we burrow into our sleeping bags. Rio struggles to wedge her way between us. The steady drum of raindrops lulls us all to sleep.

A fine mist rises from the lake at dawn. Squaretop sits above it all, luminous in pale yellow light. We linger in our bags, avoiding the morning chill until the sun breaks over the ridge of White Rock's cliffs and turns the somewhat lurid dirty green water to its more friendly creamy turquoise. Time seems larger in the wilderness. We take time to listen to the birds—woodpeckers, gray jays, and nutcrackers.

Breakfast is the usual—oatmeal with nuts, raisins, and maple syrup. Coffee is the usual—organic Bolivian with foamed milk. Service is the usual—I make coffee and cook while Dana stays in her sleeping bag. Gone are the days of cowboy coffee and plain oats on the tailgate of my truck!

The hike up canyon past the second lake is easy—this is, after all, the main thoroughfare into the northern Wind Rivers. Then, bored with the trail, we wander dense, waist-high meadows and ford the Green River, now a creek, climb onto a pine-filled ridge, and sit and do nothing—another uneventful day in the wilderness. I stare long-ingly up the canyon where it disappears behind Squaretop. Some-day, I promise myself, I will walk that trail all the way to South Pass. But not today.

We head for home. The descent of the channel is considerably easier than the ascent. On the once-deserted southern beach are a red tent and aluminum canoe. On the lake, two skiffs troll for lake trout, their gnashing motors obliterating our silence.

I bet sage grouse hate motorboat engines, too.

The weekend is upon us. No matter. Our little venture is nearly over. Again we hug the western cliffs to evade a brisk wind; again we enjoy the dark pools and ribboned falls. I spot a big fish lying in the depths at the side of the slight current where a stream enters, its tail gently caressing the water.

"I want to be like that fish," says Dana.

"I want to catch that fish. The state record brook trout was caught here not long ago. Just under ten pounds. Nothing like eating aliens."

Dana spots another moose and we stop to watch it browse. It is sleek and black and fat, a healthy wild beast ready for winter, for tri-als with wolves and cold.

It is dusk when we reach the highway. To the east, Pinedale and its suburbs shimmer with light. To the south, red beacons casually flash from high towers. A giant smokestack belches black smoke into a pale, empty sky.

Omens.

9. Chasing Cutts

--►

I love trout, and of all the planet's many kinds of trout I love cutthroat trout the most. Cutthroat trout are native to the Rocky Mountains. It was the first native fish described by European explorers. In the spring of 1541, Francisco Vasquez de Coronado's expedition found, in the upper Pecos River near Santa Fe, New Mexico, "a little stream which abounds in excellent trout and otters." This would have been the Rio Grande cutthroat, one of fourteen subspecies that once inhabited the American West, from southeastern New Mexico to Alaska's Kenai Peninsula. Sadly, two of these subspecies are extinct, and the others survive in greatly reduced numbers in only a fraction of their historic range. For instance, the Rio Grande cutthroat enjoyed by Coronado's men now occupy only 1 to 15 percent of the habitat they once graced, depending on whom you ask.

The first trout of Greater Yellowstone known to Europeans was the westslope cutthroat, caught by one Silas Goodrich, a member of the Lewis and Clark Expedition. Lewis described the fish in his journal on June 13, 1805, noting its most distinctive feature, the "small dash of red on each side behind the front ventral fins," a rather simple description that suggests nothing of its beauty. Today the westslope cutthroat has been reduced to 2.5 percent of its original habitat.

In 1998, the Wyoming Game and Fish Department initiated a program to educate anglers about the state's cutthroat species. It was awkwardly entitled "Wyoming's Cutt-Slam." If you document catching all of the state's cutthroat sub-species, then you receive a colored certificate saying "The Wyoming Game and Fish Department recognizes [name here] for completing Wyoming's native cutthroat trout Cutt-Slam."

The certificate shows only four of Wyoming's native cutthroat, even though five subspecies of cutthroat exist within the state's borders—the westslope, Yellowstone, Snake River fine-spotted, Colorado River, and Bonneville. Most anglers don't distinguish them, even though their coloration and markings are dissimilar, and more technical differences, such as the number of gill rakers, are distinctive.

I have enough certificates, but the program served its purpose. It piqued my interest in learning about the different subspecies, which for me meant catching and admiring them. It also provided an opportunity to gage the health of species that were widespread in the ecosystem. An ecosystem's health is often measured by the presence of all the original large mammal species, especially predators. But by the time ecosystem problems show up in predator populations the ecosystem itself has radically changed. I wanted to look at something lower in the food chain that might indicate the dangers the ecosystem faces. The cutthroat is a good canary.

Cutthroat trout are commonly called "cutts." The name of the species, *Oncorhynchus clarki*, is intimidating to pronounce, and by the time you add the subspecies tags every time you refer to a fish—as in *Oncorhynchus clarki bouvieri*—you sound foolishly pretentious. For the same reason, anglers who pay attention to such things usually nickname other trout—browns (brown trout), bows (rainbow trout), brookies (brook trout), or Mackinaws (lake trout). However, since there are five subspecies of cutthroats in Greater Yellowstone, sometimes "cutts" won't do and further naming is necessary to mark important differences.

Like many anglers, in the past I was not well informed about diversity of trout subspecies in Greater Yellowstone and didn't pay attention to the finer distinctions between native, alien, and hybridized trout. This changed with the 1983 publication of John D.

Varley and Paul Schullery's *Yellowstone Fishes* (reissued in a new edition in 1998), and Patrick C. Trotter's 1987 *Cutthroat: Native Trout of the West*, the first modern treatment of the species. They were followed, in 1992, by Robert J. Behnke's *Native Trout of Western North America*. Behnke is now the world's authority on matters pertaining to trout (and salmon, too) and his magisterial *Trout and Salmon of North America* (2002), beautifully illustrated by Joseph R. Tomelleri, is one of the finest pieces of natural science you will ever lay your hands on—period.

Taken together, these works provide everything one needs to know about the West's native trout and the numerous challenges they face. If the cutthroat survives the combined effects of warming river temperatures, pollution, massive industrial development of energy resources, erosion from clear-cut forests, livestock grazing, and ever more roads, it will be due in no small part to the labors of these men. But despite their efforts—plus the work of state and federal agencies, and numerous conservation organizations—the survival of the cutthroat is by no means certain. Each of their native habitats is in jeopardy.

The Yellowstone River is a national treasure—the origin of the name "Yellowstone"—and home of the Yellowstone cutthroat trout. At 671 miles in length, it is the longest undammed river in the lower forty-eight states. Its upper reaches in the Teton Wilderness are arguably the wildest in the ecosystem. The river flows through Yellowstone Lake, the largest body of water above 7,000 feet in the country, occupying an ancient caldera created by the park's largest volcanic eruption. The wildlife viewing along the river is among the best in the park. I've seen more bison, elk, trumpeter swans, white pelicans, black bears, and grizzlies along the river than anyplace else during my forty-seven years in the ecosystem.

Along the section of river upstream from Yellowstone Lake is a small creek named Atlantic Creek. Its headwaters lie on a wet meadow on the Continental Divide. To the west lie Pacific Creek, the Snake River drainage, and the Pacific Ocean. It is believed that what would come to be called the Yellowstone cutthroat crossed this saddle during the last ice age, when melting glaciers created numerous lakes. Similar situations allowed the westslope cutthroat to cross the Continental Divide into the headwaters of the Missouri, the Colorado cutthroat into the Colorado River, and the Bonneville into the Bear River.

I always fish the river between the outlet of the lake and Sulphur Cauldron, usually in the canyon above Le Hardy Rapids, sometimes along the islands above the Cauldron.

I avoid the picnic area at Buffalo Ford, a place so crowded with anglers that the trout have formed a symbiotic relation with them. If you stand in the river along the bank where there is fine gravel, monster cutts will tail a foot or so behind your boots, gulping insects you dislodge as you scuffle along. They are quite disconcerting, especially if you aren't catching fish.

This stretch is the most popular fishing destination in the Yellowstone. Since much of it is paralleled by road, it provides easy access for everyone: the elderly, kids, and anglers in wheelchairs.

Until recently the lake and river were protected from alien fish species introduced into waters outside the park by the two famous waterfalls at the entrance to the Grand Canyon. Unfortunately, lake trout were discovered in Yellowstone Lake in 1994. It was very likely an illegal introduction, though exactly how it was carried out remains unknown.

Recent research based on otoliths, the small stones found in the ears of trout, suggests that the intruders came from Lewis Lake, that there were two introductions, in 1989 and 1996, and that 300 lake trout were moved into Yellowstone Lake. This would not be a minor operation and I find it difficult to believe that it was achieved without discovery. Nonetheless, the fish are there and that's a big problem. Yellowstone cutts are under pressure in other parts of their habitat and the last thing they need is pressure here in their ancestral home.

The lake trout in Yellowstone Lake have devastated the native cutthroat population. Lake trout are big and predaceous. Eighty to

90 percent of their diet consists of small cutthroat trout. The park is gill-netting the lake trout and encouraging anglers to fish for them. You are legally required to kill every one you catch and I encourage people who are fishing for food to harvest these lake trout. They taste just like salmon.

The cutthroat's plight is exacerbated by whirling disease, an alien (European) parasite that destroys cartilage, eventually leading to death. As a result of these alien invaders Yellowstone cutthroats have suffered a drastic decline in the very heart of their already much reduced habitat. We sometimes speak casually about alien species—more than dot 200 in the ecosystem and the number is rising—but we don't often look at the consequences of their presence.

Trout numbers for spawning creeks around the lake tell the story best. Pelican Creek, a stream once famous for its trout fishing, had 30,000 spawning cutts in the 1980s; in 2004 park fishery biologists found nine—yes, *nine*—fish. During the 1970s more than 70,000 cutts spawned in Clear Creek; in 2005 biologists found 917. In 2000 they counted 2,500 spawning cutts in Bridge Creek; in 2005, they found one.

These losses have affected other wildlife, including grizzlies, white pelicans, eagles, and osprey, all of which depend in varying degrees on the cutthroat population.

The Yellowstone cutthroat is also suffering environmental indignities elsewhere in the ecosystem. The Yellowstone cutthroats in the Salt River are suffering toxic levels of selenium dumped into the river by phosphate mines. In the Teton River, which flows through a valley on the west side of the Teton Range, native cutts have declined 95 percent since 1998 while alien trout and hybrids have doubled and redoubled. It is widely accepted that the Yellowstone cutthroat continues to decline throughout the remaining 17 percent of its historic range.

Nonetheless, two attempts by conservation organizations at getting an ESA listing for the Yellowstone cutthroat have failed, most recently in February 2006, for the usual (though never confessed) reason: listing the fish would wreck havoc with economic expansion, agricultural water use privileges, mining, and energy development. Which suggests why Yellowstone Lake is the focus in the fight to preserve the species.

I head for the Yellowstone as soon as I can after it opens for fishing on July 15. The earlier the date, the better the fishing. By late August the larger fish have moved back to the lake. By late September the river is deserted by anglers; those in the know are stalking big browns along the Gibbon and Madison.

I have a late breakfast at the Lake Hotel, my favorite hotel in Yellowstone, and arrive at my parking spot just in time for the midmorning hatches. A short walk through open lodgepole pine forest leads to a bluff from which I can survey the river and its legions: I count twenty-six anglers on "my" section of the river. Stream etiquette requires that I take my place only after having determined that I am not infringing on anyone else's water, either where they are or where they are going, a determination that, given the crowd, is as simple as a differential equation. Having made my decision, I descend to the shore and quietly wade into the river with my rod, smiling at those whom I may have faintly offended.

There are bugs all around me—Pale Morning Duns, Green Drakes, and, most important, Gray Drakes. They are so big you can't miss them, and they're falling into the river in what anglers call a spinner fall. I tie on my favorite Gray Drake spinner pattern—one I originally got from Jimmy Jones at High Country Flies, in Jackson—and cast. With the third cast comes a hard tug, a nice Yellowstone cutt rolls, flashing its golden pelvic and anal fins.

I catch two more within the hour, better than average—my average or the mythical statistical angler's average. Catch rates this time of year on this stretch of river are among the highest in the park. The cutthroats here are perhaps the most beautiful fish in the ecosystem, and I hesitate to say anything disparaging about them, but the park has tagged fish here and discovered they are caught an average of 9.7 times every summer. That's enough to make a Snake River fine-spotted trout or uppity European brown cringe with embarrassment for their hapless relative.

Nonetheless, if you like to fly-fish, the first couple of weeks after opening day are marvelous: big water, big flies, and lots of big fish. And by midafternoon it's over—except for slews of smaller bugs. I am home in Lupine Meadow by dinnertime. Like many anglers, I find fishing the Yellowstone River in late July to be eminently civilized. The big question is whether we are wise enough, and determined enough, to protect our much beloved prey.

Westslope cutthroat are the most seriously imperiled trout in Greater Yellowstone, occupying—it is worth repeating—less than 2.5 percent of their historical habitat. I've caught westslope cutts before—most memorably in Kelly Creek, Idaho, one of the prettiest ribbons of water in the Rockies—but finding genetically pure westslope cutthroats in Greater Yellowstone is not a simple matter. After talking to guides and fisheries biologists I realized that most of the westslope cutts I had caught in Greater Yellowstone were in fact populations of westslope/rainbow hybrids.

Indeed, catching a westslope cutthroat was not even required for Wyoming's Cutt-Slam, even though populations exist in a few remote creeks in the northwest corner of the state. When I called Game and Fish and asked why, they responded that they had discussed that issue when the Cutt-Slam program was created and had decided that: 1) the subspecies was not within their jurisdiction, since all the remaining populations were within Yellowstone National Park and thus under federal jurisdiction; 2) there were so few fish and those few so difficult to reach that catching one might make the Cutt-Slam too difficult; and 3) encouraging anglers to catch them might further imperil already marginal populations. This strongly suggests that their status in the ecosystem is indeed grim.

But I was now obsessed with my little project, so I began my search for genetically pure westslope cutts in what was once their home water, a disconcerting task when you consider that westslope cutthroats once extended nearly 1,000 miles down the Rockies (with a few scattered populations farther west). The westslope cutthroat is even gone from its most important habitats in Yellowstone National Park—the Madison, the lower Firehole, and Gibbon rivers, replaced, as usual, with hybrids, rainbows, browns, and brook trout. This is tragic, for those rivers were among the finest cutthroat rivers in the ecosystem.

I talked and talked with guides and biologists. There were a few remnant populations in Grayling Creek, people claimed, and perhaps in Specimen Creek. Or the North Fork of Cabin Creek. Maybe in one of the forks of Tepee Creek. I had never even heard of these streams. Or Fan Creek?

"Maybe."

"Perhaps."

"I think."

I remember catching a few cutts in Fan Creek many years ago, in the meadow above where it joins the Gallatin River. I made some more calls. Yes, there were pure westslope trout in Fan Creek.

On the next available weekend, I drove to West Yellowstone, Montana. There, as is my custom, I stopped at Blue Ribbon Flies. I wanted a bit of advice since Craig Mathews (with author Clayton Molinero) wrote a guide to Yellowstone fly-fishing, and no one knows more about fly-fishing in the park. However, Craig was not there and I did not know the salesperson.

"Tell me about the pure westslope cutts in Fan Creek," I asked.

"They aren't in the main creek. The ones there have been hybridized by rainbows and pressured by browns. To reach them you gotta walk up to the North Fork of Fan Creek, up toward Sportsman's Lake."

"How far up?"

"Way up."

Well, OK, I can do that, I thought. Just bivouac and walk out the next afternoon. As long as I don't mind curling up in my bivy sack in densely populated grizzly habitat.

"And," he added, as an afterthought, "not everyone agrees the ones in the North Fork are genetically pure."

Fan Creek is twenty-two miles north of West Yellowstone. Even though it is a major highway, Route 191 is as lovely as any road in the park. About seventeen miles north of West Yellowstone it crosses a ridge and drops down to Grayling Creek. I always stop here and take a look, though I'm not looking for grayling.

The Montana grayling is found in only 8 percent of its historic range and has been extirpated from its home waters in Yellowstone National Park—including, yes, Grayling Creek. At present it survives in a few isolated lakes, even though lakes were not its original habitat. This is sad. The grayling is a beautiful, silvery fish—I've caught them in the Yukon and Northwest Territories.

The forest lies close to Grayling Creek; it's not an easy place to fish. But today I am pondering, not fishing. Staring downstream at the dancing creek as it disappears into the forest, I decide that I am cutting too close to my principle of being nice to native fish and killing aliens. There are simply too few pure or almost-pure populations of westslope cutthroat in Greater Yellowstone to be harassing them. Indeed, we should be making more strenuous efforts to increase their distribution to all their historic waters. The two hundredth anniversary of the Lewis and Clark expedition (in 2005) seemed an opportune time to increase our efforts to preserve the fish named for them—*Oncorhynchus clarki lewisi.*

And with that thought I head for home.

In the spring of 2006, the Park Service announced that 700 genetically pure westslope cutthroats had been discovered in an unnamed stream in Yellowstone. Plans were announced to poison alien fish in the East Fork of Specimen Creek, protect it with a weir, and begin restocking natives.

The unnamed tributary where the pure strain of natives was discovered was a fragment of Grayling Creek, remote from a road, untouched by trails, and well protected by grizzly bears. I like to think the wild was protecting its own, and, as usual, it was doing a good job. As Thoreau famously said, "in wildness is the preservation of the world."

According to the conservation organization Trout Unlimited, the Colorado River cutthroat trout currently inhabits less than 5 percent of its historic range. Many of the most important remaining populations are in tributaries of the Green River, at the southern end of Greater Yellowstone. The preservation of these trout and the health of their aquatic ecosystems remain a top priority of Wyoming Game and Fish. Often the most genetically pure populations are in tiny isolated creeks where the fish grow to only eight or ten inches in length. Again, conservation organizations sought an ESA listing for the remaining fish. In April 2004, the U.S. Fish and Wildlife Service announced that this most colorful subspecies of cutthroat would not receive a listing. They had lots of good reasons, of course—none of them particularly relevant. No one mentioned that the Green River is in the middle of the most intense industrial energy development in Wyoming and that an ESA listing would be about as welcome as a brain tumor.

If you want to catch a Colorado cutthroat in Greater Yellowstone, the best place to go is North Piney Lake, a narrow slice of water that provides brood stock for restoration efforts. There are sixteen-to-eighteen-inch fish in the lake, but it is a fair hike to reach it—which is nice.

When I want to fish for Colorado cutts I head for North Horse Creek, a tributary of the Green River west of Daniel Junction. Although there are some rainbows and brook trout present, most of the fish are Colorado cutts.

I have Rio and her brother Scout with me. Because it is fall, both are outfitted with blaze orange safety vests and red handkerchiefs tied around their necks. I bring my own blaze orange safety vest instead of my fly-fishing vest. This is not wilderness, so out-of-state hunters aren't required to have a professional guide. Many will be from California and, in my experience, hunters from California and Texas are dangerous.

Like most of the Green River Basin, North Horse Creek is loaded with history. A monument commemorating Old Fort Bonneville is hidden among the willows in a turnout. It was established in 1832 by Capt. Benjamin L. E. de Bonneville, who was on leave from the United States Army and eager to enter the fur trade. The mountain men called it "Bonneville's Folly." It was abandoned four years later and has remained in well-deserved obscurity ever since.

The gravel road passes through open ranching country with a few trophy homes atop a ridge to the north. There are ranch houses and old barns and an occasional log cabin, silvered with age and surrounded by broken fence and collapsed buildings. On the porch of one such cabin sits a woman with two teenage girls; her face is gaunt, the kind of haggard farm wife face you see in Walker Evans's photographs of the Depression.

Cows sleep alongside the road. Pronghorn wander among them and through people's backyards. Hunting pronghorn in this country is about as hard as hitting the ground with a tennis ball and no longer a sporting proposition, to my way of thinking.

On a map, Merna looks like a town, but it is not. Once a center for cutting ties for the Union Pacific in southern Wyoming, it is now another sleepy ranch, off the main road and out of mind.

Beyond Merna the road enters the mountains between Outlook Peak and Prospect Peak and crosses the national forest boundary near the abandoned Sherman Guard Station, a cluster of four buildings, painted the world's least interesting brown and topped with pale green metal roofs. The entire area has been leased to energy companies by the Forest Service and its apparent future as a Superfund site makes me visit as often as I can, now, before it disappears.

The road begins to hug the creek. There is forest above the sage flats, especially on north-facing exposures that hold spring snow. The southern exposures have aspen in the gullies that are beginning to turn a pale lemon. Much of the forest is charred. The Mule Creek Fire burned 1,100 acres here in the summer of 2002.

The creek is small, sometimes seemingly buried beneath willows. I first fished North Horse Creek in 1960 and have returned many times since. I tick off familiar features as they pass. Memories flood back as I drive along, of narrow two-tracks and axle-deep mud, things that were more common in this country forty-seven years ago.

There are few people about on this fine September day, though I pass many hunting camps with the usual assortment of ATVs and trailers that can now travel the graded road with ease. The people I do see are women who are sitting in plastic lawn chairs beneath canopies running off the trailers. They are reading books, talking. I think of them as hunting widows, fishing widows.

Farther up the road I pass an elderly couple bucking several cords of wood onto a flatbed trailer hauled by an old pickup. A battered Stihl chainsaw sets on top of the logs next to a five-gallon gas can. Cutting, bucking, and splitting your own firewood with the benefit of a twenty-dollar Forest Service permit is hard work at any age. Seeing them both work at it at their age makes me wince, and it reminds me that not everyone in this country is an Ivy League rancher or a top-dollar-an-hour worker in the gas fields.

Rio and Scout are sleeping, knowing there will be no action until I pull off the road.

At the dead-end circle near Rowdy Creek is a camp with pack mules, wall tents, and not an ATV in sight—a sign someone knows what they're doing. When I stop, Rio and Scout hit the truck's windows, snarling like savage beasts—a prelude to their conversation with the stock dogs protecting the mules.

I'm too far upstream. The creek trickles among rock gardens with nary a pool or run in sight. The stream is suffering from the effects of drought and a warming climate. This bodes ill for cutthroats in Greater Yellowstone: they cannot tolerate warm water.

I stop and pitch sticks into the creek for the dogs. No hatches, no shade. I head farther downstream, looking for pools and shadow and find both at a narrow bend in the creek.

The three of us cross the sagebrush flat and drop to the creek. As I join my rod, Rio slinks away to hide under a big sagebrush. As a puppy she had a bad experience with killer bees along the Mexican border that prevents her from being my fly-fishing companion. She will swim rapids, wade deep snow all day, calmly accept the sound of gunfire. But bugs? No way. Scout joins me and proceeds to do what he is named for.

Mahogany Dun mayflies are about, gracefully dancing from just above the surface of the creek to high in the air. They are medium size, the color their name suggests, and, in my experience, never plentiful. Since there are few hatches this time of year, they are always welcome. And the trout can't afford to ignore them.

An occasional trout feeds between a trunk of downed timber and a tangle of exposed roots hanging from a steep bank. The water swirls through boulders. Lots of good trout security. I cast.

Scout dutifully sits on the gravel bar beside me and evaluates my progress. He is a serious, noble dog with the classic black-and-white markings of a border collie, whereas Rio is merled—gray, white, black, tan—in classic Australian shepherd style. He follows the drift of my fly knowing perfectly well what is going on. Occasionally he cocks an eye at me. He could be a member of the House of Lords evaluating a debate. Rio watches from beneath her sagebrush, panting.

I am certain the feeding fish are Colorado cutthroat; the cutts in North Horse Creek have to a large extent avoided hybridization with rainbows and successfully competed with the brook trout. The main problems for the population are siltation and loss of habitat from livestock grazing.

I wander down the creek, the dogs follow. In the next two hours I catch two brookies and three cutts, all eight or so inches each. As usual I don't know what to do with the brookies. Killing them seems mean-spirited, and they wouldn't provide a glimmer of a meal. Putting them back is not good for the ecosystem. They are so beautiful, vivid, and alive. What to do? I put them back, muttering about what an egg-sucking milquetoast-weenie I've become in my old age. Scout stares at me: guilty.

Each of the Colorado cutthroats seems a perfect being, glowing in various shades of yellow, gold, and orange offset by the characteristic vermilion slash and reddish patches on the gill plates. I admire each one as they float lazily in the net and thank these survivors for enriching this intimate creek all these years.

By the time we head for home, long shadows have stretched

across the valley. Mountain bluebirds are flocking and heading south on their way to Mexico, extending the ecosystem, as it were. We pass two fishermen standing by a bridge holding spinning gear and a landing net suitable for thirty-pound steelhead.

"Any luck?" I ask.

"Nope. You?"

"Three."

Flat Creek is a modern trout stream. It rises in the Gros Ventre Wilderness, passes through a private ranch closed to the public, then tumbles down a long narrow canyon and out into Jackson Hole, where it vanishes into the ground leaving a bone-dry arroyo as barren as anything in Death Valley, the water having been removed by irrigation canals on the National Elk Refuge and used to grow grain. An environmental impact statement consultant and riparian expert claimed that this section of stream was the worst he had ever seen in North America.

Several miles farther downstream, on the western edge of the Refuge, ooze from springs is augmented by water stolen from the Gros Ventre River via a ditch. Flat Creek rises again, though not for any reason involving conservation. No, it is resurrected to satisfy the irrigation needs of ranchers south of the town of Jackson. A three-mile section of this water is reserved for fly-fishing, the only such water in the state.

After the creek crosses the main highway north of Jackson, fishing is restricted to children under the age of seventeen, who can fish with anything they please, even worms. Every year one of them will land a monster that is the envy of the pros.

Then Flat Creek flows through Jackson. In most towns a creek this beautiful would be considered a treasure, but not here. It is usually hidden behind trailer parks, eateries, and unsightly residues of urban existence; it is held in place with continuously "improved" dikes designed to protect the priceless real estate from returning to its natural riparian state. There is a Flat Creek Watershed Management

Plan—yes, even creeks must endure management plans. Some people want to pump warm water into the creek in the winter to prevent anchor ice from forming, sending the creek over its banks and into the neighborhoods. Trout Unlimited builds artificial undercut banks to improve habitat. Runoff from the town's streets dumps accumulated debris into the creek. Inner-tube floats are popular in the summer, complete with lots of beer and noise.

It passes through a new city park, parallels a popular bike path and more urban debris, runs through miles of suburbs and ranches, and finally (with relief, one wants to say) joins the Snake River near the bridge over Highways 191, 189, 89, and 26, south of Jackson.

The three-mile fly-fishing section of Flat Creek is magnificent water, its banks free from annoying willows, courtesy of early homesteaders. It resembles a spring creek—though, obviously, this glorified irrigation ditch is anything but a spring creek. Most of the trout in Flat Creek are wild, native Snake River fine-spotted cutthroat, *Oncorhynchus clarki behnkei,* named in recognition of Robert J. Behnke's efforts on behalf of the subspecies identification and preservation. Of our ecosystem's five subspecies of trout, the Snake River fine-spotted population is faring best, even though it originally had the smallest distribution. I still put them back so they will continue to fare well.

Despite the dazzling artifice of it all, this short stretch of Flat Creek is one of the finest places in Wyoming to fish, and it evokes in local anglers a sense of reverence. The resident fish are big and smart and hard to catch. If you think cutthroats are dumb and easy to catch, a day of postdoctoral fly-fishing on Flat Creek will adjust your attitude.

The naturally difficult fishing is further augmented by a refined ethic of what is fair to use to pursue these fish: no flashy attractor flies, no big nymphs, no streamers, just dry flies, caddis emergers (flies that imitate a fly shedding its husk), and terrestrials—ants, beetles, and grasshoppers. Nor does the conscientious angler flail about scattering casts and flies in shotgun fashion. No, you search for a feeding fish and present your most delectable imitation of what it's probably (that's the rub) feeding on, with a light rod and a long leader ending in a fine tippet. Aficionados dye the ends of their fly lines mossy green and tie their own leaders. It's a refined game for pros—sort of like playing poker in Las Vegas.

I usually don't fish Flat Creek until fall because of the crowds. There are two parking lots for Flat Creek. I choose the northern one, near the National Fish Hatchery, so that when I am particularly depressed by being skunked I can visit the big fat cutts in the concrete tanks at the hatchery—a masochistic exercise that is strangely therapeutic.

An early snow has pressed flat the fields of grasses surrounding the creek into a wavy sea of tans, through which a well-matted path passes on its way to other well-matted paths paralleling the stream. It is evening. The sun is gone from the creek but illuminates Sleeping Indian (called Sheep Mountain on the maps), still crowned with fresh snow from the same storm. I spot two other anglers slinking along the banks—so I head in the opposite direction. I am looking for Mahogany Duns and am thankful for the few I see. I walk a bit away from the stream so as not to betray my presence by subtle shocks.

The sky is an ethereal blue, the wind has dropped, the little creek slurps and glides. All is well. I amble along slowly, looking for the telltale sips and fins and dimples and subtle swirls that betray a presence. I couldn't be happier: silence, solitude, beauty, and the focus, attention, and awareness of fly-fishing.

Hmmmm . . . perhaps a glimmer of a swirl. What to do? I always feel a bit like Hamlet when I fish Flat Creek: I never know quite what do. I mutter to myself, I ponder, I finally tie on my favorite beetle imitation. The little Winston rod throws it to the opposite undercut bank with ease.

"Not bad, Turner," I tell myself.

I fiddle with the drift. Nothing.

This process repeats itself until dark. I haven't seen one damn fish and the hatchery is closed for the day. Alas, another evening in paradise.

------------>

The Smith's Fork of the Bear River system flows south from the end of the Salt River Range at the southern tip of Greater Yellowstone. The easiest way to get there from Jackson Hole is down U.S. Highway 89 past old Mormon towns with quaint names: Etna, Thayne, Afton, and, finally, Smoot, whose sole claim to fame is one I imagine residents would just as soon forget—a brief mention by Vladimir Nabokov in ("fire of my loins") *Lolita*, when Humbert Humbert discovers a new species of butterfly in the vicinity.

As usual, I don't go the easy way. It's a general principle with me. I intend to leave U.S. 89 at Alpine Junction and head down the sixty-mile-long, dusty, sometimes narrow Greys River Road.

Wits maintain there are two seasons in Wyoming: winter and road construction. It's October. No snow yet, so road construction is still in full swing. The Wyoming Department of Transportation is rebuilding the road through the Snake River Canyon south of Jackson, a massive project cutting hundreds of feet into hillsides and projecting the roadway out over the river canyon. Flashing signs warn of thirty-minute delays.

I end up sitting behind a Ford 250 4×4 truck with bumper stickers that announce HUNT TO LIVE, LIVE TO HUNT and I'M AN ELK-A-HOLIC. The driver gets out to check the tie-downs on his ATV; I notice he's decked out in full camo with a Bowie knife that might be useful for carving up opponents in Nogales but is quite useless for carving up an elk in Wyoming.

Around us is the screech and roar of heavy machinery—D-8 cats, earthmovers, front-end loaders, and dump trucks that look like they were stolen from the set of *Terminator* movies. Steel mesh hangs from the cuts in the hillsides to control rock fall. On the other side of the Snake River the same machines are turning miles of an old ranch into access to the Snake River Sporting Club, an enclave of trophy homes surrounding a golf course where the ultra-rich can chase little white balls for a very few months each summer.

The Snake is running low. Every hundred yards or so is a drift boat with a guide at the oars and one or two clients casting to the banks. I wonder if anyone bothered to tell them they would be casting into the shadows of giant earth-grinding machines.

The road up the Greys River passes hunting camps, hundreds of them. Some are in old-style canvas wall tents, with a crooked pipe sticking out at an odd angle. Tired horses stamp away in campfire smoke. Men sit on upturned logs, smoking. Battered pickup trucks are parked off to one side amid the trees. Wyoming county number 12 license plates—which means Lincoln County. Locals.

More commonly the camps are modern, with trailers, Winnebagos, or campers, a few horses, portable steel corrals, SUVs, elaborate barbecue grills, portable toilets like the ones at construction sites, portable chairs, boom boxes, cell phones, and ATVs with mounted GPSs and ABS scabbards holding scope-sighted rifles. Pods of ATVs occasionally pass me on the road, the drivers in full camo, replete with camo helmets and goggles. Looks like we've gone to war against the elk.

Grandpa sits in one camp, wearing red suspenders, watching preteen kids chase each other through the sagebrush on ATVs, oblivious to their destruction.

I see few dead elk hanging in the trees. It's dry and there is little snow in the mountains, so the elk and mule deer are still high. Stalking elk on an ATV is like stalking an elk with your weed whacker howling. Although common sense, not to mention Wyoming Game and Fish statistics, suggests it is foolish to hunt from an ATV, such details have not impressed these modern Daniel Boones.

But these hunting camps are often not about killing elk or deer. They serve a social function, bringing families together into the mountains to reenact a dying tradition—the hunting camp. As a ranger in Big Piney once told me, "Why spoil a good hunt by killing something?"

As I look around I remember hunting with my father, uncles, and grandfather in the Appalachian Mountains and the importance of bringing home meat. I never once ate store-bought meat at my grandparents' house. I was raised to believe you hunted to kill and you killed to eat, so I see social-function hunting as a bit weird.

I keep going, trying to get clear of it all.

Two men in a 4×4 truck wave me down at the turnoff to Mc-Dougal Gap. The man riding shotgun is holding a volume I recognize as DeLorme's *Wyoming Atlas and Gazetteer*. The driver gives me a fey smile and asks: "Do you know where you are?"

"Yep."

"Good, then you can tell us where we are."

I spot only two anglers on nearly sixty miles of the Greys River. It's time to hunt, not to fish.

I keep going until dark, driving like an escapee from the modern world, even if the modern world I'm escaping is in one of the least populated spots in the United States.

I know several places up near the divide ahead of me that are hard to reach, even with a 4×4 truck. They are away from streams, not really good camps, but they have a fine view of the long crest of the Wyoming Range. I will be alone.

I cook a simple dinner on the tailgate of the truck and enjoy the evening light, the subtle gradations from pale blue to the faintest pink and lavender that makes land seem so mysterious. Rio chases sticks.

Early the next morning we cross the Tri-Divide, one of the many areas in Greater Yellowstone where water from one point drains into three major river systems—the Snake, the Green, and the Bear. It's a cold, wintry morning. Frost on the sage, dirty ice in the mud puddles. And empty; not a sign of traffic on the three roads that merge here. I watch a herd of pronghorn graze along the summit of a sagebrush-covered ridge. I glass them with my binoculars, mentally calculating the shot with my Winchester .270. But they are safe today—I have a different prey in mind.

I cross Commissary Ridge under heavy cloud cover and immediately strike the headwaters of the East Fork of the Smith's Fork. It is barely a creek here, but soon the valley opens and tributaries add enough water to make it a proper fishing stream. Several miles can be fished before the river meets another fork and disappears into a canyon. It will emerge as a beautiful, full-fledged Western river that flows through private property and BLM land leased to ranches until it meets the Bear River near Cokeville. Big Bonneville cutthroat trout—to twenty-two inches—inhabit the lower section of the river. It's hard to fish, though, because of all the NO TRESPASSING signs, and because what is public land is so mauled by grazing under BLM leases that I'm distressed just walking around on it. One grazing report wondered if the cows there ate dirt. The BLM admits that only nine of the fifty-eight miles of streams on the allotment are in "functioning condition" and that none of it is suitable cutthroat habitat.

However, the upper Smith's Fork is an excellent place for an endangered species of trout to survive. During spring runoff the big fish from the lower river migrate upstream through rushing, muddy water to spawn in tributary streams—a migration now abetted by fish ladders. By the time the spawners reach suitable habitat, they are forty or fifty miles from home and most of the modern world.

The Bonneville cutthroat was thought to be extinct in the 1930s. Since then small populations have been discovered and nursed back to a semblance of sustainability in the Bear River system, and it now occupies 5 to 17 percent of its historical distribution—depending on whom you believe. It appears they have successfully resisted hybridization, at least in some areas. The tributaries of the Bear River are littered with dams and irrigation systems that bleed the river of water, disturb natural hydrologic regimes, and create barriers to spawning migrations, plus the usual populations of alien trout, but the Bonneville cutthroat is still hanging on.

The degree to which they are genetically pure is a matter of debate, but that the upper Smith's Fork is presently one of the best habitats for the Bonneville is not in question. It is also threatened with a dam that would destroy 90 percent of its spawning habitat.

Conservation organizations sought ESA listing for the Bonneville cutthroat, but the U.S. Fish and Wildlife Service denied the petition in October 2001. I won't bother to give you their reasons.

I prefer to remain in the upper, wilder part of the river, which here is a series of small meadows and bogs covered with dense thickets of yellow, orange, and russet willows and spotted with numerous, sometimes elaborate, beaver dams. Behind the dams are ponds—some quite deep—that shelter fish. These meadows end abruptly and the river enters several narrow canyons choked with downed spruce and fir. Then more willow thickets and bogs. The upper Smith's Fork is not your friendly blue-ribbon trout stream.

I join my Winston rod, set the reel, and shake out some line. The usual assemblage of vest and flies are left in the truck. One small box of flies and a roll of tippet will do.

As soon as she sees the rod, Rio hides under the truck.

I'm hoping that the few hours of sun in this narrow valley will bring out midges or—one can pray—a hatch of blue wing olives. Although there are no hatches in sight, I try various small dry flies on the surface. I'm one of those snobs who will fish subsurface only if compelled to. No action, so I'm compelled.

I shorten the leader and switch to a small nymph. The willows are so high and so close that all I can do is cast up- and downriver, and it's so shallow my line keeps snagging on the tips of rocks.

I drift the nymph through a succession of shallow pools until I catch a fish, a very little fish, perhaps seven inches at best. I work the trout into my landing net and remove the barbless hook. It rests quietly in the water inside the net while I study my minuscule prey.

I like catching trout and looking at them. Sometimes I eat them, but I admit that I much prefer to eat other species, especially salmon and whitefish. Looking is another matter. Trout are among nature's most beautiful creatures. Few beings have received more aesthetic attention and praise. And my ravishing little Bonneville cutthroat trout does not disappoint me in this regard.

Its general color is subtle, neither a pale yellow nor pale orange. Trotter, in *Cutthroat*, describes it as "pale fawn," and I can't improve on that. The fins are orangish; the spots black, bold, and distinct; the slashes at its throat pure vermilion. Again, Trotter's description is excellent: the Bonneville are "delicately colored little creatures, almost like pieces of fine bone china."

I lower the net and the trout flashes away. Then I splash back up the stream to the truck, avoiding the willows since they are a mess of trampled branches covered with cow shit.

I continue upstream into the canyon. This time Rio comes along, though she keeps her distance. I catch another fish, even smaller, and in my heart of hearts I don't think I'll find anything larger here this late in the season.

Yes, the Bonneville is a very beautiful, distinctive trout, but I don't think I'll inconvenience them anymore today. Instead I paint a watercolor of the autumn meadow, the road, and the mountains, while sitting in my Crazy Creek chair on the tailgate of my truck, sipping tea. Rio lies in the sun in front of me, much happier now.

10. Grizzly Bear Heaven

- →

I stare at Jackson Reservoir in disgust. The mudflats are the worst I've ever seen. Brown, brown, brown.

Most of the water in what everyone from the Chamber of Commerce to the National Park Service insists on calling "Jackson Lake" has gone to Idaho to grow potatoes. The swarms of summer tourists are gone, too. Not many people see the reservoir in such sad shape, so few people complain.

No one says a word. Since the driver, Dan Burgette, is a sub-district ranger at Grand Teton National Park, I might try complaining to him. But there is nothing he or the National Park Service can do about the water, and we both know that. Idaho has the water rights. Burgette knows the mudflats bring out the worst in me. Dana and Rio have heard it many times. Our friend Dick Dorworth has not, and that's my excuse to rave about it.

Dan, Dick, and I intend to traverse the Teton Range from north to south. Dana will drive the truck back from the Grassy Lake Road, an obscure byway sandwiched between Grand Teton and Yellowstone national parks, and then pick us up at Teton Pass, west of Jackson, in a week. Despite the mudflats, we are in high spirits, except for Rio. For some irredeemably lame reason the park service has a problem with dogs traversing national parks, and she already knows that she's not going on a trip.

At the trailhead Dana puts Rio into the truck so she

won't sneak off to follow us and hugs us all good-bye. I get a kiss, too.

We shoulder our packs and look at the path leading into the burned forest, the remains of the Glade Creek Fire that burned through here during July and August of 2000. Dick bows slightly and motions to Dan to go first. Dan bows and motions to Dick to do the same, saying, "No, no, you go first. I walk too fast." Dick snickers unintentionally; he can't help himself. Forty years ago in Portillo, Chile, Dick set the world speed record on skis: 106 miles an hour on a pair of metal Head skis, leather, lace-up Hierling boots, and wrap-around Geze bindings. At sixty-five he still leads harder rock climbing than Dan or I have led in our lives, even though we're both professional climbers. Not many people anywhere near Dick's age go faster in the mountains. On the other hand, Dan has ten years on him, and his ministep-gait-that-never-quits is legendary. There is a buzz of energy, as at the line of opposing currents in a river. Everyone smiles.

I adjust my knee brace and pop four ibuprofen. No matter who goes first, there will be a harrowing of the flesh.

The northern Teton range (north, that is, of Leigh Lake and Indian Paintbrush Canyon) is wilderness, not legislative wilderness created by institutions—though it is managed as such—but de facto wilderness, which one of my friends defines as a place where you don't see anyone but yourself or the few friends traveling with you. Not exactly the language of the Wilderness Act, but it will do.

There are good reasons for this de facto status. First, like every paradise, it's hard to reach. On the east it is isolated from the rest of Jackson Hole by Jackson Reservoir. You must be dropped off and picked up, assuming weather permits, or leave your boat. Now, with the mudflats, boats can't approach the shore and no one wants to wade in the seriously deep mud. Second, few trails penetrate this paradise; there are no trails at all in much of it, and the trails that do exist don't go where you want them to go—down the crest of the range—and others simply dead-end. Third, it's lonely. Very few people enter the northern range in a given summer. If you run into trouble, no one's going to run into you and help you out. Cell phones are worthless in the upper cirques and valleys. And fourth, the northern range is a haven for grizzly bears—perfect habitat and few people. The park's chief resource biologist, Steve Cain, estimates that between fifty and one hundred grizzlies roam Grand Teton, and most of them are in the northern third of the park.

Soon the burned forest gives way to open meadows and lush riparian habitat along the Snake River. Walking is easy. The willows look pretty in their autumn dress.

At a muddy stream crossing we scare some boreal chorus frogs: inch-long, tan, each with three dark stripes on its back. These amphibians are common in Grand Teton and Yellowstone. So are spotted frogs. I see a fair number of garter snakes, but I've never seen a rubber boa or blotched tiger salamander in all my years here. I haven't seen a boreal toad in a long time and I miss them. Some are monsters—up to five inches. The northern leopard frog is thought to be extinct here. The bullfrog is an alien, introduced to a hot spring on the eastern side of Jackson Hole, probably a released pet. Frog and toad populations have plummeted worldwide, but these species remain present here, even though no one seems to know much about their numbers or distribution in Greater Yellowstone.

Dan is looking for something else, wandering off the trail, turning, turning again. Since we are walking on top of the Teton Fault, I think he's looking for fault scarps, small slips of land created by earthquakes. Finally he points to an isolated lodgepole pine. "I shot three six-point bull elk in three consecutive years from beneath that tree," he says. "Then the Davis Hill Fire came along and ruined my game. I hauled them in a snow sled to my canoe and paddled down the Snake and across the Jackson Reservoir to the Lizard Creek campground."

We are close to the national park boundary.

"Dan, is that legal?" I tease. "Poor elk were only minutes from safety."

"Yep."

The names of nearby features suggest prime elk habitat. "Tusker's

Island"—a charming mound of volcanic ash left over from the explosion that created the hole filled by Yellowstone Lake. "Elk Ridge." "Harem Hill." I name Dan's tree "Three Elk Tree." Like a child, I prefer to create my own maps based on my experience. Events like Dan's story anchor them in memory. I will always think of this as place as "Three Elk Tree."

We meet a park-service packer leading a string of five horses who is returning from the Moose Basin Patrol Cabin. There, he delivered provisions for park-resource biologists who will conduct their annual mountain-sheep survey. There follows the usual banter of travelers: Where you coming from? Where you going? What's the trail like? See any critters?

One mile later we cross the boundary into Grand Teton National Park and begin a gentle climb onto the glacial moraine at the end of Berry Creek. By the time we reach Berry Creek Meadows, four miles from the river, we have gained only 800 feet. This gentle terrain continues right across the range into Idaho. The trail parallels the old mail route from Ashton, Idaho, to Jackson. When the government decided to dam the old Jackson Lake to create Jackson Reservoir, they considered building a railroad through here to supply the project. They built the Grassy Lake Road instead. One is grateful for small favors.

Three hunters on horseback pass us at a rest stop. One has a Cabela's rifle case tucked under his right leg. It's zipped closed. It looks empty, and I hope for his sake that it is empty. Dan asks polite questions; he's the consummate professional.

"Just riding around, looking," the oldest hunter replies.

They are subdued, dour, and obviously surprised to encounter a park ranger. Poachers? Hard to say. The park has a problem with poaching in these remote areas, but they could just be riding around, as he said. The ambience in this part of the park is unlike the heavily visited areas to the south. The folks on horses, a paucity of hikers, the absence of spectacular granite peaks, and especially the presence of grizzlies all make it seem like a different part of Wyoming. In the south you wander the mountains with your mind on autopilot, un-noticing, inattentive. Here you pay attention—and even that may be insufficient.

Somewhere near this spot, at 9:30 at night on March 7, 2001, an adult grizzly attacked park service employee Jim Olson as he was skiing into the Berry Creek Patrol Cabin. Just after Olson spotted the bear with his headlamp, it charged. The bear knocked him down, driving his hands, still looped to the straps of his ski poles, deep into the snow. He was helpless. The bear bit him on the shoulder and buttocks, then left. Olson managed to ski on to the cabin where he received first aid. He was evacuated by helicopter the next morning. A cautionary tale for those who don't expect grizzlies to be about in the winter.

Since there were no cubs involved and the bear was not caught off guard but intentionally changed direction to approach Olson, park investigators decided the attack was predatory. Why the bear left its downed and helpless prey remains a puzzle.

Predatory attacks by grizzlies on humans are exceedingly rare. I've heard that only seven people have been killed in Greater Yellowstone since the 1870s, although records on this subject are neither exact nor complete. On the other hand, grizzlies occupy more territory in Greater Yellowstone—especially south of Yellowstone National Park—than they did when they were listed in 1975 as threatened under the Endangered Species Act, and conflicts with humans and livestock are increasing. The State of Wyoming paid a record amount to ranchers who lost stock to grizzlies in 2006. All the losses were in Greater Yellowstone.

How we should go about living with grizzlies is not an easy subject. Half of our population considers grizzlies to be serial killers and the other half considers them a cross between Yogi Bear and Winnie the Pooh. But they are not serial killers, they are not harmless, and they are not our friends. They are wild beings, with all that connotes. For reasons I don't understand, many people have a hard time accepting that fact. As Aldo Leopold put it: "Only those able to see the pageant of evolution can be expected to value its theater, the wilderness, and its outstanding achievement, the grizzly."

On the other hand, no one should underestimate the horror of a grizzly attack. A small library of books describing such attacks is likely to keep you from ever hiking in grizzly country, especially alone. It is the stuff of nightmares. One factoid I can't get out of my head was reported by Dr. Steven P. French, a biologist who worked for the Yellowstone Grizzly Foundation: a grizzly may begin eating you before you die.

Nonetheless, I think grizzlies deserve credit for their restraint. We are a ready prey for them, abundant and easy to kill. But as far as I know, no one has ever been killed by a grizzly bear in Grand Teton National Park.

"Dick, have you ever seen a grizzly?"

"No, but I'd like to." Pause. "At about three hundred yards." I can tell he's already quite happy with our little adventure.

We wind for three miles above the dense willow thickets skirting Berry Creek. The sun is low, the willows backlit to a vivid citron yellow. It's hard to see much, but we work at it, taking our time, looking hard. I believe we are obligated to not provoke a confrontation with a bear.

Through the willows runs a pellucid stream with native Snake River fine-spotted cutthroat trout. The cabin sits at the edge of dense forest across from the grassy slopes of Survey Peak, a jumble of Madison limestone, Darby formation, Bighorn dolomite, Gallatin limestone, Death Canyon limestone, and Wolsey shale, cakelike layers of sedimentary rock. It's here because a former superintendent liked to fish this meadow.

"Patrol cabin" fails to adequately describe this luxurious lair. The cabin is roughly sixteen by twenty-four feet of handsome log work topped by a high ceiling with Plexiglas windows in the peaks, a loft, bunks, thick sleeping bags, clever gas lights, mouse-proof metal cabinets and lockers, a shelf of books, and a serious woodstove. An old axe handle has morphed into a chin-up bar. The cabin would house a platoon in comfort.

"A lot bigger than where I live," says Dick. "Me too," I chime in. Neither of us lives in what most people would call houses.

We are impressed that the park went to all this trouble to build a palace in such a remote spot. Dan instantly deflates our balloon: the materials were hauled in by helicopter, even though the area is supposed to be managed as wilderness. Dan is still peeved about it. "The superintendent *really* loved this meadow."

After eleven miles with heavy packs in an afternoon, we're beat—and delighted with the comfort. Tents? Who needs a tent in the wilderness? Soon we are sipping tea, feeding the stove, watching the sunset from the porch, and talking about the easy stuff—mind, nature, wilderness, religion, and grizzly bear encounters. Funny how when you are in grizzly country the conversation turns to grizzlies, how they dominate our minds in the way only a top-of-the-food-chain predator can.

Ranger John Carr, who was the backcountry ranger at Berry Creek for many years, had a nice encounter right on this porch. John was sitting in a chair studying a book of chess problems (he was the chess champion of Idaho) and sipping a glass of Scotch when he heard a large mammal gallop past behind him. He got up, with book in one hand and Scotch in the other, and walked to the other end of the porch to see what was up.

He saw the tail end of a moose speeding away from him. He turned in the opposite direction and saw a large grizzly sprinting out of the willows beside the creek and heading straight for him. The bear was low to the ground, its chest heaving. It was virtually upon John when it executed a 180-degree turn—what bikers call a "brodie"—its butt continuing in John's direction as it tried to run the other way. Evidently the bear was as surprised as John was. Then it turned and stared at John, still heaving from its efforts. John backed calmly across the porch and through the cabin door, closed it, and surveyed the situation through the cabin window. The bear left. John downed his whole glass of Scotch.

We are up early, preparing for a long day, most of which will be off trail. Survey Peak is inviting in the early light. I glass for bears. Dan chops more wood to replace what we used. Then he removes all ash and coals from the pan of the stove, sets newspaper and kindling for a one-match-don't-even-have-to-think-about-fire, and leaves three matches stacked in a neat triangle on the shelf in front of the stove door.

"Dan, were you an Eagle Scout?"

"Nope, not even a Boy Scout. My Mom wouldn't let me join a gang that carried knives."

We loll about, not wanting to leave this patch of paradise. Some lucky ranger gets paid to live here all summer.

The start of our path south is obscure, but Dan has traveled here many times before and he finds it easily. It often vanishes in the meadows. We wander about, searching, find it again, and climb steeply for a thousand feet. Water bottles are filled in the last trickle of a stream. One imagines the Tetons filled with glaciers, snow banks, and tumbling streams, but Greater Yellowstone is in a drought, it is late in the season, and streams disappear rapidly in porous limestone. You have to know where water is to travel this country in autumn.

At the Forellen Divide, a saddle between Berry Creek and Owl Creek, we eat as much of our pack weight as we can stuff into ourselves while glassing for elk, sheep, and bears. Nothing. I'm a bit surprised and disappointed, since sign is everywhere. This is such splendid big-game country the local poachers in Idaho call Forellen Peak the "elk factory."

Off to the north the westernmost extension of Greater Yellowstone—the Centennial Range—stretches into the haze. We are a mile and a half from the park's western border. To the west is the Jedediah Smith Wilderness; in the direction I'm looking—Jackass Pass—the wilderness area is only three miles wide, an easy lope for a grizzly. It is the combination of both the park and the wilderness that is big enough to support a population of grizzlies. Beyond the Jed Smith is the valley of the Henry's Fork of the Snake River, filled with farms and ranches. Since grizzlies have lost ESA protection, this is one of the places they will be killed, by both hunters and ranchers.

Only one half-time ranger patrols the Jed Smith, and only during the summer. In the winter, illegal snowmobiling is rampant; miles of both de facto and de jure wilderness are flagrantly traveled. Some intrepid riders have even traversed the range through Grand Teton National Park, exiting at the road head south of Jenny Lake.

Why doesn't the government do something? Recent budget cuts for the national parks have essentially neutered the park's ability to enforce the law. The park decided not to use snowmobiles to chase snowmobiles in wilderness. Helicopter time is too expensive, and the fines are minor—it's a misdemeanor. Snowmobilers will throw a beer party benefit to pay a convicted snowmobiler's fine.

The Jed Smith is what I call a "peekaboo wilderness": look in one direction and you see wilderness; cant your head a few degrees and you're looking at farmland. Three miles is a pretty attenuated protection. I'm glad it abuts a section of a national park that is managed as wilderness.

Since the grizzly bear was protected as threatened, the population has grown; now approximately 500–600 bears inhabit the ecosystem— no one knows for sure because no one has actually counted them. The government uses an estimate derived from a complex formula involving the number of sows with cubs sighted in a given year. The formula has proved unreliable, and the government's numbers show that grizzly mortalities exceed the limit set by the U.S. Fish and Wildlife Service's recovery plan. Furthermore, the government scientists have not released their grizzly data for peer review by other scientists, which leaves the public and the government's critics in the position of staking the future of Yellowstone's grizzlies on faith in the government, their scientists, their data, and their complex formula—the "trust us" policy again. Environmental organizations refuse to bet the future of the grizzly on faith in any government entity. I agree with them.

Whatever the number is, according to some authorities it is plenty to insure a healthy population, and the State of Wyoming wanted the bears delisted as soon as possible. In 2007, the USFWS complied. Other equally credible authorities insist it isn't plenty, and that the grizzly population will again decline because of a combination of factors: the decline of whitebark pine, global warming, diminished habitat, increased conflict with expanding real estate and industrial development, increasing recreational use of Greater Yellowstone, and increased human-caused mortality.

Why delist grizzly bears? One simple answer is: because the law requires it. If the grizzly population has indeed reached a predetermined number (and that is what is at issue), then they can be removed from ESA protection. Another answer is: so the grizzly population can be managed by states, not the feds. When management of the grizzly population reverts to the states, hunting seasons can be reestablished, and hunters, ranchers, and developers can kill "problem" bears without seeking approval from the U.S. Fish and Wildlife Service or be restrained by stiff penalties. Again, you don't have to be very cynical to conclude that wildlife management amounts to killing wildlife in order to keep things "natural."

I mutter something about hoping for the best for the bears. Dick, who always has an appropriate quotation at hand, immediately quotes a famous climber's saying: " 'Hope' is a vain word in the mountains." Climbers are not by nature optimists. Most of the optimistic climbers our age are dead.

The trail ends at the Forellen Divide; except for a few hundred yards at the top of the next divide, we won't see another one for three days. We face a traverse of the open basin at the head of Owl Creek. We don't want to lose elevation, so we highline, avoiding the canyons, picking our way across enormous slabs of deeply grooved and etched Madison limestone. The stone is so sharp I imagine several weeks on it would shred Vibram soles. Scattered here and there are islands of whitebark pine. As grizzly habitat goes, this is as good as it gets.

The whitebark pines here haven't been much affected by blister rust and the cone crop is excellent this year. The bears are up high, right here, feasting, which is good. When the pine and berry production is poor, bears go downhill into civilization and get into trouble. Compared with good cone-crop years, a bad crop leads to six times more management actions (trapping and/or killing problem bears), twice the mortality of mature females, which are so important to a healthy population, and three times the mortality of subadult males.

Where will they go when the whitebark pines are lost or diminished by blister rust, pine beetles, and other adverse effects of global warming? Answer: they will soon lose their most important autumn food source and be forced from their relatively safe habitat.

A big mule deer buck bounds downhill, spooked that we got so close to him.

"You better run," says Dan, smiling.

Then, beneath Red Mountain, three bighorn ewes drift through a slot in the cliffs beneath us without sound, gray phantoms amid gray stone. "Like a dream," I say, but no one hears me.

The sky is utterly clear, the sun hot—like a pleasant day in August instead of a day in late September. We are hot, nearly out of water. The rills and streams shown on the topographic map are dry. The terrain is strewn with shards of limestone and summer's flowers, gone to seed. When the wind picks up the dry flowers rattle and rustle. My knee hurts and I'm moving slower than I expected. Traversing a hillside with the bad knee downhill stresses it more than with it on the level.

Just before we reach the top of the Moose Basin/Owl Creek divide, two park-resource biologists who are part of the crew counting mountain sheep pass us. We ask one, a young woman, what they've seen.

"Ten sheep yesterday, four today," she says.

When we tell her of our three ewes, she removes a small notebook from the cargo pocket of her pants and carefully adds our sighting and the location. She's a very fit young lady who is well ahead of her male companion. They are heading down to the Moose Basin Patrol Cabin for dinner.

We must traverse another basin before dinner and we're running late. There is no water and won't be until we reach a little pond—I call it "Poacher's Pond" because it's right on the border of the park and the wilderness, where hunting is allowed.

I'm sad to leave the divide so rapidly, though there is not much here but a single post stuck in the rubble with a sign partly propped up with an elk's skull. The limestone cliffs to the northeast harbor a magnificent cave I've always wanted to visit. There are sheep and elk and bears to glass for and familiar peaks to study from an unusual angle.

It's bizarre to be nearly 10,000 feet in the mountains with no source of water. Then, as we drop into Moose Basin, Dan finds a half-full water bottle! The water is hot and tastes of plastic, but we don't care. Dan always says he is a lucky man; now we believe him.

The traverse is long and wearying. We are alert for bears, both because of the hour and because one of the Teton's best grizzly stories occurred in these remote hillocks.

On July 26, 1998, while on his way to climb Glacier Peak, John Carr had an infamous encounter with grizzlies. Carr, who has rangered for years in Grand Teton and Denali National Park and who is a very careful man, saw a sow grizzly and her two yearling cubs about 200 yards away. He thought he was OK. Then all three bears charged.

Carr pulled his pepper spray. There was nothing else to do, no trees to climb, no reason to run—a grizzly bear can outrun a horse. For a few moments the bears disappeared under the hill in front of him and he hoped they had simply left. But no. They came tearing over the crest of the hill, the cubs in front, and came straight for him.

The cubs took up a position on either side of him and snapped at his legs like dogs. The sow stopped ten feet in front of him, reared on her hind legs, and, in John's memorable description, "scissored the air with her claws." She faced him but didn't come closer. Carr raised his sunglasses for a better look at her eyes. She was looking off to the side and he knew not to stare directly at her. So they both sort of pretended the other might not be there. He decided not to spray her because he thought it might make the situation worse.

The sow dropped back down and began to feed and one cub followed suit. The other cub kept snapping at him. Carr kicked it and started walking backward. The sow and cubs charged again. The same scenario was repeated.

Again the bears drifted off to feed and John kept backing up. Finally the distance between them became comfortable, at least in the sow's judgment. Carr, in an eloquent act of equanimity, continued his ascent of Glacier Peak. The adrenaline rush made him feel like a youth; he claims he has never climbed a mountain so easily.

Later that day he returned to the Moose Basin Patrol Cabin and wrote up the event in the cabin's log. I've read it. As stream of consciousness goes, it's right up there with Faulkner. Still discombobulated by the adrenaline rush, he spent a sleepless night. The next morning he called park dispatch for a boat and walked nine miles down to the Jackson Reservoir, still pumped. I know of no other grizzly story that so thoroughly confirms why one must remain cool when confronted with a grizzly and expect the unexpected.

At dusk we climb onto the long ridge south of Moose Mountain. The park boundary follows it and is marked by metal stakes. Dense groves of krummholtz fall off to the east. The last bit of light illuminates the higher peaks, the main chain of what we call the Tetons, even though this lower sedimentary ridge is the real watershed.

Dan is ahead now. I thought we were going to hang lower, and I would have, but we want to stay together as darkness nears. Reluctantly, Dick and I climb to the top of the ridge again. I'm trying to remember the way off this ridge before it ends in the steep cliffs above Poacher's Pond. Then I remember: west down a nasty slot filled with steep scree. Dick and I head down the grunge, then along an equally nasty traverse at the base of a cliff. I am always startled at how nimbly Dick moves through difficult terrain. Though weary he still has his winning smile, a smile that has charmed the socks off a lot of ladies.

By the time we reach the pond, darkness is upon us.

To the north the cliffs are limestone; to the south the long ridge leading to Glacier Peak is gneiss. Poacher's Pond is on a geological seam; you can put one foot on sedimentary rock millions of years old, the other on granitic rock billions of years old.

We cook and eat in the dark. Too tired to put up the tent, and lacking a nearby tree to hang our food in, we simply crash among the hummocks of grass amid a disarray of food, pots, clothes, and empty packs. We hope the local grizzlies don't notice three old fellows snoring in a meadow.

High clouds stream out of the west, harbingers of changing weather. The night is warm, too warm for me to have clothes on or sleep inside my bag, so I throw it over me and lay with the grasses on the hummocks prickling my legs like needles.

Dawn brings more feathered lenticular clouds that indicate strong winds up high. We eat, pack, and leave hurriedly, anticipating the familiar granitic landscape before us.

The walk south is across slabs of gneiss interspersed with meadows which are filled with thick grasses and sedges and bordered by lines of conifers and gleaming lakes of pale green turquoise water. There are flowers again: lavender harebells, asters. Above us is the bone-white glacier for which Glacier Peak is named. After a day of dry limestone hills we are happy to see water, happy to be back on gneiss. Nice gneiss, as climbers say. We loiter, enjoying the warm sun and dreading the climb before us. The path is all too obvious: straight up a narrow slot for several hundred feet, then a traverse south and another climb to a pass at 10,400 feet. We go at it without comment. At the top we find two piles of bear scat, one large, one small. The larger is about 2½ inches in diameter. Probably a sow grizzly with a cub.

For the first time we can see most of the peaks I think of as home: Mount Moran, the Grand Teton, Teewinot, though they are still several days' travel to the south. Twelve hundred feet below us, the meadows of the South Fork of Snowshoe Canyon beckon. We head down, cautiously. The drop is so steep in places you can't see much before you, and small clumps of whitebark provide food and cover for critters. Ten years ago Dan and I ran into a sow grizzly with two cubs on this slope, and we don't want to be surprised again. We stop often, scrutinize the terrain, and then slowly descend until we arrive at a little chunk of paradise. I call it "Fairy Meadow."

Although it is early, we camp. I could stay for a month at this very spot without complaint. Rolling Thunder Mountain and its miles of open, colorful slopes offer opportunities for glassing. Our camp is on grass and sedge through which wanders an archetypal boulder-and-slab-strewn brook, gurgling and clear. Around us are steep rocky walls. A dipper greets us with its sharp call—*dzik, dzik*—as it scurries down stream. We laze about in the grass, Dick and I writing in our journals, Dan glassing for game. A hatch of mayflies dances on the water.

I do not think I will pass this way again, certainly no time soon. It's been twenty years since I did this traverse alone and ten years since I last walked this valley, even though it's one of my favorite places on the planet. I want to absorb its impeccably simple beauty.

The sun sets at 4:25 in our narrow canyon. Immediately the cold becomes unpleasant. We pile on clothes and gather for tea and dinners, each of our own preference and making. More rested than we have been for the past two nights, we fall into conversation, our backs propped against packs and boulders, drinking more tea. Eventually we are silent, on our backs, staring at the stars. Dan falls asleep with his usual irritating rapidity—a minute or two and he's snoring softly. A few more minutes and Dick is gone, too. I lay awake with my brain burning jet fuel, envious as hell.

I arise early and meditate for an hour until the sun rises through a notch in Rolling Thunder. We move about in silence, not wishing to break the spell of a perfect morning. With the warmth, a caddis hatch comes off the brook, crowding my parka. One perches on the peak of the tent like a weather vane and refuses to move, even as I take down the tent. I manage to transfer it to my finger and blow warm puffs of air at it but the bug clings tenaciously. Finally it lifts off my finger like a tiny kite, and disappears into the sky.

Then Dan's stove runs out of fuel. I heap abuse on him, his ranger-hood, his reputation, the National Park Service, and so on.

Dick is very serious about coffee. He travels in the mountains with a small French press. He is also not one to complain, but he stares forlornly at his lukewarm coffee and does the funny thing with his mouth he does when he's perturbed. I'm not happy, either. Fortunately, Dan says he knows of a secret park service cache we will pass before dinner.

"A secret park service cache! Probably has Scotch, too! Paid for, no doubt, by the American taxpayer!"

Our route is again obvious: another notch in a ridge, this one leading into the next basin. We angle up the steep slope for 1,400 feet, each at our own pace, often on slightly separate routes. The world shrinks; space becomes a matter of an inch, a foot, a yard, only occasionally farther. Attention is a matter of the body's reach. We all like this. It is the condition of a climber searching and testing a handhold or foothold, the sculptor's touch, the skier's feeling the snow through his skis, the painter's stroke. Although we all spent too many years in college and are anything but anti-intellectual, we are happiest when we completely occupy our bodies.

The gully narrows into a hodgepodge of ice, boulders, and frozen snow. We kick steps the last hundred yards to the notch. Then, a surprise: we are not at the top. Like Survey Peak, this area is a mishmash of different rocks, in this case gneiss with dark intrusions of hornblende. We thrash upward through steep, heartbreaking scree until we reach the crest. And lo, where do we go? Why, a thousand feet straight down to a lake in the North Fork of Moran Canyon.

"Straight down" is only minor hyperbole. The first 500 feet or so is scree so steep that Dan and Dick "ski" blithely down in a controlled landslide. Dick—as befits a former director of the Aspen Ski School and a coach of the U.S. Ski Team—is particularly agile, making perfect parallel turns on his boots, knees bent, poles gracefully carving the air. I am considerably less graceful, painfully so.

The second 500 feet takes us down grassy ribs to what is arguably the most beautiful spot in the Tetons: a small lake, fringed on one side with healthy whitebarks, offering a stunning view of the Grand Teton, Mount Owen, and Middle Teton rising into a band of cirrus clouds. The scene is framed by Mount Moran to the east and Cleaver Peak to the west. From this angle, Cleaver is, as the kids say, awesome—like a tower in Patagonia.

We lunch with the splendid view attended by three goldeneye ducks. Dick says, "This is among the most magical and lovely places of my mountain life."

I would spend more time here too, but, alas, we have miles to go before we sleep. Hard miles.

As before, we are loath to drop into Moran Canyon and lose our elevation, so we descend a bit and begin a seemingly endless traverse (bad knee down again) across rocky slopes broken by the usual stands of conifers. Dan has an altimeter on his wrist. If we can hold at 9,200 feet we will have to climb only 400 feet to our night's camp, a lake beneath the divide one mile west of Window Peak.

Bear scat and more bear scat. Little bear scat, big bear scat. We keep a sharp eye, stopping, looking. A few clear-winged grasshoppers are clacking about, a slight breeze refreshes; vast stretches of vermilion huckleberry bushes and miles of talus. But we see no bears.

They're here, though. Another major food source for the grizzly is the army cutworm moth. These moths migrate to Yellowstone Island from as far east as Kansas; some survive farmers' efforts to eradicate them. Upon arrival they feed during the night in the flowered meadows and hide during the day under talus. Grizzlies love moths: it has been estimated that grizzly bears will eat up to 40,000 moths a day. Most of the moths that survive return to parts east about now, but we bet the bears are still picking up a few.

"Warming will cover the talus with trees eventually, knocking out another grizzly food source," I comment. No one replies. We don't want to ponder the future in detail right now; we just want to be present. Dan knows all this, he knows more about bears than I will ever know.

Trying to be a bit more positive, I say, "It is heartening to see such superb grizzly habitat—grizzly bear heaven."

"Yep, grizzly bear heaven," Dan repeats.

At a rest stop in the shade of a whitebark pine a shadow glides over us. Overhead, a golden eagle—its size precludes it being anything else up here. After studying us intently, its head cocked, it swerves downhill, stoops into the canyon beneath us and disappears into the forest. No sooner has it gone than another shadow appears, this time a sleek bird with a long tail and pointed wings—"dapple-dawn-drawn / Falcon in his riding / Of the rolling level underneath him steady air," as Gerard Manley Hopkins so memorably put it.

"A peregrine?" I ask.

"No, it's too light to be a peregrine," says Dan. "A prairie falcon."

I don't argue with Dan about birds. In his sculpture he specializes in birds carved from wood or forged from stainless steel or titanium. And he's good, a master carver. In 2001 he took "Best in World." It's a prairie falcon.

We traverse, yet again, into the open meadows of the North Fork, through more bear scat, and reach our lake, small and still unnamed. Its eastern bank is a perfect spot: a level stretch of short grass and sedge only a foot above the lake's surface. We set about making camp before the sun drops over the ridge.

A languid breeze rises with the setting sun. The lake laps against the shore, its soft patter shattered occasionally by the screeching of Clark's nutcrackers collecting the last of the year's nut crop.

To the west an odd, slightly angled band of dark rock several hundred feet wide cuts through the ridgeline—a seam of some sort? While Dick and I seek spots to meditate, Dan strides off at his famous clip, obviously on a mission. He returns to inform us that the dark rock is the same vein of igneous rock, technically known as diabase, that slices through Mount Moran—the so-called "black dike." I had no idea it went clear through the range.

Tonight's discussion rambles from religion and the creation of the universe to the impossibility of controlling the extremes of environmental destruction if we refuse to accept limits. Dick and I are Zen Buddhists and our belief system lacks a creation myth; Dan is trying to reconcile his hard-headed scientific education with God's handiwork. Dan and I rant about the absence of limits to growth—god-given or otherwise. Dick, his glasses perched professorially on the tip of his nose, searches his journal and reads us an apt passage on the subject by Wendell Berry. I finally put them both to sleep explicating in detail the plot of my novel.

Morning arrives accompanied by a raucous chorus of nutcrackers, dancing in the whitebarks and squawking like politicians.

We head southeast over a low divide to another lake, then angle back west on another traverse, heading for the crest of the range. It seems we're passing large piles of bear scat every hundred yards or so. Then we find two sets of fresh prints. The bears were running uphill.

A hundred yards later Dan starts chortling, followed by howls of laughter. He lifts a can of pepper spray off the ground. The holster lies nearby. The safety plug is still intact but the can is empty. Two sets of teeth marks explain why: it has been chomped twice by a bear. We don't know the story (and never will), but obviously someone either dropped it, or threw it, or . . . No difference. Dan is bursting with mirth.

"I'm going to ticket them for littering the park. I'm going to ticket them for feeding animals."

Dick and I are laughing, too, as much at Dan as at the can—and studying the surrounding forest.

"Dan, I'm not sure it's a good idea to laugh about a bear getting a lung full of pepper spray—bad karma," I gasp between laughs.

"Very bad karma," adds Dick.

Soon we are on the crest enjoying new views to the west, admiring the orange and yellow stands of aspen. The crest is easy walking. When I did some of this trip in reverse twenty years ago, I walked most of the way on trails west of the crest, finally crossing a pass to the Moose Basin Divide and down Owl Creek to the Grassy Lake Road. It was a lovely trip, but no comparison to our route, in beauty or difficulty.

We stroll south for three miles through open meadows at 10,000 feet toward Little's Peak. A trail leads over its summit but we traverse around the side onto a flat plateau. Now the Grand Teton dominates the view, more so than from any other place in the park, I think. Huge, isolated, magnificent, uncluttered by the lesser peaks, its western face glows in golden light.

The route off the plateau down to Lake Solitude is grim. I cannot remember the way I climbed up years ago, so we wander off to the east a bit and then down, down, down along a series of ledges, steep talus, and grassy meadows. My knee is shot. I limp slowly, painfully, bowing in my mind to the ski-pole gods and modern pharmaceuticals. When I finally catch up I reluctantly admit I shouldn't continue on to Teton Pass.

On our last day we descend the North Fork of Cascade Canyon to the trail coming up from Jenny Lake, the most popular trail in the park. This is to say we descend into humanity, its authority, works, and pleasures, a descent rather like an astronaut's reentry from space. For a few days we've managed to get Thoreau's "dead dry life of society" out of our heads. Perhaps at no time do we appreciate the wilderness more than when we leave it.

The trail is wide now. Sturdy bridges cross the streams, bridges that were constructed for horses carrying a now nearly forgotten kind of tourist—the Dude—from the valley to picnic and fish at Lake Solitude.

We meet Goldie Morris, a ranger on patrol who will reverse our route, ending up at the Berry Creek Patrol Cabin. A quartet of young hikers march past with regimental vigor, their constitutional bringing them little pleasure, it seems. Then a young couple, vague in the way Generation X always seems vague. Then a couple running hard in skimpy shorts, he carrying his shirt rolled up in his hand, she in a sports bra. Then crowds of hikers.

Beneath Storm Point I hear the cries of climbers on Guide's Wall. We stop for a drink, a snack, and to fill our water bottles. Lying with our backs to our packs and enjoying the Indian summer day, we watch the climbers on the route, one of our own favorite climbs.

At Inspiration Point and Hidden Falls the number and kinds of people increases exponentially. Although officially designated to be managed as wilderness, the area is a "sacrifice zone," a place where visitors are funneled by trails and boats to diminish their impact on surrounding country. Tots and grandparents and everything in between vie for space on the trail, moving unconsciously into their "lanes" as they pass, pausing often to breathe. They are here to enjoy the view out over Jenny Lake, the Absarokas, and the Gros Ventre ranges to the east. They have struggled a mile and 500 feet in elevation from the boat dock; some look and act as if it took all they had. As we trudge past with our huge packs, they stare.

This is home ground, the location of the Exum climbing school, the place where I work most of the summer. I know the trail by heart, every step, root, and rock. I grow accustomed to the crowds of people during the summer months; now, after our little adventure in the boondocks, the crush of humans is depressing, a spectacle with all the ambience of a circus.

On the boat ride across Jenny Lake, the other sixteen passengers study us like we're aliens.

"Where did you come from?" one asks.

"Up near Yellowstone," I reply. "Down the crest of the mountains."

The woman next to me turns to her husband and says—loud, clear, and rude—"I don't believe that."

"How long did it take you?" another man asks.

"Parts of five days."

"See any bears?"

"No, but we saw lots of sign—both black bears and grizzly."

A long silence.

"Which one is the Grand Teton?"

"Well, the Grand Teton isn't visible now. We just lost it behind that mountain, Teewinot. 'Teewinot' is a Shoshone Indian word meaning 'many pinnacles.' It was their name for the whole range."

More questions follow. I am civil and informative. I am a professional mountain climbing guide who works here. Like the hit man Tom Cruise plays in *Collateral* says, "It's what I do for a living." On the one hand, it irritates me that they are so ignorant and disengaged from the place I love; on the other hand, their patronage will determine the future of Greater Yellowstone, and I intend to be pleasant and support that cause.

With his park-service shirt, badge, and hat, Dan is fielding even more questions than I am. Dick contemplates the mountains, studiously oblivious. He is practicing his beatific smile.

From the dock we walk a dusty road for a half mile to the compound of cabins where the Jenny Lake climbing rangers and Exum guides live during the summer. Rangers greet Dan with smiles—he is their much beloved leader. Exum guides Rod and Mark Newcomb are remodeling a cabin. Dave Carmen is building a bunch of beautiful picnic tables. Saws grind, a radio blares. Rio runs in circles around me, whimpering and trying to find a stick. More kisses from Dana.

Then it is over. We shake hands and agree, formally, that it was a great trip. Ranger Jack McDonald gives Dan a ride home to Moose. Dick and I take showers. I check my e-mail: seventy-three new messages.

We go to Moose to shop. Space and time collapse, albeit in a different way than in the mountains. At Dornan's store, we buy coffee from Colombia, chocolate from Switzerland, and water from France. On the radio I hear the voice of a man in New York, then the voice of a man in Iraq. This is the heat, the friction and drag of reentry into what we so casually call the world. As though there is no other.

The next morning Dana makes Dick a celebratory breakfast of oatmeal. Today is the fortieth anniversary of his world-record breaking ski run in Portillo, Chile. Then he is off—to Aspen to see friends, to New Mexico to read from his great book on the ski-racing scene in the sixties, *Night Driving*, and finally to Utah for hard rock climbing at Indian Creek. As he drives away down the dusty road, Dana and I enact an old Japanese custom: we wave until he is out of sight. Over the top of his van I can see the summit of Rolling Thunder Peak, rising gracefully above a hidden Fairy Meadow. So near, so far.

Dan calls. The resource biologists saw a total of eleven bears. A party on horseback along the Moose Basin Divide nearly rode into a grizzly sow with two cubs only a day after we passed. The northern end of Grand Teton may not be the wildest place in Greater

Yellowstone, but in combination with the Jedediah Smith Wilderness it is still pretty wild and a fine example of what the grizzly bear needs to survive—if only we can keep it big and wild.

Yes, we were among grizzly bears. I am sure they watched us closely from their piece of grizzly heaven and let us pass, at their pleasure, in peace. That's the best way. A Zen master once said: "The deep sky never obstructs the floating white clouds."

II. Red Rock Lakes

---------------------------------➤

Late autumn. The green world vanishes; winter eases the passing with new snow. Human transportation in the ecosystem is closing down. On November 1 the roads in Grand Teton close; a few days later fishing season closes in Yellowstone and the roads there begin to close, too. The Beartooth Highway has been closed for a month. Many dirt roads in the backcountry are impassable. The trailheads are empty. There is too much snow in the mountains to hike and too little to ski or snowmobile. Hunters are still getting around on horses but they are leery of early winter storms. There is an edge to the weather. Late autumn in Greater Yellowstone is a time for care.

We travel where we can, driving the few roads that remain open, usually because someone needs them to be open for more than mere recreational interest. One place we like to go is Red Rock Lakes in southern Montana at the northwestern tip of the ecosystem.

"Shall we do a last overnight?" I ask Dana.

We pack the truck with winter camping gear and cross the Teton Range to the Henry's Fork of the Snake River in Idaho, then follow it north to its source, Henry's Lake, in a valley on the northern border of Idaho that is surrounded on three sides by the state of Montana. Justly famous for its fishing, the lake is popular, its shore speckled with summer homes of both the modest and the gothic variety. I often drive by the lake on my way to favored fishing holes on the Madison River, just over Raynolds Pass. Now we turn west, heading for Red Rock Pass and the Centennial Valley.

This is not Dana's favorite time of year to be out and about. She is a person of spring, of flowers and sunshine, and balmy winds. I, on the other hand, love late autumn—the time of classical Chinese poetry, of pale skies and muted colors, of fallen leaves lying in the ponds and along the braids of shrunken rivers. But we both look forward to Red Rock's silence and serenity, something that is guaranteed this time of year.

The paved road ends after two and a half miles. There will be no more asphalt until it reaches Interstate 15 near Monida, Montana, approximately fifty miles west. As we ascend through aspen forests, we pass a few trucks with horse trailers but no cars. Though the road is graded and maintained, this isn't car country. One can go for a week here without seeing a car on this road. At night you might never pass a vehicle. There is the solitude of the open road, a passage through an endless tunnel of light. It's hard to find those kinds of drives now. Sometimes when I travel this road at night it seems I could drive off the end of the earth and no one would know.

The road is said to be open all year but it was often closed by snow when I first passed this way nearly half a century ago. I came through here in the sixties driving a VW. Grim. I was afraid they wouldn't find me until spring. Now, with milder winters, it may indeed be open all year, but one should check with the Highway Patrol before crossing the valley in midwinter, and carry good sleeping bags, water, food, a stove, and extra gas—there are still no gas or services available. A century ago it was a busy thoroughfare for the stageline that hauled tourists to Yellowstone National Park from the railroad stop at Monida. Not many places in America have seen so little growth.

Beyond the pass, at a gentle crossing of the Continental Divide 7,120 feet high, the country opens into the Centennial Valley and the Red Rock River, the ultimate source of the Missouri River. The much-traveled mountain man Osborne Russell crossed the valley in

1835. He guessed, correctly, that Red Rock Creek was the headwaters of the Missouri. From a gorge in a mountain to the south it is 3,745 miles of river to the Gulf of Mexico, making the Missouri/Mississippi the third longest river in the world.

Russell found the valley "full of Buffaloe." And Indians. The Indians—Shoshone and Bannock—are gone. There are no bison now, either, save an occasional wanderer from Yellowstone that is immediately killed. There haven't been bison here for more than a century. Fishers haven't been seen since 1900; no pine marten since the 1920s. The last bighorn sheep in the Centennials was shot in 1912, and reintroduction would be a waste of time as long as there are domestic sheep in the area. No pygmy rabbits since 1940. Mountain lion, lynx, wolverine, black bear, grizzlies, and wolves remain rare despite the fact that this is perfect habitat for them.

This is as big as Big Sky country gets—600 square miles of it, 6,600 feet high, and one of the least populated areas in the lower forty-eight states. The valley is a mosaic of fragmented ownership: U.S. Fish and Wildlife Service, Forest Service, Bureau of Land Management, the State of Montana, and 100,000 acres of private property, most of it controlled by fifteen long-established ranching families. The valley's population is less than it was fifty years ago.

The diversity of habitat is impressive by any standard: sand dunes, grasslands, wetlands, lakes, sagebrush flats, alpine meadows, forests, and alpine cirques. As one would expect, the diversity of flora and fauna is equally impressive. Both the Nature Conservancy and the U.S. Fish and Wildlife Service have active conservation programs in the area, and for good reasons—it is among the largest wetland complexes remaining in Greater Yellowstone, and the most critical corridor linking it to similar habitat in the Selway/Salmon/River of No Return Wilderness in central Idaho and to the Northern Rockies of Montana. The threat to this vital corridor is the development of private property with a resulting fragmentation of habitat, and what happens here may well determine just how healthy the island of

Greater Yellowstone will be in the future. With so many species already gone it is imperative we try to hang on to what's left.

The air seems brighter, the aspens along the lower slopes of the mountains more vivid, white skeletons etched against the darker forest. The creeks that will eventually form Red Rock Creek and feed Red Rock Lakes are lined with muted yellow willows. Everything is a lyrical blend of crystalline clarity and restrained hues of dull gold, gray-green, dusty-rose, russet, white, pale cobalt blue—the colors of the autumnal West.

To the south and north are mountains, the Centennial Range on our left, its slopes now plastered with frozen snow, and the Gravely and Snowcrest ranges to the right, remote and lonely, silent and grave.

Studying the Centennials, Dana says, "Looks like a good place for hiking."

She is determined that this will not be just a road trip and that we'll get in one last hike before the snows come. The Centennial Range is indeed attractive. Sixty miles of the 3,100-mile-long Continental Divide Trail, stretching from Canada to Mexico, follows the crest of the Centennial Range.

"I don't like it up there—too much Twilight Zone for me," I say. "Too scary."

Some of the trail passes through a U.S. Department of Agricultural, Agriculture Research Service (ARS) Sheep Experiment Station on the southern side of the main peaks. The map of the area carries the following warning:

> ARS sheep flocks carry a disease organism that can be passed to humans using the area. The Q-Fever disease can be serious for persons with heart conditions and women of childbearing age. The Experiment Station has trained dogs guarding the sheep and these dogs are trained to protect the sheep from anything they perceive as a threat to the flock. They can cause harm to people or their pets.

Q-Fever is spread to humans by airborne contaminated dust. Since I don't think I've ever hiked a trail in Greater Yellowstone that wasn't dusty, my desire to walk the crest of the Centennial has been considerably dampened. I've been told that many of the dogs are Great Pyrenees, three feet tall, 125 pounds, bred to deal with wolves and bears, and trained to be aggressive.

Oh well, welcome to your national forest—"Land of Many Uses." A place where you can catch a weird disease and get ripped to shreds by a pack of dogs.

Occasionally we pass a mailbox on a post, an indication there is a ranch nearby, though not necessarily close to the road.

More common are tiny birdhouses nailed to the tops of fence posts, an invitation to mountain bluebirds. Why so much effort on behalf of bluebirds? See that stunning patch of cerulean blue fluttering above the snow after a long winter and you will understand. The boxes probably outnumber the mailboxes 20 to 1.

For ten miles we don't even pass a truck.

"Where do the kids go to school?" Dana asks.

"I don't know, but I imagine many are still schooled at home."

Rio is usually alert in new country; now she sleeps. She knows. I'm in driving mode, going fast enough to level out the washboard bumps.

After fifteen miles we enter Red Rock Lakes National Wildlife Refuge. Except for the sign and a modest exhibit you wouldn't know anything had changed. But it has changed, because it is protected land, the majority of it wilderness with few trails. The refuge's headquarters is in Lakeview, a—well, I don't know what to call Lakeview, with a population of ten souls—a village? a ghost town? It lacks facilities. Nice trumpeter swan display, but that's it.

Only 15,000 people visit the refuge in an average year, compared to Yellowstone National Park's four million. It was not created for tourism. The official literature is lofty on this point: "Physical facilities are limited and commercialism is minimized . . . formal trails are not maintained or designated. In keeping with the wilderness spirit, visitors are free to explore the country and follow numerous game trails, seeing the country the way wildlife see it, and follow in the trails and tracks of moose, elk, and deer."

President Roosevelt established the Red Rock Lakes Refuge in 1935 specifically to protect trumpeter swans. At the end of the nineteenth century trumpeter swans were thought to be extinct. Then in 1918 two nests were discovered in Yellowstone National Park. A thorough survey by the National Park Service followed. In 1932, sixty-nine trumpeters had been located in the United States, although unknown to biologists there were hundreds more in remote areas of Alaska. By the 1950s there were more than 500 swans and birds from Red Rock Lakes, and some were relocated to sites in other states to establish more widely distributed breeding populations. Then in the 1980s the population dropped precipitously.

Before colonization, trumpeters bred from Pennsylvania, Arkansas, and Oregon east to Nova Scotia and north to the Northwest Territories and Alaska. European settlement reduced the population by destroying wetlands habitat, trapping, hunting, and human development. During a sixty-year period in the 1800s the Hudson Bay Company alone sold 108,000 swan skins—mostly trumpeters—and tens of thousands more were no doubt killed. The commodities produced from trumpeter-swan parts were writing quills, fancy hats, and ladies' powder puffs. By 1935 they were on the brink of extinction.

In E. B. White's charming children's story *The Trumpet of the Swan,* the male trumpeter, called a cob, announces to the young swans, the cygnets, that now that summer is over they are flying south to Montana.

> "Montana," said their father, "is a state of the Union. And there, in a lovely valley surrounded by high mountains, are the Red Rock Lakes, which nature has designed especially for swans. In these lakes you will enjoy warm water, arising from hidden springs. Here, ice never forms, no matter how cold the nights. In the Red Rock Lakes, you will find other Trumpeter Swans, as well as the lesser waterfowl—the geese and the ducks.

There are few enemies. No gunners. Plenty of muskrat houses. Free grain. Games every day. What more can a swan ask, in the long, long cold of winter?"

There, in one paragraph, is much of what you need to know about why Red Rock Lakes are so closely associated with trumpeter swans. *Warm water.* The many springs and thermal features here, and in other areas of Greater Yellowstone, helped the species to survive even though the winters were severe. Not only did they prevent the formation of ice, they were rich in aquatic flora upon which swans feed. *There are few enemies.* By the 1930s we had killed off most of the predators in the ecosystem. *No gunners.* Hunting swans was illegal in the refuge and in Yellowstone National Park. *Plenty of muskrat houses.* Swans like to build their nests on the top of a muskrat house because it is one of the few solid bases in marshy areas, it is high enough to serve as a good observation point, and it is up to nine feet in diameter. Since the muskrats use an underwater entrance, everyone is happy. Since the area was remote and much of it was protected, there was good riparian habitat for muskrats and trapping was either forbidden or restricted. *Free grain.* From 1935 until 1992 trumpeter swans were fed grain at Red Rock Lakes. The feeding was stopped because too many trumpeters came to occupy too small an area, disrupting aquatic growth and increasing the odds of a disease spreading among the still-threatened population. The trumpeter population was increasing as their habitat was decreasing.

Perhaps it is a tad much to say that nature designed it for swans, but it was a damn good place to preserve the few that remained and build a larger population.

The centerpieces of the 45,000-acre refuge are two shallow, marshy lakes—Upper and Lower Red Rock lakes—surrounded by miles of marshy, dense willow thickets, ponds, and quagmire through which wind little creeks. Great moose habitat, and unlike the bison and the mountain sheep, moose are still present. Indeed the refuge allows a hunt to keep their numbers down.

Dana has an eye for moose, and sure enough, she soon spots several.

"I don't like to see them so close to the road," she says. I find moose hunting on a refuge to be particularly distasteful. They are so easy to kill, the word "hunting" should not be used. You drive along the refuge road and look for moose in the willow flats. The moose are near black, the willows dull yellow this time of year. When you spot one, you park, walk out into the willows, and shoot it.

The campground at Upper Red Rock Lake is empty. We drive to our favorite site and open the doors of our truck to the din of thousands of birds—ducks, geese, and swans.

"Trumpeter swans?" asks Dana.

"Tundra swans."

Trumpeter swans are aristocrats. Their voice has been compared to a French horn, though *The Sibley Guide to Birds* suggests the less delicate "honk of a European taxi." Tundra swans are, in comparison, peasants; they hoot, they honk, they bark. David Allen Sibley likens the sound of a distant flock of tundra swans to a pack of baying hounds. And that is what it sounds like now—a thousand baying hounds. To make things more complicated, the voices of both species vary with age and the time of year, making vocal identification difficult. Fortunately for our sleep tonight, they are— whatever they are—on the other side of the lake. I can't imagine sleeping among a flock of tundra swans.

We get out binoculars and our spotting scope. A myriad of big birds pop into view, certainly hundreds—perhaps more; so many are hidden it is impossible to know. Birds landing, taking off, birds flapping their wings and hooting.

At a distance, a tundra swan looks like a trumpeter swan: a white body, neck, and head with a black bill. We need more glass. I look through our 30-power spotting scope. The end of the lake where it enters, or, more accurate, becomes, the River Marsh, is filled with various swans and geese. This year's cygnets can fly now. You can identify them from their smaller size and gray color, but they are all too far away to become involved in identification, particularly this late in the day. We set about making a camp.

The view from the campground is simplicity itself. A band of dull orange willows separate us from the lake. On the other shore is another thin band of orange willows, beyond which raise several bands of mountain ridges dimmed by the evening light. To the northeast, perhaps twenty miles away, a forest fire pumps a lavender plume thousands of feet up into the evening sky.

A spring near the lake offers sweet water from a pipe gently placed among rocks. The outhouse has a rock to prop open the door with. Beyond is a marvelous view of lake and mountains. In the old days the stagecoach to Yellowstone stopped here and a bar offered refreshments. I've looked, but I can't find a sign of its ruins.

It's cold and the wind starts blowing a gale. For some reason that I cannot adequately explain to Dana, I brought our floorless Megamid tent. Dana disappears into it and buries herself in her forty-below-zero sleeping bag. After squinting into the blowing dust for a few minutes, Rio joins her in the tent.

I labor at my tailgate kitchen. The stove blows out the instant it is lit; the pots and pans blow off the tailgate and tumble about in the dirt. I curse and nurse. An elaborate barrier against the wind helps the stove some; I make tea and start dinner—our usual fare of boil-in-a-bag rice with several cups-of-soup on top. "Hippie food," I call it. Dana cheers my efforts from the shelter of her sleeping bag.

When we go to bed the forest fire is still roaring. Occasionally we see flames flash against the dark purple sky through the door of the tent. The wind howls through the gaps at the bottom of the tent, blowing dust and leaves over us. Dana and I try to snuggle with only the tent pole between us, leaving Rio at the edge. She will have none of it. She climbs on top of us until we wiggle around enough to give her a well-protected warm spot between us, and there she settles in for the night, ignoring my depredations about her ancestors. The swans squawk, we try to sleep.

Dawn is icy cold and thankfully windless. The lake reflects the distant mountains like a mirror. I think of Keats.

> *Thou still unravished bride of quietness!*
> *Thou foster-child of silence and slow time.*

Tiny cracks in the mirror appear—the wakes of ducks and geese. I work at coffee and oatmeal on the tailgate, stomping my feet and trying to hold my hands around the stove at the same time. Dana and Rio remain buried in down. Dana urges me on: "You are my hero!" Rio barks for her morning bones.

"Don't you want to go hiking, my dear?" I ask Dana.

Silence.

Diffuse smoke from the fire fills the eastern sky, suppressing details. The scene is one of vast planes of earth and sky in subtle colors. For a moment I have a sense of déjà vu: Haven't I seen this before, in just this way? Then the "ah-hah": Chatham.

Some artists so completely capture the essence of a place and make it their own that to imagine the place or hold it in the mind's eye of memory is to see it distilled through their art. We are not free to do otherwise: it dominates our inner vision. I imagine the Italian hill country with Corot, I think of Provence through the mind of Cezanne, I see Russia with the eyes of Levitan, I remember the Maine coast through the labors of Homer. And like many people I now see Montana through the paintings of Russell Chatham. My recognition and appreciation of this morning's offering of space and color derive from Chatham. The visible silence, the dense stillness, the simplicity that eludes language and yet remains rich in allusive depths, the colors beyond the reach of naming, the marrow penetrating beauty—all of this I feel standing next to the tailgate of my truck.

What to do this lovely autumn morning? There are no manufactured spectacles in Red Rock Lakes. Not much to do unless you want to watch birds. Or sit in silence. Or read. The sun is finally up. Dana has moved from the tent into the sunlight and now occupies a chaise lounge—still in her sleeping bag. Another folding chair holds her binoculars and a second mug of coffee. She is working on the second volume of the complete Sherlock Holmes and sees no reason to move. "I can see the lake and birds from here," she notes, concentrating on her story and barely noting my presence.

I wander away with Rio in tow, tripod and spotting scope over my shoulder. Since I'm not carrying a fishing rod, she follows along willingly, staying close. She's supposed to be on a leash, of course, but she's too smart to bother wild things at her age. Her days of nipping bears are over.

Four trumpeter swans are lounging at the edge of the western shore of the lake. Reaching them will not be easy. We wander into the willow thickets, following game trails. We don't get very far: there are too many other birds to see.

A blue grouse sitting in a nearby tree causes me to set up the scope for a closer look. They are a common bird at home, but this one is close and looking straight at me. Through the scope it is so close I can see the hazel iris and watch the tiny feathers on its face rise and fall in the freshening breeze. It stares at us, unabashed at our presence. Rio sits and watches it—the perfect lady.

We keep moving, sometimes in the willows, at other times through ruddy autumnal turf. I see a kestrel and a belted kingfisher, the usual chickadees, and what must be the season's last killdeer. I look for golden and bald eagles. I miss the shorebirds. This is the only place I have ever seen a black-crowned night heron or a solitary sandpiper. Red Rock Lakes is a paradise for birds and for birders.

The number of bird species found here is a matter of debate. Some sources say 232, others say 261. No matter what the number, that's birding paradise and the main reason the American Bird Conservancy lists Red Rock Lakes as a globally important bird habitat.

The Centennial Valley has the densest populations of peregrine falcons and ferruginous hawks in Montana and a good population of sage grouse. The peregrines here are another great success story for conservation. By 1970 few peregrines remained in the United States despite their having once been common in every state. By 1980 there were no breeding peregrines in Montana. The Peregrine Fund worked to reestablish the species through artificial insemination and incubation. The chicks were raised in captivity and released into the wild at artificial nest sites in areas of excellent habitat—including the Centennial Valley. The population, though about as artificial as you can get, has flourished.

Sandhill cranes are common in the summer, but they've left for the winter. So have the white pelicans. Lots of ducks are still here, though, and it's hunting season.

Although Red Rocks is a refuge, fishing and hunting are permitted in certain areas. Fishing does not compare to the blue-ribbon waters of the nearby Beaverhead, Madison, and Henry's Fork rivers. And, as usual, the fishery is a mess because of past management policies that stocked alien trout. Brook trout, to quote the official literature, are found in "nearly every inhabitable lake and stream in the valley." The rainbows have hybridized with the local cutthroats. Native fish are rare and the few that remain will be invaluable for the creation, probably far in the future, of a truly native fishery. Genetically pure westslope cutthroats are confined to isolated brooks in the Centennials where they must compete with brook trout. A rare indigenous lake trout in Elk Lake has suffered from decades of genetic mixing with Mackinaw trout from the Great lakes. The native lake-dwelling form of the Arctic grayling is barely hanging on—the sole population in the contiguous United States. The lingcod, properly called "burbot," are abundant and the population here has been used to restore other populations in Montana.

Hunting is more popular, especially for ducks and geese, though elk, pronghorn, and deer are taken, and a few moose. Most people are surprised to discover that hunting is allowed on national wildlife refuges. There are ninety-five million acres in the refuge system. Hunting is allowed on most, and slightly over half allow trapping.

Sixty percent allow other forms of resource extraction, including gas and oil drilling, logging, grazing, farming, and mining. The negative effects require little explanation: reduction of water levels, erosion from irrigation, oil spills, sedimentation of streams, toxic wastes in groundwater—the list is long. All of which adversely affects flora and fauna and uglifies the landscape.

Despite all that I can't get too upset about Red Rocks Lakes Wildlife Refuge because of the four stunningly beautiful trumpeter swans swimming slowly before me on the lake, their graceful necks continually dipping underwater to eat. Watching them, one can understand why they were creatures of myth and why Audubon waxed eloquent about them.

Then there is their size. Trumpeter swans are the largest of North American wildfowl. Sibley gives twenty-three pounds as an average weight, but males have been known to exceed thirty pounds. The average length is sixty inches, the average wing span is eighty inches. Fred A. Ryser Jr., in *Birds of the Great Basin,* mentions specimens over thirty pounds with wingspans of 120 inches—that's ten feet! For comparison, a bald eagle weighs a diminutive ten pounds, is half as long, and has an eighty-inch wingspan. Only the California condor and white pelican approach the size of the trumpeter swan.

Trumpeter swans fly low and you can hear them coming. Anyone who has had one pass thirty feet overhead with a whoosh will attest to its size and power. Sometimes I have actually felt their disturbance of the air. All this made them easy targets for hunters.

Trumpeter swans cannot be hunted in the United States, but Nevada and Utah still offer hunting seasons on tundra swans, even though they are not considered good eating, and every year trumpeter swans are mistakenly killed. Bizarrely, each state has an official limit on mistakenly killed trumpeter swans. When that limit is reached, all swan hunting ceases for the season. I am a hunter, but I cannot imagine killing a swan; it would be like killing a unicorn. Nonetheless, just as there are people who hate wolves and kill them, there are people who for absolutely no reason kill trumpeter swans. In 1995, some wacko shot and killed two nesting swans on Lilly Lake in Jackson Hole.

Like the peregrine falcon, the trumpeter swan is a Centennial Valley success story. Sort of. Unlike the peregrine, the trumpeter swan is, let us say, sensitive. A peregrine can live on a skyscraper in a city; a trumpeter requires a more specialized habitat, especially during winter.

Like pronghorn and sage grouse, swans are shy and do not tolerate human disturbance. They need lakes, ponds, and streams that do not freeze and offer an abundant supply of aquatic plants. Basically that means riparian, lake, and marshy habitat—precisely the places we have planted with alien crops such as alfalfa (a native of Iran that arrived in the United States via Chile), and littered with condos, subdivisions, and log castles.

We had a growing population of trumpeter swans, but not habitat for them. Hence the conservationist's common refrain—habitat, habitat, habitat. Both the Wyoming Wetlands Society and the Trumpeter Swan Society are devoted to restoring breeding populations of trumpeter swans to Wyoming. It will not be easy.

The problem is that more swans need to migrate further south to where they are not so dependent on Greater Yellowstone's diminishing supply of waters that are impervious to freezing temperatures. Unfortunately, with the severe decline of the trumpeter populations a century ago went the loss of the species memory of its migration routes. Animals that don't continue to migrate lose the memory of migration routes, the memory of migrating. The same is true for pronghorn and mountain sheep in the ecosystem. I've heard it said that the oldest females carry the memories. If they die without migrating, the migration stops. This happened to the Jackson Hole pronghorn population. Scientists believe they discovered it again by accident. If this loss of memory becomes a recurring problem with numerous species, then the ecosystem will be in trouble. An ecosystem need species, habitats, migration corridors, and, oddly enough, memories.

We can't have healthy wildlife populations and healthy ecosystem without these things, and yet we continue to destroy what remains of Greater Yellowstone's already diminished habitat at an astounding rate even as we nod, wring our hands, give our twenty bucks to a nonprofit, and preach conservation. Indeed, the conservation community is rife with members who continue to develop land even as they preach the importance of habitat, and many more conservationists profit from that development. The movement suffers its full share of hypocrisy.

Despite the many problems facing the trumpeter swan the U.S. Fish and Wildlife Service has steadfastly refused to grant it threatened status. Their excuse is the usual smoke-and-mirrors move, refusing to grant status to different population segments. Why worry about trumpeter swans in Yellowstone when there are thousands along the Pacific coast? Why indeed.

Although the Fish and Wildlife Service adopted ecosystem management in 1994, the Endangered Species Act is not sufficiently based on ecology. The act was created in 1966 and amended in 1973—before the full implications of ecological dependence were recognized. Which is why we need an Endangered Ecosystems Act, or better, a constitutional amendment that mandates the preservation of ecosystems. Otherwise more and more parts—sage grouse, trumpeter swan, lynx, fisher, riffle beetle—will go missing and Greater Yellowstone will end up with the integrity of Swiss cheese.

I can no longer ignore the harsh fact that it is very windy and very cold and that even watching trumpeter swans is no longer comfortable. I'm sure Dana is not very happy, either.

Rio and I head for camp. She leads, sniffing her way home through the dense willows.

We pack up and head for Lakeview. The refuge headquarters is a quiet building with a few folks working at desks in back rooms. We look at the trumpeter swan display, pick up some literature, and leave. We're going to take the long way back to Jackson Hole and the weather is threatening.

Several miles west we see a fire burning in a forest south of the road. After some discussion we decide to return to Lakeview. We drive back to the refuge office to report it, but the office is closed—everyone seems out to lunch. Then I notice a grinding noise coming from what appears to be a maintenance shed and I walk over. A man is hunched over a tire, working. I make some noise so as not to startle him.

"There's a fire burning down the road a few miles, off to the south." I'm feeling ambivalent. I like forest fires but this one is downwind from a community.

The man doesn't even bother to look at me. "It's been there all summer," he says.

And that is the end of the conversation.

"What did he say?" Dana asks when I return to the truck.

"He said its been there all summer." I shrug. "No good deed goes unpunished."

We drive west and I now feel free to admire the beauty of the wildfire. The road is long, desolate. The wind is up. Dust devils cruise the road; blowing clouds of dust sweep along the sides of mountains. The truck shudders when we drive through them.

After we pass a dilapidated ranch two dogs run onto the road to greet us, happy Labs smeared with mud and shit, their tongues dragging on the ground. Up to mischief, no doubt about it. Chasing, digging, rolling, chewing, barking. Dogs free to be dogs. No doubt it's dangerous being a dog in this wild country, what with the occasional wolf, mountain lion, wolverine, and packs of coyotes passing through. But then danger is the price of freedom—even dogs know it and think it's worth it. Freedom is always dangerous, and perhaps the most important is the freedom to make mistakes and endure the responsibility of your mistakes. "Wild and free," we say, knowing full well they go together even as we slither into our layers of security.

We leave the Labs to their happy life. Rio barks madly out the window. The Labs are too exhausted to bark back.

Dust storms have turned this high desert bleak. We have left Island Yellowstone and entered another ecosystem.

"I feel like an exile," I remark.

A band of low gray clouds to the west is trailing veils of snow. The horizon looks like winter.

12. Christmas at Old Faithful

Christmas at Old Faithful! It sounds so romantic—Bing Crosby, sleigh bells ringing, walking in a winter wonderland. I had promised myself this trip for years, and the years passed. Then I married a genuine romantic. Reservations at Old Faithful duly followed.

There has been such protracted controversy about the environmental consequences of winter travel in Yellowstone— snowmobiles versus snow coaches—that I no longer want to hear about it. I wanted to believe that solid science would decide the issue, but after reading Todd Wilkinson's *Science Under Siege: The Politicians' War on Nature and Truth*, a detailed account of how science in federal agencies has been repeatedly twisted or ignored in the interest of political expediency, and, worse, how courageous scientists who have published politically incorrect research have been maligned and punished—a process that began with Rachel Carson and her famous book, *Silent Spring*—well, after Wilkinson's book I lost faith in the ability of science to settle the issue. At root, the controversy concerns values—solitude, silence, self-reliance, the natural, the health of other beings, the integrity of an ecosystem, the wild.

What is a nonspecialist to do? The first thing is to go look for your self.

Our trip begins at Flagg Ranch, a resort near the south entrance to Yellowstone National Park that caters, in winter, to snowmobilers. It is one o'clock in the afternoon, and the temperature is 10 above 0, the sky somber. A crowd stands about nursing cups of coffee and stomping their feet. Since we are strangers, conversation is limited. People smile pleasantly, some seem to guard their pile of luggage, as though there might be robbers in the shoulder-high snowbanks.

Instead of sleighs and stomping Clydesdales there stands idling before us a pair of bright yellow Bombardier snow coaches, named for their designer, Joseph-Armand Bombardier, an inventor responsible for a number of motorized recreational craft including snowmobiles and what would become Jet Skis. Bombardier designed the snow coaches for use in rural Quebec, where they served as school buses and ambulances in areas where roads were not plowed. They hold ten passengers each. The name sounds vaguely warlike, and the vehicle confirms that impression: it looks like a Bradley M2 Fighting Vehicle without the turret gun or the camo paint job.

Our coach was built in 1969, well before the line went extinct in 1982. The drivers load our luggage onto the top and back of the coaches, and direct us to spartan benches along the sides and back of the interior. Dana and I are joined by four couples from Denver, including a pair of honeymooners.

The windows are small, the heater is noisy, and so is the strident grind of the engine. Our driver must yell her introductory lecture at us. Dana smiles. She's on an adventure.

We leave with the lurch common to tracked vehicles and are soon coasting along at thirty-five mile per hour. The windows immediately fog up, blocking what view there is—of the tops of trees. The noise makes ordinary conversation impossible. We yell at each other, a peculiar way to achieve familiarity, but required. The gas fumes become so annoying that we agree to open the hatch in the roof—another vaguely martial feature. As the 10-degree draft rushes in, people bundle up with provided blankets and nestle closer. We all smile now but in a grin-and-bear-it fashion.

The drivers clearly love their Bombardiers the way people inexplicably love their ancient Jeeps. Even though they were to be outlawed in the park because of their noise and pollution, their historical status has, like the Jeep, made them an icon seemingly immune to regulations. So they still ply the park's snowy roads along with modern coaches that are more or less buses fitted with tracks instead of wheels. When locals learn you went to Yellowstone in the winter, they ask cheerfully, "In a Bombardier?" If you say no, they look disappointed.

After rumbling into the park, we make the first of three stops, a short scramble down Crawfish Creek to see frozen Moose Falls.

We pile back into the snow coach. Everyone claims their original seats and blankets and proceeds to cuddle.

We lurch north above Lewis River Canyon and stop again at a turnout. People take photographs. I know from fishing this part of the river in summer that there is a family of otters living here, and we look for them but don't see them. The driver says she saw four otters, a coyote, and swans at West Thumb this morning, West Thumb being a parking lot with toilets and a warming hut.

Near West Thumb we spot an old bull bison shoveling snow aside with his massive head. A bison's head and neck weigh 500 pounds. A 500-pound shovel effectively moves all but the deepest snow and that never occurs here because the hot springs either melt it entirely or significantly reduce its depth. Areas in the park with geothermal activity thus act as a magnet for large animals, especially bison.

More photographs.

The third stop is the warming hut at West Thumb, a sturdy cabin with a monster wood-burning stove, icy outhouses, and a parking lot with idling snowmobiles spewing plumes of exhaust. We crowd around the stove and make forays to the outhouses.

Dana, borrowing one of my favorite lines, says, "We could have gone to Maui." She is no longer amused.

I do not envy the snowmobilers. The temperature is now 6 degrees above 0 with what sailors would call a moderate wind, capable of producing whitecaps. The wind-chill factor is probably 12 degrees below 0. Since these snowmobilers are racing along at thirty-five miles per hour or more, they have experienced wind chills of around 20 below 0, even colder if they started early. They look, and act, frozen. Several women express reluctance to leave the stove, even for the outhouse. The ranger on duty cheerfully informs us that the temperature last night was 38 below 0.

A boardwalk leads to the edge of Yellowstone Lake. Because of the presence of hot springs at West Thumb, some water near the edge of the lake is free of ice, though most of the lake is a frozen shelf of white disappearing east into clouds. On the ice, fifty feet offshore, lies the front half of a pine marten surrounded by a corona of fur and blood. Evidently a coyote found it away from the protection of a tree and killed it.

"Our arrival chased the coyote off," our guide says, "but it'll be back to finish its meal."

"What is a pine marten?" the new bride asks, to no one in particular.

"It's basically a sable," I reply, "like the critters Karl Lagerfeld uses to make fur coats for Fendi. That should be a felony punishable by public castration, disembowelment, and quartering."

"Aren't your watercolor brushes made from sable?" Dana asks. I'm being punished for bringing my romantic to this very unromantic spot and acting in such an unromantic fashion.

Three trumpeter swans are cruising gracefully near the edge of the ice, two adults and a cygnet. They look gorgeous against the steely blue lake. I also count eleven Canada geese, five mallards, and two common goldeneyes in winter plumage, their white bodies again gorgeous against the lake. A lone dipper hops from rock to rock along the shore, perfectly adapted to a frigid environment. They offer quite a contrast to the tribulations of freezing humans.

We climb back into the Bombardier, don our blankets, and snuggle for the final run to Old Faithful. At 4:30 p.m.—dusk this time of year—we arrive at the Snow Lodge, a modern building that opened in 1998 to accommodate the increase in winter visitors to Old Faithful. The old Old Faithful Lodge is closed in the winter because it lacks insulation.

Bellhops unload our luggage, skis, and snowshoes, and a staff member hustles us into the lobby, which is replete with blazing fire-place, prominently displayed snowshoes of ancient vintage, over-stuffed chairs, and sofas. The contrast with the Bombardier is disorienting, but sure enough, it is Christmas. There are wreathes, and red and white things, and Bing Crosby crooning through every speaker in the building. One must be thankful for small things. I am thankful it is not Janet Jackson screaming about Santa Claus.

Our room is luxurious and anything but rustic, with cream-colored walls, vertical-grain fir trim, and stainless-steel hardware. Dana tests the bed and smiles. "I'm not going to do anything until I take a long bath." A bath is a treat for her, given the five-gallon camp shower and galvanized feed bucket she usually bathes in dur-ing winters at our cabin. I've hung a Degas painting of a bather on the wall above it in an effort to induce the appropriate spirit, but it does not replace a real tub.

I return to the lobby to survey the scene. To my surprise, the road to West Yellowstone is still open to vehicle traffic, though not to the public. Guests are arriving in ordinary buses and vans. Lines of other Bombardiers stand fuming; they have arrived from Mammoth Hot Springs with more guests. Others are returning from snow-coach tours of the park.

Outside, the high-pitched whine of snowmobiles is nearly con-tinuous. Although the roads and many walkways are clear, people use snowmobiles for trips of only a hundred yards, as though walk-ing were prohibited. The roads are well groomed, safe, and much wider than ordinary snowmobile trails. Combined with all the pa-trols and warming huts there is probably no better place, and cer-tainly no more beautiful place, to ride a snowmobile.

The ambience in the Snow Lodge is chic, rather like a private club in New York. Along the halls and around the fireplace are men, some trussed in ties and sport coats; elegantly turned-out women occupy tables and comfortable wicker chairs. Most are absorbed in games—bridge, poker, hearts, chess, Monopoly. Others are reading. Snippets of French, Italian, and German fill the room. A man in a floppy beret is writing postcards with a Montblac ink pen. Directly in front of the hearth a lovely woman clad in fashionably cut wool slacks and a black silk blouse is reading through diamond-studded glasses. The boy next to her is playing a DVD reruns of a football game on an Apple laptop balanced on his knees. His ears are buried in thick headphones. We might be in Davos, Banff, or Portillo.

There appear to be few athletes present. As far as I can tell, the only people fit for backcountry travel are the coach drivers, the rosy-cheeked women running the ski-rental shop, and the backcountry guides. I cannot help wondering what all these swank folks thought of the Bombardier ride, though they are undoubtedly smarter than I am and arrived via heated bus on the comparatively short ride from West Yellowstone.

Not everyone is swank. There are college kids in drooping shorts and long jerseys, and flocks of children being children. Ethnic diversity is close to zero.

I duly admire the Christmas tree and ask the staff if there is television.

"No," she replies. "And many guests complain about that. That and no Internet access."

Cell phones work, however, and they are commonplace. I spy two satellite phones.

"Why do you think these people come here?" I ask. I am genuinely perplexed and curious.

"Most people come to snowmobile or go on tours to see animals," she says.

At the Snow Lodge's ski shop I ask one of the rosy-cheeked women about business.

"A few people rent skis and snowshoes for day trips, either with guides or alone. Not many. Some trails leave directly from the Snow Lodge, others require a snow-coach drop-off at nearby trailheads from which one can ski or snowshoe back to the lodge. Business is definitely not booming."

Dana arrives, fresh from her bath, beaming and hungry.

The Obsidian Dining Room, described as "a fun environment with something for every taste," is filled with laughter and revelry; everyone indeed seems to be having fun.

"It's Christmas," Dana reminds me.

"I know, but I'm a Buddhist."

In an attempt to enter into the festivities, I order the Christmas Special—turkey, mashed potatoes, veggies, and pumpkin pie. Dana orders vegetarian fare and wonders out loud how all these vegetables make their way to this frozen speck on the planet.

"Where does all the food come from to feed a staff of one hundred and fifty people plus hundreds of guests?" I ask the waiter.

"We stock the essentials before the road closes in the fall," he replies, "and we bring fresh produce by snow coach from West Yellowstone."

"Really? That's a lot of snow-coach trips. Does anyone complain about that the way they complain about snowmobiles—the gas, the exhaust, the noise?"

He smiles and shrugs. We go to bed early.

What does one choose to do on a winter day at Old Faithful? We brought skis and snowshoes with us, but the scant snow is too icy for good skiing, and snowshoes are gratuitous. After an afternoon in a Bombardier we don't relish the thought of a whole day in another coach, even a new one, especially after a woman tells us she got sick riding in one. Our options are thus reduced to renting a snowmobile or walking.

It has been my experience that people who love machines do not like to walk, and people who love to walk do not like machines. The gulf separating them is deep. Once when I flew to an airfield near Mount Everest, a passenger, the wife of the director of the national park there, asked the French pilot if he would like to have tea at their nearby house before flying back to Katmandu. He replied, "Thank you, Madame, but it is against my principles to walk." No snowmobiler could say it better.

I have used snowmobiles on various winter jobs in Jackson Hole over the years and I do not question their utility. I simply hate their sound. Spending a day on one is like spending a day in your freezer cutting metal roofing with a table saw. When the former secretary of the interior Gale Norton visited Yellowstone on snowmobiles accompanied by her husband, he wore earplugs. Rangers at the entrance stations wear protective masks to reduce their exposure to the pollution snowmobiles spew. What more do you need to know?

In terms of recreational vehicle use in national parks, the great snowmobile debate is for me a nonissue. The National Park Service and the Environmental Protection Agency have spent millions of dollars and concluded—several times—that snowmobiles do not belong in Yellowstone. Further research is a cynical and transparent charade designed to make science fit political pressure from the current administration.

True, the newer snowmobiles are quieter and cleaner, but not enough to change the point: they are still noisy and they still pollute and they still harass wildlife.

Forbidding snowmobiles in Yellowstone isn't elitist, either, despite rabid claims by snowmobilers to the contrary. The cost of a snow-coach tour of Yellowstone is about $100. A new pair of cross-country skis with boots and poles cost $400. Snowshoes cost $200 or less. Used skis and snowshoes are much less expensive, and the rental of either at the Snow Lodge is dirt cheap. A new snowmobile costs $10,000–$12,000.

What is snowmobiling about? Does it have anything to do with national parks or their ideals? Here is a typical Polaris advertisement: "The 2006 Fusion sled is the epitome of controlled aggression." "Experience the dominance." Not a word about a winter wonderland.

I am, however, no particular fan of snow coaches, either. Visiting Yellowstone in a Bombardier is like visiting Paris in a tank: there may be compelling reasons to do so, but they must be, well, compelling. Having tried it, I can find no compelling reasons to revisit Yellowstone in a Bombardier.

The new snow coaches are better in many ways. They have windows you can see out of and the heating system keeps them clear. They are high enough so you can see something other than a snowbank or the tops of trees. They are quite clean. Some have a TV that shows videos of wildlife, which saves you from having to look out the window. Digital bison and elk are closer, clearer—why bother with reality? A guide will deliver a canned lecture of factoids predigested and approved by the park service.

If polled, I think most Americans would say they don't want to ride in a snow coach or drive a snowmobile. The vast majority want to drive their cars. The true egalitarian solution for winter access to Yellowstone is obvious: plow the roads in Yellowstone all winter. The surrounding states plow their roads all winter, and the park already plows one road through the park—from Mammoth to Cooke City. The expense of grooming Yellowstone's roads for snow coaches and snowmobiles is already significant—not to mention the ongoing cost of litigation over snowmobile use, litigation that will not end in our lifetimes. It is perhaps noteworthy that no faction advances this entirely feasible solution.

My own view? Close the park every year for six months. Every critter and chunk of land deserves a rest from *homo sapiens commercialis*.

Since Dana and I are walkers, we'll walk and visit the local geysers and hot springs. There is excellent skiing and snowshoeing trails leading to them from the Snow Lodge, but with so little snow it is easier to walk.

Amidst the clamor over snowmobiles and snow coaches, it is easy to forget that Yellowstone was preserved as the world's first national park because of its thermal features—10,000 of them. Even the park's borders were created to embrace the majority of geothermal features in the area.

From the Snow Lodge and the nearby Visitor Center, a series of trails extend for two miles northwest through the Upper Geyser Basin. One is a bicycle path, others are boardwalks strung above the sometimes thin crust of characteristic white sinter surrounding the geysers. The boardwalks serve a purpose: people and their pets have been injured or killed after falling into hot springs or breaking through the crust of sinter covering the area.

This sinter is a manifestation of the Yellowstone Hotspot, an underground heat source that feeds not only the thermal features here but a live volcano. Its first major eruption, about 2.1 million years ago, was 2,400 times larger than Mt. St. Helen's eruption in 1980. It dumped ash on Missouri. A more recent eruption 640,000 years ago created the caldera that is now Yellowstone Lake. The volcano is still active; according to recent research, the surface of the caldera is rising at the rate of eight centimeters a year. It is accurate to say that Yellowstone National Park is the top of an active volcano.

A geyser is an intermittently erupting hot spring. Why particular hot springs erupt and others don't is due to the unique plumbing beneath them. Not only must water seep into the system from rain and snowmelt, it must make contact with a source of intense heat. That heat is provided by magma. A chamber of magma—the Hotspot—lies beneath the park and is unusually near the surface.

When water percolates down to this magma chamber it is heated to more than 400 degrees Fahrenheit—well above the boiling point. But because water and rock are pressing on it from above, this hot water remains trapped—and primed for release. Convection currents bring the superheated water up near the surface via shafts and holes in a layer of rhyolite left by the volcanoes' eruptions. Rhyolite contains silica that is dissolved by the superheated water. The resulting solution seals the walls of the rhyolitic shafts and holes, creating a smooth, impervious surface that prevents the pressurized, superheated water from dissipating into the porous rock.

The shaft of a geyser is constricted somewhere near the surface. The constriction in Old Faithful is slightly more than four inches in diameter. As the superheated water is trapped below, the entire system begins to act like a pressure cooker: trapped water with a constant high heat source. Eventually the plumbing system is full and the constant heat produces ever-increasing pressure until the hot water blasts through the constriction as a column of steam and water—a geyser eruption. The siliceous solution evaporates, leaving sinter, that pale, slightly lunar landscape that surrounds Yellowstone's geothermal attractions.

The conditions to make all this happen are so rare I am utterly awed. More than half the world's geysers are found in Yellowstone, 200 geysers in the Upper Geyser Basin alone, the densest concentration known. Appreciating them seems to me far more interesting than spending a day in a freezer with a saw.

The geysers and other thermal features here—hot springs, mud pots, and fumaroles, are all the more valuable because many of the planet's other thermal areas—on Russia's Kamchatka Peninsula, in New Zealand, and in Chile—have been exploited for energy production with the usual calamitous consequences. Even Yellowstone's vast thermal system is vulnerable to thermal energy developments outside the park.

Thermal areas north at Corwin Springs and to the west at Island Park connect to Yellowstone's geothermal system, and development at either location would affect its geysers. Oil or gas development in the region will also cause problems because wells affect water levels and pressures underground. Like bears, bison, pronghorn, elk, and wolverines, the unique underground plumbing of Yellowstone's thermal wonders do not operate according to state, federal, or private boundaries. They are yet another example of the park's dependency on a Greater Yellowstone area.

And, unfortunately, some of the thermal features within the park have been despoiled by thoughtless human behavior. In his book *A Field Guide to Yellowstone's Geysers,* Carl Schreier describes what was found in Morning Glory Pool in 1950: socks, bath towels, seventy-six handkerchiefs, 8,627 pennies, and $8.10 in other coins.

We time the beginning of our walk to see a predicted eruption of Old Faithful, which is only a short distance from the Snow Lodge. The paths and boardwalks are clear of snow and walking is pleasant despite the overcast skies, temperatures near 0, and a brisk wind. As we approach Old Faithful we see that the eruption has already begun. I check my watch.

"Damn, and we are right on time."

But this is not too surprising since Old Faithful is not completely predictable. The average time between eruptions can vary from 45 to 120 minutes, although the average is 92 minutes and the time of the next eruption can be quite accurately predicted from the force of the previous one. But not to the minute. Old Faithful's fidelity, like fidelity in general, is a matter of degree.

The statistics on Old Faithful provided by the park service are as impressive as the eruption: the spout—8,400 gallons of 204-degree water—can reach over 180 feet high in less than five minutes. During winter, cooler air temperatures react with the boiling water to produce more mist than during the summer, and the eruption is indeed a misty affair, with the stream of water rising from the earth like a wraith. The eruption lasts for several minutes and is gone, leaving water streaming down the sinter cone.

During the summer, crowds surround Old Faithful and the eruption is celebratory. People cheer. Now oddly, at Christmas, with hundreds of people in the area, Old Faithful has performed to a nearly empty house. The most surprising thing about Christmas at Old Faithful is that we are alone. I find this disconcerting.

The number of people visiting our national parks every year is declining, a fact that worries many thoughtful defenders of the national-park idea. Although some of us may prefer fewer people on the roads and trails and rivers, it is hard to believe that the decreasing numbers of people who have actual contact with the parks will in the future prove sufficient to provide continued support for the parks' maintenance and existence, much less for the additions we need in Greater Yellowstone to protect the ecosystem.

Part of the reason is our culture's creep toward virtual reality. The park's Webcam of Old Faithful clocked an average of more than 200,000 hits a month for the first four months of 2006. At that rate virtual viewers may well surpass the number of people who actually watch the eruption. An increasing number of ethnic minorities seem to lack interest in national parks, so much so that some parks are setting up special programs to educate them about their value. Lastly, we are an increasingly urban society that both fears and misunderstands the natural world—and only 18 percent of us believe in evolution. Research at Cornell University by Nancy Wells and Kristi

Lekies found that "participating in such wild nature activities as camping, playing in the woods, hiking, walking, fishing and hunting" before the age of eleven strongly correlated with actively caring about the environment as an adult.

Needless to say, fewer and fewer children participate in such activities. Richard Louv's excellent book *Last Child in the Woods*, documents what is now called "nature deficit disorder," the decline in our children's direct contact with nature. At one time those kids in the Snow Lodge watching DVDs would have been building snowmen and rolling in the snow, even in these temperatures, but the majority have come to prefer computers to snowmen, machines to campfires. I cannot but think that all this portends ill for national parks. And for the sacrifices required for intact ecosystems.

"Shall we keep going?" I ask Dana. "I want to show you the colors in some of the pools. They will remind you of the ocean off Kauai."

"Great. I want to walk."

We head north, up Geyser Hill, and wander above the boardwalks along the Firehole River.

From the remains of old camps archeologists know that Indians occupied the geyser basins, probably because of the concentrations of wild game, though there is evidence that they also used them to bathe in and to cook with. Mountain men described the geysers in such extravagant terms that no one believed them; indeed, Yellowstone was first known as "Colter's Hell," after John Colter, who was the first European American to visit the area, or as "the place where hell bubbled up." Two hundred years later this hell has become a fragment of heaven.

Three of the West's great surveying expeditions—Folsom-Cook-Peterson (1860), Washburn-Langford-Doane (1870), and Ferdinand Hayden (1871–72)—confirmed their reality, as it were, renamed many of them, and initiated scientific studies that continue to this day.

Scientific interest would, however, prove insufficient to create the first national park. Legend credits the creation of Yellowstone to members of the Washburn expedition, who, while sitting around a campfire in Madison Meadow (at the junction of the Firehole and Gibbon rivers), acted as farsighted, public-spirited citizens concerned with conservation and beauty and gave birth to the national park ideal. This, historians have demonstrated, is false. In *Searching for Yellowstone*, park historian Paul Schullery concludes, "The campfire conversation may not even have taken place, and if it did, it hardly mattered in the history of the park." No, the creation of the park lies in a deeper, nearly mysterious union of greed, art, and biology.

In 1871, the painter Thomas Moran joined Ferdinand Hayden, head of the U.S. Geological and Geographical Survey of the Territories, on a trip to Yellowstone. Moran's position on the expedition was secured by a letter of introduction, and a loan, from Jay Cooke, he of Cooke City fame and chief financier of the Northern Pacific Railroad. Moran received further backing and another loan from *Scribner's Magazine*. Both his supporters were attracted to the commercial opportunities in the Yellowstone region. At the birth of Yellowstone was tourism.

Moran was relatively unknown but enormously ambitious, and committed to painting the American landscape. He painted for six decades and his oeuvre had a profound effect on our national psyche, our conception of what was significant landscape worthy of preservation. The Americans making decisions about land conservation viewed what would become their iconic landscapes through the eyes of an artist.

In 1862, when he was twenty-five years old and already an artist who had exhibited accomplished work, Moran traveled to England to study, and copy, the paintings of J. M. W. Turner, the English landscapist famous for his Romantic watercolors and oil paintings. Moran was also to absorb the ideas preached by Turner's friend, John Ruskin, ideas that valorized nature, attention to detail, and an emphasis on the sublime, especially in the mountains. The most influential volume of Ruskin's numerous works was entitled "Of Mountain Beauty." Both men emphasized the importance of color.

Moran never outgrew their examples and teachings. By the time he painted Yellowstone for Hayden's expedition, Romanticism and detailed, naturalistic mountain scenery was dead in Europe. Modern painters had moved on. Manet had scandalized Paris with "Olympia," Whistler was painting wispy Nocturnes nearly devoid of detail, Monet was stabbing his canvas with painterly touches, and Cézanne was at the edge of that most modern of phenomena, abstraction. In contrast, Moran's painting—both his watercolors and his oils—were regressive in both spirit and emphasis. And yet it was precisely the Romantic spirit, an attraction to the sublime, and emphasis on grandeur and color that were to prove decisive in persuading Congress to pass the Yellowstone Park Bill and establish the world's first national park.

In his official report Hayden remarked that the expedition spent five days on the upper reaches of the Firehole River "exploring its wonders, making charts, sketches, photographs, and taking the temperatures of the springs." Moran even made a tiny pencil sketch of Old Faithful entitled "Stream from Faithful." There are also sketches of two of the most famous geysers, Bee Hive and Castle. All three of these geysers are visible from the boardwalk on Geyser Hill upon which Dana and I stand.

We are never away from the drone of snowmobiles. From the height of Geyser Hill I notice something I didn't notice below. A slightly yellowish haze veils Upper Geyser Basin. I know the color well from my youth in Southern California: smog. It is an environment completely at odds with Moran's crystalline views.

Moran often did not have time to finish many watercolors, so there are many pencil sketches. Written over the sketches are color references he later used to complete some of these drawings and to construct the exquisite paintings made in his studio upon his return East. There can be no doubt that Moran was sensitive to color.

Moran's Yellowstone sketches were displayed on Capital Hill along with photographs by William Henry Jackson, the Hayden expedition's photographer. Their work conveyed both the oddity and beauty of Yellowstone to those who would decide its future. As *The*

New York Times noted, "While only a select few can appreciate the discoveries of the geologists or the exact measurements of the topographers, everyone can understand a picture."

The color in Moran's watercolors proved decisive. Jackson's photographs were black and white. They could not represent the subtle colors of hot springs, their mineral deposits, and their aquatic flora. Hayden acclaimed the area's mineral deposits for their brilliancy— "like the most delicate of our aniline dyes." He praised Moran's "delicate perception of colors" and noted that he was "justly celebrated for his exquisite taste as a colorist." Writing in *The New York Times* a year after the exhibit on Capital Hill, a critic concurred and emphasized Moran's color: "The drawing is necessarily slight, and not especially remarkable in any regard. But the color is very beautiful."

In March 1872, Congress established the world's first national park and laid the foundation for what would become the administration of Yellowstone. Searching for the factors responsible for this early conservation victory I find commercial greed and Romantic idealism, art and color, the sublime—and mats of thermophilic algae that produce the color.

Many of Moran's Yellowstone watercolors hang in the Visitor's Center at Mammoth. They were indeed notable for their color— exaggerated, it is true, but, I want to say, even truer to the spirit of the place. Moran's sketches of Yellowstone were my inspiration for adding small watercolor paintings to my writing journals. Later I did watercolors for their own sake, and later still oil paintings, so I am indebted to Thomas Moran for many things in my life. And by some complex strands of causal good fortune I will never understand, the beautiful colors in the springs remain, even on a cold, gray, overcast, blustery day 130 years later.

We walk the trails, admiring each hot spring. We pass perhaps a dozen people in two hours, some elegantly dressed, some clomping along in their huge snowmobile boots. We play one of our favorite games.

"Is it a green or a blue?" Dana asks as we peer into Beauty Pool. When confronted with an aqua tint, I tend to see greens whereas Dana tends to see blue.

"Too green for cobalt teal, too blue for viridian. I don't know. Aqua, somewhere between green and blue."

"Turquoise," she announces.

As Hayden said, the colors are divinely delicate, quite beyond our color vocabulary. What produces all this vibrant color? Refracted skylight accounts for the myriad blues. Pigments in the pool's bacteria contain different levels of chlorophyll and carotenoids. Chlorophyll produces the greens, carotenoids the reds, oranges, and yellows. In winter, with less sunlight, the balance between the two changes and the colors are less vivid.

In the end so much comes down to bacteria and minerals. Because we read the labels on our vitamin bottles we know that we need minerals and that they are good for us. We are less tolerant of bacteria. Bacteria are not, we like to think, us. But, of course, they *are* us. Ninety percent of our body's cells are bacterial cells. The human genome of which we are so proud is completely dependent on the 100 trillion bacteria inhabiting our body. We are a hybrid of minerals, human cells, and, mostly, bacteria cells, all working together in often unpredictable ways to make a larger living being— which is to say that our body is like a wild ecosystem.

Although these hot springs seem barren, they are teeming with life, with what is called "thermophilic life," life that has evolved in extreme temperatures. Beneath our feet are ephydrid flies who survive by eating the algae that produce the colors we so admire. Spiders eat these flies, beetles eat the spiders, birds and fish eat the beetles. It is thought that there are thousands of species in these thermophilic mats, all interconnected with the larger species we visit Yellowstone to admire, the food chain in action, the codependence of vast communities we barely know exist.

And at some deeper and as-yet-unknown level they are connected to us. Some have not changed much since life began on Earth. We have evolved to different destinies but we began in the same primordial muck.

NASA, universities, and major corporations are studying Yellowstone's thermophilic microorganisms. These hot springs are responsible for some of biotechnology's most lucrative commodities. The reason is simple and marvelous. Every hot spring is unique—that's the rub about Being: everything is unique and everything is dependent. Each hot spring manifests subtle differences in chemistry and temperatures that produce subtle differences in the bacteria and algae they accommodate. Why should an enzyme in a thermophilic bacterium in Yellowstone National Park be useful to the technological process known as "polymerase chain reaction"? This is the artificial production of DNA that has led to DNA fingerprinting and proved useful, in turn, to so many scientific endeavors, from criminal identification to the diagnosis of AIDS. Why are drug companies aggressively plucking microorganisms from these hot springs? And why aren't the park and the American public getting a fair share of the profits?

All life is connected at many layers and at many scales in many ways we have yet to fathom. One layer mirrors all layers, and I believe the health of one layer is reflected in all layers. From Geyser Hill we can see bison. Elk are near, and deer. Grizzlies are sleeping; wolves are on the prowl. Flies and spiders scramble about. Microbes convert inorganic chemicals to energy; bacteria convert sunlight to energy; all those plant chloroplasts doing their thing. They get on quite well without our management goals, values, or assistance, each in its wild fashion, and no doubt many of them will be here when our species has passed into history. Evolution clearly works.

At times I think of Greater Yellowstone as an ecosystem of bacteria that are collectively smarter than we are. It is not so clear that human artifice works, even for such a sacred institution as a national park. But to believe that is to take a narrow view of where we are in the battle to preserve Greater Yellowstone. Flip the view from the very small to the very large and we are again confronted with ongoing fragmentation and loss, and its effects on thermophylic mats and geysers are unknown. Einstein said that God does not play dice with the universe, but we are not God and we are playing dice with Greater Yellowstone. It is folly to think otherwise.

Dana and I return to the Snow Lodge, to the fireplace, the warm baths, the fresh vegetables, the games, the cell-phone conversations. Eventually we climb into the Bombardier and sit next to the same people we arrived with, in exactly the same order. We ask the usual questions about their visits and receive the usual answers. I talk about color and thermophilic mats of algae—not a subject my fellow travelers seem much interested in this afternoon.

The Bombardier careens and rolls along the groomed road, its headlights blazing even during the day, lights searching into blinding snow. Snowmobiles pass with a roar we barely discern above our own roar, steered by silent figures in snowsuits and Darth Vader helmets. Dana and I snuggle under our blankets. No one asks to stop.

After the Bombardier ride, driving our old truck through Jackson Hole seems like a treat. We'll be home, it's still Christmas, which is where one ought to be.

"I'll be home for Christmas / You can count on me / There'll be snow . . ."

There is snow and it is snowing. Spring seems far away. We no longer live in our little cabin in Lupine Meadow during the winter, though we are still there during the summer. Now we are caretakers of an eleven-acre inholding in the park. Rio is freer to be a dog. Moose and elk and coyotes and pine martens and red squirrels and chickadees are still our neighbors. Once home we drink eggnog spiked with Kentucky bourbon whiskey. Dana stares out the window at the lodgepole pines laden with snow.

"Beautiful. Just beautiful," she says.

"We don't need wreaths and Christmas trees," I tell her.

Yes, it is beautiful, and the power of that beauty may be Thomas

Moran's greatest gift to us. It was beauty that preserved Yellowstone in the first place and regardless of the plight of so many ecosystems, the beauties of Grand Teton and Yellowstone remain. Perhaps, ultimately, that same wild beauty will prove the best defense of Greater Yellowstone.

Bibliography

-----------------------------------➤

Introduction: The Greater Yellowstone Ecosystem

Chittenden, Hiram Martin. *The Yellowstone National Park: Historical and Descriptive.* Cincinnati: Robert Clarke, 1903.

Gaines, Ernest J. *A Gathering of Old Men.* New York: Vintage, 1992.

Leopold, Aldo. *The River of the Mother of God and Other Essays by Aldo Leopold.* Edited by Susan L. Flader and J. Baird Callicott. Madison, WI: University of Wisconsin Press, 1991.

Noss, Reed, George Wuerthner, Ken Vance-Borland, and Carlos Carroll. "A Biological Conservation Assessment for the Greater Yellowstone Ecosystem: Report to the Greater Yellowstone Coalition." Corvallis, OR: Conservation Science, 2001. A copy of the report can be obtained by writing them at: 7310 NW Acorn Ridge Corvallis, OR 97330.

Prichard, James A. *Preserving Yellowstone's Natural Conditions: Science and the Perception of Nature.* Lincoln, NE: University of Nebraska Press, 1999.

Schullery, Paul. *Searching for Yellowstone: Ecology and Wonder in the Last Wilderness.* Boston: Houghton Mifflin, 1997.

U.S. Department of the Interior. National Park Service. *Yellowstone Resources and Issues,* 2006 edition.

Wuerthner, George. *Yellowstone: A Visitor's Companion.* Harrisburg, PA: Stackpole Books, 1992.

1. The View from Blacktail Butte

Clark, Tim C. W. *The Natural World of Jackson Hole: An Ecological Primer.* Moose, WY: Grand Teton Natural History Association, 1999.

Craighead, Charles. *The Official Guidebook of Grand Teton National Park.* Moose, WY: Grand Teton Natural History Association, 2006.

Craighead, Frank C., Jr. *For Everything There Is a Season: The Sequence of Natural Events in the Grand Teton–Yellowstone Area.* Helena, MT: Falcon Press, 1994.

Love, J. David, John C. Reed Jr., and Kenneth L. Pierce. *Creation of the Teton Landscape: A Geological Chronicle of Jackson Hole and the Teton Range.* Moose, WY: Grand Teton Natural History Association, 2003.

Luoma, Jon R. *The Hidden Forest.* New York: Henry Holt, 1999.

Madsen, Chris. "On the Wild Side: Keeping the Wild in Wildlife Should Be a Primary Goal of Modern Conservation Efforts." *Wyoming Wildlife* 67, no. 1 (January 2004).

Smith, Robert B., and Lee J. Siegal. *Windows into the Earth: The Geologic Story of Yellowstone and Grand Teton National Parks.* New York: Oxford University Press, 2000.

Stamets, Paul. *Mycelium Running: How Mushrooms Can Help Save the World.* Berkeley: Ten Speed Press, 2005.

2. *Opening Day on the Firehole River*

Back, Howard. *The Waters of Yellowstone with Rod and Fly.* New York: Lyons Press, 2000.

Brooks, Charles E. *The Living River: A Fisherman's Intimate Profile of the Madison River Watershed—Its History, Ecology, Love, and Angling Opportunities.* New York: Winchester Press/Nick Lyons Books, 1979.

Juracek, John, and Craig Mathews. *Fishing Yellowstone Hatches.* West Yellowstone, MT: First published 1992 by Blue Ribbon Flies, West Yellowstone, MT.

Schwiebert, Ernest G., Jr. *Matching the Hatch: A Practical Guide to Imitation of Insects Found on Eastern and Western Trout Waters.* New York: Macmillan, 1955.

Varley, John D., and Paul Schullery. *Yellowstone Fishes: Ecology, History, and Angling in the Park.* Mechanicsburg, PA: Stackpole Books, 1998.

3. *Modern Wolves*

Askins, Renée. *Shadow Mountain: A Memoir of Wolves, a Woman, and the Wild.* New York: Doubleday, 2002.

Coleman, Jon T. *Vicious: Wolves and Men in America.* New Haven: Yale University Press, 2004.

Debord, Guy. *The Society of the Spectacle.* Translated by Donald Nicholson-Smith. New York: Zone Books/MIT Press, 1995.

Halfpenny, James C. *Yellowstone Wolves in the Wild.* Helena, MT: Riverbend Publishing, 2003.

Leopold, Aldo. *Game Management.* Madison, WI: University of Wisconsin Press, 1986.

———. *Round River.* New York: Oxford University Press, 1993.

McIntyre, Rick. *A Society of Wolves: National Parks and the Battle over the Wolf.* Rev. ed. Stillwater, MN: Voyageur Press, 1996.

Russell, Osborne. *Journal of a Trapper.* Lincoln, NE: University of Nebraska Press, 1965.

Smith, Douglas W., and Gary Ferguson. *Decade of the Wolf: Returning the Wild to Yellowstone.* Guilford, CT: Lyons Press, 2005.

"Special Issue: The Wyoming Wolf." *Wyoming Wildlife* 67, no. 11 (November 2003).

4. *Alpine Tundra: The First Domino*

Anderson, Bob. *Beartooth Country: Montana's Absaroka and Beartooth Mountains.* Helena, MT: American & World Geographic Publishing, 1994.

Arno, Stephen F. *Timberline: Mountain and Arctic Forest Frontiers.* Seattle: Mountaineers Books, 1984.

Craighead, John J., Frank C. Craighead Jr., and Ray J. Davis. *A Field Guide to Rocky Mountain Wildflowers: From Northern Arizona and New Mexico to British Columbia.* Boston: Houghton Mifflin, 1963.

Gellhorn, Joyce. *Song of the Alpine: The Rocky Mountain Tundra Through the Seasons.* Boulder, CO: Johnson Books, 2002.

James, H. L. *Scenic Driving the Beartooth Highway.* Helena, MT: Falcon Publishing, 1997.

Moen, Jon, Karin Aune, Lars Edenius, and Anders Angerbjörn, "Potential Effects of Climate Change on Treeline Position in the Swedish Mountains," *Ecology and Society,* no. 19 (2004).

Plants of the Alpine Tundra. Estes Park, CO: Rocky Mountain Nature Association, 1981.

Schneider, Bill. *Hiking the Beartooths.* Helena, MT: Falcon Press, 1996.

Scott, Richard W. *The Alpine Flora of the Rocky Mountains,* Vol. 1, *The Middle Rockies.* Salt Lake City: University of Utah Press, 1995.

Singer, Mark. "The High Mark: Mountains, Grizzlies, and the Smell of Exhaust in the Morning." *New Yorker.* March 25, 2002.

Strickler, Dee. *Alpine Wildflowers: Showy Wildflowers of the Alpine and Subalpine Areas of the Northern Rocky Mountain States.* Columbia Falls, MT: Flower Press, 1990.

Wingate, Janet L., and Loraine Yeatts, *Alpine Flower Finder: The Key to Wildflowers Found Above Treeline in the Rocky Mountains.* Boulder, CO: Roberts Rinehart Publishers, 1995.

Zwinger, Ann H., and Beatrice E. Willard. *Land Above the Trees: A Guide to American Alpine Tundra.* New York: Harper & Row, 1972.

5. *The South Fork*

Bosse, Scott. "River at a Crossroads: Development in the 100-Year Floodplain of the South Fork Snake River," A report from the Greater Yellowstone Coalition, February 2003. Available from the Greater Yellowstone Coalition, Bozeman, MT.

DeVoto, Bernard. *Across the Wide Missouri.* Boston: Houghton Mifflin, 1947.

Palmer, Tim. *The Snake River: Window to the West.* Washington, DC: Island Press, 1991.

Prosek, James. *Trout of the World.* New York: Stewart, Tabori & Chang, 2003.

U.S. Department of the Interior. Bureau of Land Management. Idaho. "Ecology and Management of the South Fork Snake River Cottonwood Forest," by Michael F. Merigliano. Idaho BLM Technical Bulletin 96-9, May 1996.

6. *The Wyoming Range*

Craighead, John J., Frank C. Craighead Jr., and Ray J. Davis. *A Field Guide to Rocky Mountain Wildflowers: From Northern Arizona and New Mexico to British Columbia.* Boston: Houghton Mifflin, 1963.

Lanner, Ronald M. *Made for Each Other: A Symbiosis of Birds and Pines.* New York: Oxford University Press, 1996.

Rawlins, C. L. *Broken Country: Mountains and Memory.* New York: Henry Holt, 1996.

Tomback, Diana F., Stephen F. Arno, and Robert E. Keane. *Whitebark Pine Communities: Ecology and Restoration.* Washington, DC: Island Press, 2001.

"Too Wild to Drill: Wyoming Range, Wyoming." A report from the Wilderness Society, 2006.

Turiano, Thomas. *Select Peaks of Greater Yellowstone: A Mountaineering History & Guide.* Jackson, WY: Indomitus Books, 2003.

7. *The Deep Winds*

Kelsey, Joe. *Climbing and Hiking the Wind River Mountains*, Second Edition. Evergreen, CO: Chockstone Press, 1994.

————. *Wyoming's Wind River Range*. Helena, MT: American Geographic Publishing, 1988.

Repanshek, Kurt. "Of Fire and Ice: The Severity of Wyoming's Drought Can Be Measured in Its Glaciers." *Wyoming Wildlife*, August 2004.

Shewey, John. "Wind River Range, WY: Golden Trout in Wyoming's High Country." *Northwest Fly Fishing*, Fall 1999.

"Too Wild to Drill: Red Desert, Wyoming." A report from the Wilderness Society, 2006.

8. *Green River Lakes*

Jensen, Holger. "The Vanishing Sage." *Wyoming Wildlife News*, November–December 2004.

Kloor, Keith. "Sagebrush Showdown." *Audubon*, January 2007.

Madsen, Chris. "A Taste for Quiet: Recent Research Shows That Sage Grouse Breeding Is Easily Disturbed." *Wyoming Wildlife*, February 2006.

"Too Wild to Drill: Upper Green River Valley, Wyoming," A report from The Wilderness Society, 2006.

Zwinger, Ann. *Run, River, Run: A Naturalist's Journey Down One of the Great Rivers of the West*. New York: Harper & Row, 1975.

9. *Chasing Cutts*

Behnke, Robert J. *Trout and Salmon of North America*. New York: Free Press, 2002.

Hunt, Chris. "Bringing Back the Bear River Bonnevilles." *Trout*, Fall 2005.

Trotter, Patrick C. *Cutthroat: Native Trout of the West*. Boulder, CO: Colorado Associated University Press, 1987.

Varley, John D., and Paul Schullery. *Yellowstone Fishes: Ecology, History, and Angling in the Park*. Mechanicsburg, PA: Stackpole Books, 1998.

10. *Grizzly Bear Heaven*

Craighead, Frank C., Jr., *Track of the Grizzly*. San Francisco: Sierra Club Books, 1982.

Herrero, Stephen. *Bear Attacks: Their Causes and Avoidance*. Rev. ed. Guilford, CT: Lyons Press, 2002.

McMillion, Scott. *Mark of the Grizzly: True Stories of Recent Bear Attacks and the Hard Lessons Learned*. Guilford, CT: Globe Pequot Press, 1998.

Peacock, Doug and Andrea. *The Essential Grizzly: The Mingled Fates of Men and Bears.* Guilford, CT: Lyons Press, 2006.

Robbins, Charles T., Chuck C. Schwartz, Kerry A. Gunther, and Chris Servheen. "Grizzly Bear Nutrition and Ecology." *Yellowstone Science* 14, no. 3 (Summer 2006): 19–26.

11. *Red Rock Lakes*

Chatham, Russell. *One Hundred Paintings.* Livingston, MT: Clark City Press, 1990.

Russell, Osborne. *Journal of a Trapper.* Lincoln, NE: University of Nebraska Press, 1965.

Ryser, Fred A., Jr., *Birds of the Great Basin: A Natural History.* Reno: University of Nevada Press, 1985.

Sibley, David Allen. *The Sibley Guide to Birds.* New York, Alfred A. Knopf, 2000.

White. E. B. *The Trumpet of the Swan.* New York, HarperCollins, 1970.

12. *Christmas at Old Faithful*

Brock, Thomas D. *Life at High Temperatures.* Yellowstone National Park, WY: Yellowstone Association, 1994.

Bryan, T. Scott. *The Geysers of Yellowstone.* 3rd ed. Boulder: University Press of Colorado, 2001.

Hayden, Ferdinand V. "The Hot Springs and Geysers of the Yellowstone and Firehole Rivers," *American Journal of Science and Arts,* 3 series, no. 3, February 1872.

——. "The Wonders of the West II. More About the Yellowstone," *Scribner's Monthly 3* (February 1872): 388–96.

Kinsey, Joni Louise. *Thomas Moran and the Surveying of the American West.* Washington, DC: Smithsonian Institution Press, 1992.

Louv, Richard. *Last Child in the Woods: Saving Our Children from Nature-Deficit Disorder.* Chapel Hill, NC: Algonquin Books, 2005.

Morand, Anne. *Thomas Moran: The Field Sketches, 1856–1923.* Norman, OK: University of Oklahoma Press, 1996.

Schreier, Carl. *A Field Guide to Yellowstone's Geysers, Hot Springs, and Fumaroles.* Rev. ed. Moose, WY: Homestead Publishing, 1999.

Schullery, Paul, and Lee Whittlesey. *Myth and History in the Creation of Yellowstone National Park.* Lincoln, NE: University of Nebraska Press, 2003.

Smith, Robert B., and Lee J. Siegel. *Windows into the Earth: The Geologic Story of Yellowstone and Grand Teton National Parks.* New York: Oxford University Press, 2000.

Spear, John R., Jeffrey J. Walker, and Norman R. Pace. "Microbial Ecology and Energetics in Yellowstone Hot Springs." *Yellowstone Science* 14, no. 1 (Winter 2006): 17–23.

Jack Turner is the president of Exum Mountain Guides and School of American Mountaineering in Grand Teton National Park. He has led treks in India, Pakistan, Nepal, China, Tibet, Bhutan, and Peru. His first book was a collection of environmental essays, *The Abstract Wild*; it was followed by a memoir, *Teewinot: A Year in the Teton Range*. He is a visiting scholar at the University of Utah, and has been honored with a 2007 Whiting Foundation Writer's Award. He lives in Grand Teton National Park with his wife, Dana, and their dog, Rio.